MEMOIRS FROM A YOUNG REPUBLIC

MEMOIRS FROM A YOUNG REPUBLIC

Thomas Keneally

HEINEMANN : LONDON

First published in Great Britain 1993
by William Heinemann Ltd
an imprint of Reed Consumer Books Ltd
Michelin House, 81 Fulham Road, London SW3 6RB
and Auckland, Melbourne, Singapore and Toronto

ISBN 0 85561 519 2

A CIP catalogue record for this book
is available at the British Library

Printed in Australia by Griffin Paperbacks

To all the robust ghosts,
some of whose names are
Dan Deniehy, John Dunmore Lang,
Henry and Louisa Lawson,
Mary Gilmore, Manning Clark

CONTENTS

AUTHOR'S NOTE

My thanks to Professor George Winterton, who advised me against legal errors. Any remaining are not his fault.

TO START

THIS IS AN account of
(1) Things experienced in a Republican lifetime;
(2) Things discovered which make up a sort of Republican history of Australia, and which turn a lot of the normal propositions about Australia and its long passion for the Monarchy on their heads.

Much has been forgotten, many glib statements have been made about earlier Australians, how they felt about Australia and the Empire, and what their motives were. My account tries not to take anyone glibly, not even the shrinking cohorts of modern Australian Monarchists.

Part of this history is the account of what has befallen me in the past two years in my life as a writer and as chair of the Australian Republican Movement. I claim no special significance for the ARM, although I think that we had the good fortune to speak at the right time and shape the debate— before any significant politician had spoken—in the direction of an inevitable Republic.

This is above all just a tale, that's all, an ordinary pilgrimage.

Its bias is—without apology—that the Republic is not a side issue for resolution at some future, happier date. The Republic is part of the mechanism of our national deliverance. If that idea offends you, you won't like this book.

CHAPTER ONE

*

OF TREASON AND UNCLE JOHNNY

IN AUGUST 1991, not long after the dull winter's morning when, on the shores of Sydney Cove, the Australian Republican Movement declared itself for an Australian Republic by 2001, I had to go to Dublin to give a long-before-arranged talk at the Joyce Summer School. The members of the Republican Movement at that stage thought that after we had made our initial statement in Sydney, the ferment would soon die. We would have a job to keep the debate rolling for the next ten years and to try to give it a visible face.

But in fact the launching of the movement in a small room (its use donated by the management) in the Regent Hotel in Sydney, had created a furore which would not diminish.

I gave the lecture in Dublin, and while I was in London waiting for a plane back to Australia I heard that a man named Bruce Ruxton, a Victorian official of the Returned Services League, the Australian war veterans organisation which had considerable political potency, had called for the arrest of a number of Republicans, including Neville Wran, a former

Premier of New South Wales, Malcolm Turnbull, the solicitor and merchant banker, and myself, a novelist and chair of the Australian Republican Movement. In making the demand Ruxton appealed to a venerable section of the New South Wales Crimes Act covering fealty to the Crown.

Ruxton's call was made to a person who at that time was something of a star in the New South Wales Liberal Party government, the newly appointed, youngish, energetic, fresh-faced Attorney-General, Peter Collins. By an irony, Collins was also Minister for the Arts, and had the respect of the artistic and literary community in the State. In the old days you would have found people with the same name as Michael Collins, creator of the Irish Free State, in the Labor Party. But increasing numbers of younger Australians of Irish derivation were to be found in the Liberal Party. I suppose this was a result of the elevation of the Irish to the mainstream of Australian society, and a reaction to the shenanigans of the New South Wales Labor Right, a faction with a remarkably Tammany Hall complexion.

In any case, though Collins was a minister of the Crown, it became apparent both that he found Ruxton's idea laughable, and that it was impossible to say so explicitly. As in all things, in every arm of Australian society, the Monarchy was a shibboleth, a sign of contradiction. If Peter Collins had publicly laughed at Ruxton, which was his private tendency, he would either have suffered political damage, or would at least have *seen* himself to suffer potential political damage.

It is an interesting proposition that a man like Ruxton, who represents the veterans of a war against tyranny, such as I remember World War II to have been, should spend his time and either his organisation's money or less likely his own, in the search for the most clear cut and punitive edict on the holiness of the Australian connection with the British Monarchy.

The edict in question, the New South Wales Crimes Act of 1900, was a law promulgated on the edge of Australia's becoming a Federation. I had learned a little of 1900, having scanned the newspapers of that year for research for a novel called *The Chant of Jimmie Blacksmith*. At that time the atmosphere in Australia was a little like that of the Vietnam years. Australian forces were engaged in the Boer War in South Africa. The columns in the *Sydney Morning Herald* regularly told the populace of New South Wales that local boys were perishing—of Boer bullets but more commonly of enteric fever—for the Empire. Most amateur Australian historians, myself counted in, also know that 1900 was the end of a decade of nationalist debate, that the *Bulletin* had not only published resounding Republican poetry by William Lane and Henry Lawson, but had heaped scorn on both Empire and Queen Victoria and the whole Imperial system. The Boer War, and the contribution various Australian States strove to make to it, had served to focus the rough Australian nationalism the *Bulletin* specialised in: anti-British, but also anti-Asian and anti-Semitic (the magazine full of Jew-mocking cartoons), and certainly arrantly Australian, even if White Australian. The Boer War, like the earlier Imperial war in the Sudan— the graves of the New South Wales contingent to that Imperial fracas lie in the scabrous Sudanese seaport of Suakin —had inevitably raised the question of where Australian loyalties resided. But as we'll see in this account, it is not possible to judge the people of 1900 as if they were unthinking British jingoists. They saw what they thought of as hardheaded political and social advantages in their British connection and their devotion to Imperial foreign adventures. Many of them were far more sensible Monarchists than the rootless, visceral Monarchists of this millennium's end.

More of all that later though.

At the time of the Boer War, Sir George Reid, later to become an Australian prime minister, made a declaration which seems prophetic in view of what was to happen in 1914–18. 'If ever the old country were really menaced, we would send our last man and our last shilling in the cause'. At the same stage, Joe Wilson, Henry Lawson's *alter ego*, in a sketch-memoir Lawson wrote in London, exalted Australian identity over that of the mother country. 'There is none of the warmheartedness and impulsiveness of the Australians here. Give me Australia and the people who are born in a sunny climate.'

I suppose you have there, as you will find again and again in this story, the eternal Australian debate, both sides often contradicting themselves as is the Australian norm.

For example, Henry Lawson's praise of a side of the Australian character which he sees as contrary to the British runs dead against the dismal picture he would give of inner-city Sydneysiders in 'The Faces in the Crowd' and other poems he wrote about a coming revolution in Australia.

But then the argument was never an entirely rational business on either side, as Bruce Ruxton was proving some ninety-two years after the utterances of Sir George and Joe Wilson.

In case anyone got any smart ideas about what it was to be an Australian, a New South Wales parliament of 1900, featuring such robust loyalists as Sir George Reid and Sir William Lyne, passed a Crimes Act with a highly Monarchist flavour. It not only provided in Section 12 penalties for anyone who tried to maim, harm or destroy the Monarch or her heirs and successors, but also set down: 'Whosoever, within New South Wales or without, compasses, imagines, devises, or intends to deprive or depose Our Most Gracious Lady the Queen, her heirs and successors, from the style, honour, or Royal name of the Imperial Crown of the United Kingdom, or of any other of Her Majesty's dominions and countries . . . shall be liable to penal servitude for twenty-five years.'

The twenty-five years was originally life, and Bruce Ruxton's press release joyously invoked life imprisonment. And as unlikely as it was that any modern court would finally interpret the Act Bruce's way, he seems to have joyously embraced the chance.

Through the officers of his department, the nimble Peter Collins thanked Mr Ruxton for drawing his attention to the matter, but ultimately declined to prosecute. Both men, I like to fancy, knew what this Act stood for. It stood for the idea that Australian identity included being subject to the British Monarch. Ruxton wanted to re-establish that as a given, and to hell with free speech. Collins knew it was an embarrassing question. They were both conjuring with concepts of *'subject'* and *'citizen'*, of fealty as against the right of free expression. They were both dancing, as we all do, around the enigma which lies at the heart of what an Australian is and has been to this point.

For when he became a minister of the Crown, Collins himself had certainly sworn the fealty Ruxton now wanted him to act on. Politicians in Australia don't take an oath to the people who elected them. They take one to Queen Elizabeth, her heirs and successors. Ruxton was being literal—he wanted Collins to act on his oath.

As always, to add holiness to his arguments, Ruxton invoked of course the hosts of the Fallen, particularly those fallen in two world wars, the names of the brave and terrified dead boys which are maintained on monuments at the centre of every Australian town, however poor. The voices of the Fallen, stilled, were not able to comment on Ruxton's primitive claims about them. But many living veterans took trouble to distance themselves from the Ruxton idea.

One of them, with a finer and wiser war record than Ruxton's, wrote to the Australian Republican Movement:

> I am delighted to hear that at last a move has been made to get rid of the British ties. I am a returned soldier Army No.—. Member of the 2/2nd Inf.Batt 6th Division. Took part in the capture of Bardia and Tobruk and thanks to W. Churchill and R. Menzies was badly wounded in Greece on 18 April 1941. Was a patient at 5th AGH when it was taken by the German Army on 28/4/41. Spent four years as a POW ... From now on we can declare ourselves and join up and encourage others to do the same.

My own father had served more than two years in the Middle East and did not particularly, then or now, seem to have the Crown in the forefront of his mind. His favourite stories are to do with the detailed strategies Australian troops resorted to to avoid saluting British officers. And it is obvious from his letters that he saw himself as representing Australia, not the Crown.

In pursuing this question, we have to admit for the moment that we have been for most of this century playing a game which equates Australian identity with male valour, and that women are beginning to get justifiably disgruntled at that. What I remember myself from childhood was the somewhat less civically hallowed and less mythically enshrined anguish, courage and grief of soldiers' women and soldiers' widows, which was all I witnessed of World War II.

Men like the old soldier quoted above have never been simplistic about the question of male valour anyhow. They have often seen the Australian myths fully tested in battle, sometimes astoundingly validated, occasionally overturned, perhaps especially on Crete, one of the most savage campaigns Australians ever fought in (and all not so far from Gallipoli either).

Who can really read the motivations of the ANZACs and the First AIF, that heroic Dominion force in whose title 'Australian' and 'Imperial' had equal billing? The conundrum written right there, on the sunrise badges they wore on the sides of their hats. The sunrise and the Crown. Can it really be claimed that all those who fought and perished—or simply perished, as half the AIF deaths were from disease—that all these lads took that dark path to defend and honour the Crown? And can it really be argued that the reasonable Australian desire for a Republic spits on their memory?

I do not believe for a moment that the boys of 1915 were quite the post-Whitlamite Republicans depicted by Chris Lee and Mel Gibson in Peter Weir's fine film *Gallipoli*. But neither were they the monochrome Loyalists of Bruce Ruxton's atrophied imagination. A lot of them, as we'll see, were a third and perhaps subtler kind of being: Imperial federalists. Again, more of that to come.

Weir's film has good solid officers and men who believe they are dying for Western Australia. Classically, they lack support from the Poms, who according to what a runner says in the film, are not bringing up the flank but are 'drinking tea on the beach'. A friend of mine, Geoffrey Moorhouse, has recently written plaintively in a book called *Hell's Foundations* that whole towns in Lancashire and Nottingham were left son-less and husband-less in the same offensive in which Australians died at Lone Pine. But it is nonetheless true that there *were* plenty of letters home to Australian cities and the bush complaining of the poor stamina and will of British troops. So that if the Australians saw themselves as subjects of the Crown, they saw themselves as different subjects than the British proper.

Most fair commentators would believe that amongst the motivations of World War I diggers who fought and perished at Gallipoli and on the Western Front, or else in the long push north through the left flank of the Turkish Empire which ended with the capture of Damascus, the following impulses ranked high.

There was certainly an Australian identification with the liberal values of the British Isles, and of being a unit in a great Empire which guaranteed the sort of world we wanted to live in. (Again, you'll see this when I get on to quoting that forgotten Australian race, the Imperial federalists.)

There was a desire to make young Australia's mark upon the world and—perhaps above all—to show the fibre of Australians. There was, as in all white colonial peoples, a desire to expiate the stain of colonialism, and even in our case the stain of convictism. (A possible PhD thesis: *The Connection Between Convict Families and Gallipoli and France*. How many of the diggers were the children or grandchildren of transportees?) Certainly, I believe that that particular stain, first identified as such by the reformer Sir William Molesworth before the Transportation Committee, a Westminster Parliamentary Committee of Enquiry in 1837, was still with us in 1915. In some people's minds, it is still with us today, since it has been frequently and recently invoked not only by the British tabloids but by BBC television in 1992, as by the London *Daily Telegraph* ('settled by the detritus of eighteenth and nineteenth century Britain', wrote a columnist in March 1992) as a means of slurring the reasonable drive towards an Australian identity.

I am old enough to have had an uncle who served two years on the Western Front in World War I. His name was Johnny. *His* great-uncle Johnny was transported on the last convict ship to Australia, the *Hougoumont*, in 1867.

Uncle Johnny number one had been Fenian centre or organiser for County Cork. Though a political radical, and one who countenanced and planned for a coming armed uprising involving Irish soldiers within the British Army, he seemed to be a civilised fellow. I would not like to sentimentalise him, as people in Dublin pubs do tend to sentimentalise the 'auld rebels', but from his expressed sentiments—some of these appear in a fine book called *The Fenians in Australia* by Keith Amos—it would certainly be hard to imagine him committing the sort of crimes the Provisional IRA is guilty of today.

In view of my Uncle Johnny's own Uncle Johnny's service in Her Majesty's prisons, and the honour that the latter had at Portland Prison in 1866 of being in the first batch of criminals ever to have mug shots taken of them, it is certain that he was not a perfervid Monarchist. But what about his nephew, Uncle Johnny number two? What was his motivation for spending his time in dangerous France in the 19th Battalion of the Second Australian Division, some fifty years after his great-uncle's shipping?

What I do know about my Uncle Johnny, nephew of the Fenian, is that in 1913 he wrote a letter from Kempsey, New South Wales, to his sisters who were on a visit to Sydney, and said that about all that had happened in the old town was that a new door had been put on the outhouse and that 'the old town is so dead they've arranged the funeral for next Thursday'.

My Uncle Johnny's letters home from France are innocent of Monarchist effusions, though they mention all manner of events. 'Sydney. I wish I was there. France is very unhealthy at times.' (4 September 1917) Of being given a food parcel from home in which the lid had come off a tin of condensed milk, he writes, 'We had been walking nearly all night coming out of the line and none of us in too good a humour falling over broken duckboards and into shell holes full of water and dodging Whiz bangs. I was building on a good tuck in and it didn't improve me when I seen the milk all over the business.' (20 November 1917) 'At the time of writing I am having a spell in hospital with trench fever ... We have a few minutes excitement now as Fritz comes over pretty regular with air raids and bombs the town.' (18 September 1917) 'I have been exceedingly lucky up to now having gone through a lot of stunts where you would think it impossible for a fly to live let alone a man.' (15 August 1918) 'You will no doubt be sad to hear that Lt. Plummer (Jack) of Smithtown who was with my Batt was killed a couple of days ago.' (6 September 1918) 'By the way, I lost one of my old mates Barney Heffernan. You have his photo I think I sent on which we had taken when we first arrived in England. He had a fairly hard knock and died of wounds.' (28 October 1918)

He writes of the conscription referendum of 1917, 'We are all waiting very anxiously for the result of the referendum and see what sort of a time Mr W Hughes has got for his trouble.' (20 December 1917)

The 19th Battalion, like the rest of the Second Division, had come out of the lines at Passchendaele to vote in the referendum. Not only were snow and ice flying everywhere during that November poll. But the shallow valleys behind the Passchendaele lines were in places so saturated with Dichlorethyl Sulphide or Mustard Gas that the earth could not be lain upon for fear of blistering the flesh.

And then there were the standard assurances of religious observance: 'We have plenty of church going over here, our padre Father Chine is always with the boys and we have the rosary nearly every night—myself and the two young Walshes from the Macleay.' He writes too of a Scottish nurse he fell for in hospital.

Though it would be foolish to project retrospectively on him the Australian identity of the 1990s and though the ethos of the times was one which saw Australians as South British, it is significant that he never invokes in his letters the Crown or the Empire. I suspect the motivation of men such as him was well stated in Les Murray's superb poem 'Ode for the Country Soldiers'.

The king of Honour louder than of England
cried on the young men to a gallant day
and ate the hearts of those who would not go

for the gathering ranks were the Chosen Company
that each man in his lifetime seeks, and finds,
some for an hour, some beyond recall.

When to prove their life, they set their lives at risk
and in the ruins of horizons died
one out of four, in the spreading rose of their honour

they didn't see the badge upon their hat
was the ancient sword that points in all directions.
The symbol hacked the homesteads even so.

In a great and perhaps fatal communal adventure, Johnny and the others were as Les Murray says elsewhere ensuring that they drank from the 'common bowl'. They were qualifying for the world beyond the war, for an antipodes fit for the last heroes of history.

But—even in Australia's holy wars—men enlisted as well for a mixture of utterly personal motives. To get a job in bad times (a powerful motivation in 1939), to escape some impasse with a woman or a parent, to avoid the drudgery of a farm or an office, or to defeat the sempiternal ennui of living in a small town.

Uncle Johnny's letters brim with the names of other Macleay boys, vessels of ambiguity since they were human, met in trenches and transit camp, on railway stations, in hospitals. Bruce Ruxton presumes to speak for the lot of them, especially for those who were unlucky in their adventure.

And Johnny is lucky therefore that his letters remain, that he does not have to depend on such a primitive voice as Bruce's but can speak for himself in a somewhat subtler one.

When Uncle Johnny returned from France in 1919, the municipality of Kempsey awarded him a certificate, signed by the Mayor and the Town Clerk, thanking him for the sacrifices he had made for King and Country. The certificate is headed ALLIES, though it preserves the biggest print for the subscription 'Municipality of Kempsey, New South Wales'. A digger, carrying the blue Australian ensign, advances in open country with other diggers. It's an unlikely scene, given what we know of trench warfare. The waratah, bottlebrush and flannel flower, so prevalent in the bush of the Central and North Coast of New South Wales, decorate the base of the picture, where there is also a medallion of a troop ship and diggers boarding it.

There is no question that many returning soldiers must have been delighted with these certificates, as Uncle Johnny no doubt was, or at least his mother, for she had it put in a handsome, dark, wooden frame. But it had often been the case with Australians that a gulf existed between one's identity and real motives, and identity and motives as stated on certificates which invoked the civic pieties of an Australia which still perceived itself, to use Sir George Reid's phrase, as 'a colony within the Empire'.

Naturally, civic documents have to achieve a formula of simple and fundamental values. 'For King and Country' was —in the climate of 1914—a reasonable summation of those few values, just as 'Liberty and the American Way of Life' served the Americans, and 'For Duty and Fatherland' the Germans. But there was a difference between the phrase 'For King and Country' as used in England and as used in Australia. The boy in Blackpool presented with a certificate like Johnny's knew exactly what the term 'Country' meant. There were no shadowy dimensions to it. For the 'Country' whose defence was referred to in British documents was certainly Great Britain. Whereas what was the 'Country' the officers of the Municipality of Kempsey honoured in their certificate, with its representation of beleaguered France as a beautiful woman, its mingling of Australian, British and French flags, and its background of young men in slouch hats boarding troop ships?

It was an Australia whose flesh was part of Britain's mystical body. It was the Britain in which we were extreme South Britons. It was the Kingdom prodigiously offshore but intimately close to heart and to Australian hopes. It was the Empire, with Australia set as a previously under-appreciated but now (surely) validated antipodean jewel in the Empire's diadem.

Amongst the cuttings in my uncle's possession is a press report from the London *Daily Telegraph* under the headline 'KING AND HIS TROOPS—Review of Australians—Proud Record'. 'It was impossible not to praise their physique, their general air of complete fitness and their fine, swinging gait as company after company, battalion after battalion, they swept by.' A number of decorations were presented by George V that day in early 1917, a day the Australians cherished since 'April was in a sunny mood'. The medals went mainly to the AIF, but also to the Seaforth Highlanders, the Inniskilling Fusiliers, the London Regiment, the Yorkshire Light Infantry, the Canadian Force, the Newfoundland Contingent, the South African Force and the New Zealand Force. There is little doubt all these men saw themselves as having some form of kinship through the Crown.

But again, though Johnny was there and proudly clipped the article, he did not go as far as ever asserting that he was in France for the Crown's sake.

These men on parade on Salisbury Plain were clearly not directly defending Australia. Except for the period when the German raider *Emden* cut loose in Australian shipping lanes early in the war, ultimately to be sunk off Cocos Island by HMAS *Australia*, and except for an uprising by two Turkish miners in the Broken Hill area, Australia had previously needed no direct defence.

A pro-conscriptionist verse of 1917 was able to say:

Should this fair land be blighted,
Should Australia meet her doom—
Befouled, outraged, like Belgium
In the shadow, in the gloom?

But geographical location made such a question ridiculous.

So the question recurs and can't be simply answered by me or by Ruxton: to what extent were the diggers campaigning for Australia and to what extent for Britain? Some of them considered the interests identical. But it was apparent that Uncle Johnny didn't, if the sole statement of strategic motivation which occurs in his letters can be believed. He wrote in mid summer 1917: 'I think the main thing is to show the world that we can stand up. We want to show the world the stuff Australians are made of.'

I suppose the only thing I am arguing for is that the motivations of these citizen soldiers were too complex, too colonial and nationalist at the same time for anyone, bare-faced in the late twentieth century, to be able to say with confidence that these holy dead who are commemorated every evening in our RSL clubs in Australia, when the lights go down and the lamp of remembrance is lit, were in sole and final essence dying for the Crown.

What many of them were doing, however, was pledging themselves to an Australian destiny under the aegis of Britain, and in terms of the period, this was a credible thing to do. They were men who wanted Britain to prevail so that Australia could go on developing its unique society in peace and without threat. That is, they were pro-British for Australia's sake, not for the sake of blind fervour towards the Crown. They hoped for a future in which the British government would consult with Australia and New Zealand as peers in making policy for the entire Empire. They were the Imperial federalists I keep talking about. They included Alfred Deakin, Andrew Fisher and Billy Hughes.

Humphrey McQueen writes about them in a much abused book called *The New Britannia*, which seems nonetheless to have the bite of some truth. 'Australia's primary concern before 1904 was that Britain should protect her from predatory European powers; and after 1904 (because of the Japanese triumph in battle over Imperial Russia) that it should protect her from Japan.' In the national mind, he argues, British supremacy was a required factor in the flourishing of Australia.

This, says McQueen, is the spirit of Lawson's early verse, 'The Distant Drum',

> Let Britannia rule forever
> O'er the wave; but never, never!
> Rule a land great oceans sever
> Fifteen thousand miles away.

There were many other early twentieth century Australians who believe that British supremacy should be the absolute given under which Australia should pursue its own white and equal society. The first Labor Premier of New South Wales, McGowen, proposed the model: 'While Britain is behind us, and while her naval power is supreme, Australia will be what Australians want it, white, pure and industrially good.'

There is a fascinating speech McQueen quotes by the Labor member for Melbourne, Dr Maloney, in the House of Representatives in 1912.

> The seat of the British Empire is in Europe; the heart of the race is in the capital of the English world. If that be injured or destroyed then all our hopes and ideals, the greatest the world has seen, must sink into the gloom of oblivion, and the world be the poorer, that our civilisation, with all its wider life and greater opportunities, were strangled ere it had a chance.

I believe that Maloney was a nationalist, and when he spoke of 'all our hopes and ideals, the greatest the world has seen' and of 'our civilisation, with all its wider life and greater opportunities', it is unlikely that he is speaking of Nottingham or Manchester. He is speaking of Australia. The Australian Utopia existed at the limits of the earth beneath a firmament in which British power was supreme and eternal.

A similar feeling—keeping Britain or Europe secure for Australia's sake is in Henry Lawson's 'For Australia', written after the Russo-Japanese war of 1905 had ended in disaster for Russia.

> Now, with the wars of the world begun, they'll listen to you and me,
> Now while the frightened nations run to the arms of democracy,
> Now, when our blathering fools are scared, and the years have proved us right—
> All unprovided and unprepared, the Outpost of the White!

And similarly in the 'Vanguard':

> 'Tis the first round of the struggle of the East against the West,
> Of the fearful war of races—for the White Men could not rest.
> Hold them, IVAN! staggering bravely underneath your gloomy sky;
> Hold them, IVAN! We shall want you pretty badly by and by! . . .
> It means all to young Australia—it means life and death to us,
> For the Vanguard of the White Man is the Vanguard of the Russ!

The radical mentor of John Curtin, Maurice Blackburn, who would ultimately be politically destroyed in the 1940s when he wouldn't accede to Curtin's desire to conscript troops for the Southwest Pacific zone, disapproved of the Easter rebellion in Ireland and threw support behind the British Empire because, 'loose voluntary unions of states with common institutions and language are a step towards internationalism'. (This 'internationalist' argument, by the way, has been refurbished with less credibility by some of today's Monarchists, who don't have a great protective Imperial fleet to point to as an excuse for their slavishness.)

If you look at early twentieth century Australia in the light of the idea of a great British federation, then perhaps British endeavours in the Hellespont in 1915, or in France and Belgium thereafter, are not as remote from perceived Australian interests as they would seem to be to today's nationalists. It is in this light that Prime Minister Fisher's pledge at the start of World War I that we would fight to 'our last man and our last shilling' should perhaps be seen, rather than by the light of national feeling today.

The devotion to this idea began even earlier in Australian history. William B. Dalley, Premier of New South Wales, child of Irish convicts, sent a contingent to the Sudan in 1885, arguing that if there was a setback for the British in the Sudan and Egypt, the security of the robust child—Australia—was thereby threatened. The same with the Boer War and the Boxer Rebellion. 'Yet again,' writes McQueen, 'we see the peculiar nature of Australian anti-Imperialism, which accepted British domination of the world as a condition for Australian independence.'

The Imperial Federation League of the 1890s was the chief organisation for those who saw Australia developing as a province within the Empire. The League believed itself to be at the other pole from the Australian Natives Association, a body which attracted those whose focus was upon Australian development in its own right, and which was increasingly concerned throughout the decade with achieving Australian Federation. Members of the Imperial Federation League

sometimes considered the Australian Natives 'narrowly jingoistic'. But some people, including the brilliant Alfred
Deakin, belonged to both.

The *Bulletin* opposed the Imperial Federation movement,
though mainly on grounds of old-fashioned racism. 'Imperial
Federation is a monstrous plot to institute aristocracy and
privilege in democratic Australia, to destroy the decency
and livelihood of the working man by opening the country to
"leprous Mongols" and every unwashed tribe of the British
dominions.'

At least in part, Australian nationalism in the days of the First
AIF *was* often inseparable from ideas to do with Irish and
English history. Immigrants from the British Isles, *other* than
Ireland, saw their Australian nationalism mainly in terms
of the Crown and the Empire. Whereas Australians of Irish
extraction sometimes based their ideas of Australian identity
on the griefs of a small, moist, and—as everyone used to rush
to tell us during Australian droughts—'emerald island'.

The outlaw, Ned Kelly, indulged massively in this Irish
reading of the Australian identity. And his values are as much
those of Gallipoli and Anzac as is Ruxton's shallow Australian
Loyalist version.

Ned and his associates held the town of Jerilderie hostage
for a weekend in 1879. It was a very jovial weekend, marked
by Ned's casual benevolence and flashness. Hostages were
entertained—literally—in a pub.

One thing Ned did that weekend was to deposit with the
office of the local newspaper a letter known as the 'Jerilderie
Letter' which most historians, Manning Clark, Ian Jones, John
Molony, John McQuilton believe to be authentic and to have
been composed by Ned himself.

Jerilderie sits on the ancient Australian river called the
Murrumbidgee. Its riverbanks are fringed by eucalypts, and
its dead flat plains are marked by calf-high saltbush. The
rainfall is around ten inches a year in a good year. Then, as
now, it had problems of its own, and Ned had problems of his
own, purely Australian problems unrelated to the history of

the British Isles. When an Anglo-Saxon looked at a place like Jerilderie, with its courthouse in whose cornice the letters VR—Victoria Regina—were carved, he might have seen a continuity with the Empire. Ned saw a continuity with Ireland.

'Is my brothers and sisters and my mother not to be pitied also,' wrote Ned,

who has no alternative only to put up with the brutal and cowardly conduct of a parcel of big ugly fat-necked wombat-headed big-bellied magpie-legged and narrow splay-footed sons of Irish Bailiffs or English landlords which is better known as officers of justice or Victorian Police.

A policeman . . . is a traitor to his country ancestors and religion as they were all Catholics before the Saxons and Cranmore yoke held sway. Since then they were persecuted, massacred, thrown into martyrdom and tortured beyond the ideas of the present generation. What would people say if they saw a strapping big lump of an Irishman shepherding sheep for fifteen bob a week or tailing turkeys in Tallarook Ranges for a smile from Julia or even begging his tucker, they would say he ought to be ashamed of himself and tar-and-feather him. But he would be a king to a policeman who for a lazy loafing cowardly billet left the ash corner, deserted the shamrock, the emblem of true wit and beauty to serve under a flag and nation which has destroyed, massacred and murdered their forefathers by the greatest of torture as rolling them down hill in spiked barrels, pulling their toe and finger nails and on the rack and every torture imaginable. More was transported to Van Diemen's Land to pine their young lives away in starvation and misery among tyrants worse than the promised hell itself.

Ned goes on to mention many convict stations in some of which his father did time, and to say 'in those places of tyranny and condemnation many a blooming Irishman rather than to subdue to the Saxon yoke were flogged to death and bravely died in servile chains but true to the shamrock and the credit to Paddy's Land'.

Towards the end of his message, he raises the prospect that in some way he is part of a universal Irish insurrection including the American Irish. 'Would they not slew around and fight her [England] with their own arms for the sake of the color they dare not wear for years and to reinstate it and rise old Erin's isle once more from the pressure and tyrannism of the English yoke which has kept it in poverty and starvation and caused them to wear the enemies' coat.'

Ned was an early illustration of Conner Cruise O'Brien's aphorism: 'To be Irish is not primarily a question of birth or blood or language; it is the condition of being involved in the Irish situation, and usually of being mauled by it.'

Ned, like the Queen-honouring Anglo, Welsh or Scots Australian, was an illustration that colonial people inevitably do not quite know where in God's name they are. Their geographic and historic sense is the geographic and historic sense of the place they come from, and their motivation derives from the same centre.

That was certainly what influenced the relationship between Uncle Johnny and his father when Uncle Johnny returned from France in 1919. Whereas many other Australians would have taken pride in their son's service, somehow Uncle Johnny's father, my grandfather, who partook to some degree in the alternative history of the British Empire favoured by Ned Kelly, saw Johnny's enlistment in the AIF as a malign thing for an Australian boy to do. One of the motivations for Irish migration to the New World was that male descendants could thereby escape the inevitability of service in the British Army. These Wild Geese—the Irish who fought in what they considered a foreign army, for a cause they didn't always believe in—are invoked in a famous song of the Easter 1916 Irish uprising, 'The Foggy Dew'.

> 'Twas Britannia bade our wild geese go,
> That small nations might be free.
> But their only graves are Suvla's wave
> Or the shore of the great North Sea.
> Oh had they died by Pearse's side,
> Or had fought with Cathal Brugha,
> Their names we would keep
> Where the Fenians sleep,
> Neath the shroud of the foggy dew.

It must have seemed an irony to an Irish immigrant to come twelve thousand miles and find his eldest born in the same fix as the Irish at home: serving in what he saw as a British Army. To my grandfather, Uncle Johnny was one wild goose too many. And would his son be cherished and respected as an individual warrior? It seemed not. Indeed so thoroughly was the Australian Army seen, at least by the British, as a mere set of interchangeable units to be inserted into and withdrawn from British divisions at will, that a separate Australian Corps of five divisions, all serving together with the one identity, was not formed until 1918, the last year of the war.

My grandfather was one kind of Australian nationalist, the same kind as that distinguished immigrant, Archbishop Daniel Mannix of Melbourne, who uttered the Hibernian alternative version of the Anglo passions people like Billy Hughes were all to ready to spout. Mannix's version then, uttered at St John's College in Sydney in the second conscription debate: 'If I put Australia and Ireland before the Empire it is not that I love the Empire less, but because I love Australia and Ireland more.'

My grandfather and Mannix sensibly enough couldn't see why Australians had to go so far to perish in such numbers. They were Australian nationalists for the sake of Irish history. Billy Hughes and many of my grandfather's British immigrant fellow citizens of Kempsey were Australian nationalists for the sake of British history. And both sets, though they did not know it, were probably more centrally Australian than they believed the other to be. This was true obviously and supereminently of their children.

In a sense too, the story of Uncle Johnny and my grandfather was a typical story of immigrant attitudes, of the way the histories of various old countries impinge on the relationship between foreign father and native son. When Uncle Johnny did return to Kempsey, New South Wales, on the rail line which had reached it only in 1917, he went through some sort of falling out with his father. Having seen Paris and London and the pyramids of Egypt, having courted a Scots nurse while he was in hospital with trench fever, having fought in General Monash's great demonstration battle of Hamel, which was designed to teach Allied generals how to advance without the loss of half a nation's gene pool; and having walked up the road into Germany on that great day in August 1918, the exhaustion of the Germans at last permitting the upright striding posture favoured by recruiting posters—Uncle Johnny was now expected to settle down, adhere to his father's world view, and drive the grocery cart, making deliveries back and forth over the Macleay River Bridge between East and Central Kempsey.

In one version of the family myth it was what he'd been through which made him unfit for return to such a banal life. In another it was the difference of politics with his father. In reality it was no doubt a blend of both. In any case, he left home sometime in 1920, casting himself adrift. He worked on cattle and sheep stations in Queensland and New South Wales, and was heard from only once or twice in the next half century. He died in Gilgandra in 1975, remembered as an honoured member of the Gilgandra RSL, the organisation for which Bruce Ruxton rushes to speak.

When people say identity doesn't really matter, that there are other questions: the economy, social justice; and whenever anyone says that under the present system we've as good as got identity, I think of Uncle Johnny. To him questions of identity were worth fifty-five years as a kinless pilgrim. His grave is in Gilgandra cemetery. By one of those coincidences which everywhere occur, it is only fifty yards from the graves of the victims of the Jimmy Governor massacres in the Gilgandra region. Jimmy Governor is the basis for Jimmie Blacksmith.

CHAPTER TWO

*

OLD MICK, YOUNG QUEEN

I HESITATE TO write about the tone of Australian society before 1960. On the one hand it is all very remote from the young. On the other a number of good novels and memoirs have already exploited the material. But since it is all germane to the Monarchy and the young Republic, I feel I must try to make something of it.

In trying to explain to interviewers how I once took the now faintly embarrassing direction of becoming a student for the Catholic priesthood, I tell people that the atmosphere of Australia earlier this century was like that of Ulster. Religion was one part of the essential definition of every Australian. To be a Protestant was to be a player at the centre of Australian society, a participant in all those potent mainstream organisations, from the Boy Scouts to the Masons to organisations which full-throatedly congratulated themselves on their place in the Empire. It has likewise often been explained by historians and memoirists that to be a Catholic was to be under doubt, except from one's co-religionists.

Australia was already working on the question, changing both sides into the one human being without their knowing it. We *knew* we were Australians, though others kept asking us whether we really were.

The things Australians innocently but stupidly wasted their time on then! I remember the family scandals when someone *took* to a Protestant, and there had to be, after enormous clan argument and soul-searching and conferences with priests, a *mixed* marriage, celebrated not before the altar, but behind it. I remember how people said both, 'She's going with a Catholic, but he's quite a nice fellow, really'; or else, 'She's going with a Protestant, but he's really quite nice'. The sentiment uttered in both cases with a faint air of surprise, as if each camp expected of the other the full forehead horns people somehow still see on each other's heads in the slums of Ulster. As if, from some shy, lank Methodist Auntie Kate had met at the Hornsby Cricket Club dance you should look for flagrant heresy and Cromwellian malice.

On both sides, and to Australia's ultimate benefit, people bravely crossed the divide for love. It is just as well for us that it happened more regularly than it seems to in Belfast or Derry.

If you went to a Catholic school, you found no picture of the then King George VI in the corridor. You were faintly disappointed there was no Empire Day celebration, since the ritual took up class time for the lucky Proddos at the state school, that centre of the heresy called secularism. You always walked home with a bigger boy or girl, someone who could deal with the gangs of stone-throwing state school children, primitively asserting Protestant identity as if we were all still in Armagh or Glasgow or Liverpool. Sensitive young state school children, now estimable citizens of the Commonwealth, confess to having been similarly ambushed by gangs of stone-chucking Papists dressed in Virgin blue.

In 1870 Pope Pius IX, the so-called Prisoner of the Vatican, compensated himself for the loss of the Papal States by declaring Papal infallibility on matters of faith and morals pronounced on *ex cathedra*. It might have been a limited definition of infallibility, but he did it against the advice of cardinals from pluralist societies, notably American, German and French cardinals and Cardinal Newman from England. The demands of the doctrine of infallibility upon the Faithful were such as to raise suspicions in the minds of the pluralist majority, and give them—if they wanted it—a stick to beat the Catholic minority with. The solid majority were therefore able to wonder aloud about the real loyalties of Irish Australians in particular, and this acted powerfully on the motives of Catholics. They wanted to prove they were fully paid up members of the Australian family. It also drove Catholics further into a corner, and made it easier for their Ayatollahs to impose on them an education system which, though sometimes of a high quality, was itself sectarian, embattled, and therefore closed-minded.

So before 1960 there was little ecumenism either in the street or in the church.

Like all Australians my age, I remember the Australian religious wars, in which Proddos clung all the more to the sane-faced Monarch George VI as a balance to the supposed prime fealty of the Papists, which was to the squinty-eyed zealot Pius XII. God Save the King, ran the normal line, and if the bloody Pope's infallible, why can't he tell us who'll win the Melbourne Cup?

In this sense, like all my kin, I was suspected of disloyalty even as my father served the Empire two and a half years in the Middle East—Egypt, Libya and Palestine, those traditional zones of combat for Kipling's soldiers of Empire. I was in a no-win situation at the age of seven. But then my tribe had put the other tribe in a no-win situation too.

This idea that there were two competing fealties in Australia, the fealty of Loyalists to the Crown and the fealty of Catholics to the Pope, was an argument pushed so successfully that at the time of writing, I have found myself in a debate with Doug Sutherland a former Lord Mayor of Sydney, and attender of the same Western Suburbs Papist den from which I came, who lightly said in the winter of 1992 that the argument that our fealty to the Monarchy is invested ridiculously far offshore does not matter, since there are many offshore allegiances, such as the allegiance of the Catholics of Australia to the Pope.

I could only say in reply, as one who feels no fealty anyhow to that preposterous institution in Rome and to the Mannix-minded Pole who at the time of writing occupies the *cathedra* mentioned in the doctrine of Papal Infallibility, that there is a slight difference. The Pope has no mention in the British Act of Parliament to which the Australian Constitution is Covering clause 9. In Section 2 of that British Act it *is* said that 'the provisions of this Act referring to the Queen shall extend to Her Majesty's heirs and successors in the sovereignty of the United Kingdom'. In other words, it doesn't say, in all fairness, as goes the Papacy, so goes Australia. But it certainly says, as goes the Monarchy of Great Britain, so—automatically, without any input from Australians—goes Australia.

Likewise Chapter I, Section 1 does not—thank God—say that the legislative power of the Commonwealth shall be vested in a Federal parliament consisting of the Pope, a Senate, and the House of Representatives. But it does say, 'The legislative power of the Commonwealth shall be vested in a Federal parliament, which shall consist of the Queen, a Senate, and a House of Representatives'. Though the Papacy—perhaps not quite the Whore of Babylon—may have frequently and ecstatically danced with that great Apocalyptic *femme de nuit*, let us at least be fair and say that it is the dead hand of the British Monarchy which lies over the Constitution now and claims our fealty willy nilly, and that in the late twentieth century the Papacy has little to do with us, while the Monarchy still—shamefully for us—claims our total loyalty.

Even the nation's near invasion by Japan in 1942 did not pause Australia's ridiculous and inherited sectarian follies. That year my family had moved down from Wauchope in the bush to Sydney, and I had a mile to walk to school and back, risking attack at every corner, all the way down Homebush Road, between St Martha's Dominican School in Strathfield and my home by the railway line at Loftus Crescent. Darwin and Broome were being bombed, and the Japanese were about to make their midget submarine attack in Sydney Harbour. The nuns believed that the best air raid shelter was a cramped storage space under the high altar, since they innocently decided that God would not permit a bomb to hit a high altar at which the Mass was celebrated. I hated that low-ceilinged, dark place into which we huddled with our little linen bags stocked with their compulsory items of air raid equipment: two halves of a tennis ball to put over the ears to protect them, a bandage, a tin of salve, and a whistle.

One day when we were lined up to practise entry, sitting down in, and exit from this improvised shelter, my mother turned up to collect me. She told the nun that a Japanese reconnaissance plane had been sighted over Sydney, and she thought that she might take me home in case an air raid developed. A few other mothers arrived, not quite enough to make me feel easy about the special treatment I was receiving. But I was intensely grateful just the same not to have to go into *that* place.

We walked home at crisp mid morning, my mother looking skyward in sylvan Homebush Road, with its imported, Council-planted evergreens. But I was not worried by the bombers. I had, after all, my little white linen shoulder bag with everything my elders told me was needed for aerial bombardment. What delighted me, I remember, was that the streets were empty of state school children. It was a free run in safe terrain. The Japanese Air Force was not as immediate to my concerns as were certain divisions growing out of the Battle of the Boyne in 1690 and the Plantations of Ireland, particularly of Ulster.

My maternal grandfather, a barrel-chested engine driver from the Northern Rivers of New South Wales was like my other grandfather a member of the Ned Kelly school of Australian nationalism. He liked to recount quarrels he had in railway barracks in Bathurst and Grafton with locomotive engineers of the Empire Day school. He was a generous, passionate man who told me with a straight face when I was very young that the House of Hanover, as he called the House of Battenberg-Windsor, was so infested with syphilis that Queen Victoria had to wear high collars to hide the sores on her neck. This, apparently, was taken as gospel in Donegal and in certain cottages in the Northern Rivers of New South Wales. So that even in 1941, when the Monarchy rode high, when George VI walked with a humane frown on his face amongst the rubble of blitzed London, my maternal grandfather was living testimony to the truth that not everyone was reconciled to monarchical Australia. Even though, for the purposes of serving the public or joining the armed forces, his family knew they had to affirm fealty.

My grandfather's name was Old Mick. On his visits down from Kempsey, he embarrassed me by not standing in the Vogue Theatre at Homebush, when that pleasant, gentle (later historians such as Phillip Ziegler would say 'wimpish') face of George VI appeared on the screen and 'God Save the King' surged out of the amplifiers. Again, he was a caution for the Ruxton world view, and yet he was an Australian nationalist. The younger of his two sons was serving in the Air Force in New Guinea, and his other son had joined the Second AIF but been sent back to the railways as an essential war worker.

Old Mick was a large, ham-fisted, ironic, bountiful man, and when he came to our place in Homebush for Christmas in the 1950s, he always arrived laden with improbable amounts of delicacies, poultry and beer, the sole drink of ordinary folk in those days. Despite this generosity, we knew that by mid afternoon there would be a fight between himself and my Aunty Annie over the question of listening to or—when television arrived—watching the Queen's Christmas message. Aunt Annie, Uncle Johnny's sister, my father's sister too, was comforted by the platitudes of dwindling Empire and burgeoning fraternity, and kept hushing Old Mick while he uttered well-polished references to the 'Saxon yoke', to 'German interlopers', 'the Potato Famine', and the 'Curse of Cromwell'—sentiments again which would not have been out of place in the Jerilderie Letter and would fit in perfectly today with the idiom and mythology of a Republican pub in a Bogside.

Naturally, I cannot personally imagine a childhood without this unfashionable, minority, Republican view of Australian history. Later, as a novelist, I would write a great deal about the impact of the old world on the new, and how newcomers, or even first or second generation Australians, habitually used the history of the old as a lens through which to look upon the new. I suppose *Bring Larks and Heroes* was a novel concerned with such questions—very much with what I've called Ulster-in-the-South-Seas. And in *A Family Madness* I wrote of a group of people who could not help seeing Penrith, an outer suburb of Sydney, as a version, another incarnation, of Byelorussian history.

One of the things that astounds me most is how pluralism and the ordinary secular values make their claim upon people who are determined to be tribal, the claim the majority values make no matter what sentiments someone like Old Mick might express when faced with the Monarch's Christmas broadcast.

And indeed pluralism is the proper preparation for the coming Australian Republic, and sectarian impulse is not. And yet the contradiction is that I cannot imagine being the sort of Australian I now am without Old Mick's passionate input.

So sometimes in my childhood I was a player in sectarian Australia, and sometimes a player in pluralist Australia. The latter perhaps during the massively attended first post-World War II Test match series between England and Australia, as those unutterably great batsman, Bradman, Barnes, Morris, and an infant called Neil Harvey, put together massive innings against Wally Hammond's pale Englishmen. I found that the other people in the crowd of course harboured the same Australian fervour as myself. In those unimaginably bitter sectarian days before the arrival of the Reffos and Balts, I saw a gastritis-stricken Bradman join Sid Barnes at the wicket, and bat nearly all day with him, both of them scoring 234. On that miraculous day, attended by armies of schoolboys wearing those little peaked caps with school badges on them which were the fashion of the time (no kid went to such events without these emblems of identification, unless they were rough trade from the state schools), the Ulster wars were irrelevant. The muttered rumours that the Don was a Mason and therefore by definition devoted to the overthrow and disadvantaging of my tribe counted for nothing.

The Order of the Christian Brothers of Ireland, immortalised by a number of their students, including Ron Blair in the play that bears that name—*The Christian Brother*—were founded by a Waterford merchant, Edmund Ignatius Rice, in the late eighteenth century. These were the grievous years in fact leading up to the Irish Rebellion of 1798, which would bring the first shiploads of Irish political prisoners to Australia, and would lead to the abolition of the Irish parliament and the union of Ireland to Westminster. In Edmund Rice's young manhood, the Penal Laws, so impressed upon the minds of all Catholic schoolchildren in the New World by Irish monks and nuns, still operated in Ireland. Priests were subject to arrest, and said Mass on stones in laneways. As Ned Kelly was willing to tell anyone, Catholics were prohibited from attending university, holding a commission in the army, owning land above a certain minuscule value or a horse worth more than five pounds.

Edmund Ignatius Rice's purpose was to absorb the slum children of Waterford, put them in a school suit, and subvert the British intention of keeping them obtuse and supine.

Much of this founding motivation, the sense of being embattled and of needing to give the untutored a chance, still prevailed at the school I attended after St Martha's—St Patrick's, Strathfield—a huge distance from Waterford. In Strathfield we were apprised of certain sectarian facts of the kind the Brother passes on to his charges in Ron Blair's play. We were given the names of companies who would under no circumstances employ one of us—Sanitarium Health Foods figured high on that list. We were told which departments of the State government of New South Wales had fallen to the Knights of the Southern Cross, our tribe's answer to the Masons.

I used sometimes to see the Masons at summer's dusk making their way to their modest yellow temples, ordinary-looking men carrying mysterious, flat little bags, full supposedly of some device designed to prevent me succeeding in any way in Australian society. I used to see the ordinary Masonic wives in their white dresses, their face powder clotting with sweat on humid nights. They didn't quite look like the children of Satan to me. Some of them must have been at the Second Test at Sydney, and seen Bradman and Barnes lash out, and felt the same Australian zeal as I had.

Nonetheless we were warned—as the Brother in *The Christian Brother* warned his charges—not to accidentally write JMJ (Jesus Mary and Joseph) or AMDG (*Ad Majorem Dei Gloriam*— To The Greater Glory of God) by accident and from habit on top of our public examination papers. And again, like the invisible students in Blair's play, if we got the question on Italian Unification, we were never to refer to the Pope as the Holy Father, only as the Pope. If possible we were to show some delight at the Pope's loss of the Papal States, just to throw the Masonic examiners off their stride.

Australian politics was looked at in these embattled, sectarian terms. Sure, Curtin was a recovered socialist and a declared agnostic, said Brother Hines, a great Labor man. But it was a God-ordained lapse, since it enabled an electorally adequate number of Masons and Protestants to feel safe voting for him. He would come back to the Sacraments on his death bed.

Indeed this happened. John Curtin, utterly destroyed by his effort in winning the war, and with his golden society not yet broached, uttered the pitiable words, 'I'm not worth two bob. I'm too tired,' and went to his deathbed. And he *did* have a priest in, and he *did* receive Extreme Unction.

For not only did we have our Creed. We had our Labor Party, the temporal arm of God's work on earth, whose ranks we swelled. For the Conservatives *certainly* belonged to the Masons and were Anglophiles.

I can remember how this political solidarity—which carried with it a grudging respect for George VI to temper a fundamental suspicion of the British Monarchy—began to break up during the prime ministership of Ben Chifley after World War II. Chifley was a former locomotive driver on the New South Wales railways, and my maternal grandfather, Old Mick, claimed to have shared barracks in Goulburn with him.

After the war, the Communist unions on the coal fields and the waterfront undertook to destroy Australia's bourgeois democracy, and succeeded only in destroying Chifley, dividing the Labor Party, and producing in Australia such a phobia of Reds that a long—indeed a record—reign was ensured for Bob Menzies. As a result of what happened at the end of Chiff's prime ministership and in the subsequent few years, our view of the world and of the undoubtedly perilous events in Asia became fatally skewed.

I was part of that skewing. The mining unions in the Hunter Valley were able to starve the coal-fired electricity stations, and in the winter of 1949 Sydney was blacked out, particularly at night. I remember cold, black, moist evenings when my parents cooked the meal primitively on a wood fire in the backyard, as everyone else was doing. At a sunnier time of year this might have been a picnic, and it was certainly not any great hardship for children. But darkness grew habitual, echoed the wartime black outs, and became associated in the minds of an innocent populace with Communism. This darkness in Sydney was matched by a darkness falling over regions elsewhere—over Vietnam, China, the Eastern Bloc. Darkness was spreading apace.

In that black winter the Boy in the Iron Lung died at the Children's Hospital. I had been in the same ward as him in 1944, while suffering from a bout of pneumonia. Doctor Connolly of Homebush had put me in there largely to save my mother from sitting all night with me, given that she was an absent soldier's wife with a bouncing, hyperactive baby boy and a pneumonic older one. The Boy in the Iron Lung had been a hero in the ward. He was sixteen and had been there since before he turned ten, his head protruding from the steel coffin which did his breathing for him. There was a slot above his head into which textbooks were placed—I remember very clearly a Verity edition of Shakespeare being slotted there. He would call for nurses when he wanted the page turned. He had been studying in 1944 for his Leaving Certificate, and in the intervening years I had followed his career in the *Daily Mirror*.

He was doing university studies by 1949. It happened that during a prolonged blackout, emergency supplies of power could not be got to his iron lung, and he asphyxiated. So this was Communism too. Darkness and murder.

In the same winter the Boy in the Iron Lung went, a martyr to class warfare, my mother's brother, Old Mick's son Jack, who worked in the shunting yards at Merewether, was crushed to death between carriages. He was a universal favourite, my father's best friend amongst his inlaws, berserkly generous like Old Mick and with an anarchic sense of humour. My father stayed home to keep my brother and me going to school, and cooked us inept stews which we ate in the unheated darkness. So not only were Communists murderers of boys in iron lungs, they did not permit the casting of a light upon a mourning household.

Amongst the Brothers, I remember, this year signalled a change in the attitude towards Labor and the Monarchy. Some old timers who had known Premier McGirr and Joe Cahill, Billy McKell and Ben Chifley personally, remained loyal to Labor. It was a case of poor Mr Chifley crucified by the Reds. Others believed that the enemy was already within all the structures of Labor and must be fought. The Industrial Groupers were gearing up—Catholic men of Labor background to fight for democracy in union elections, if necessary by force. In dour post-war Sydney, the Industrial Groupers— telling their tales of union ballot-box protection, of braving gangs of Reds armed with bike chains, of going into battle themselves armed with cricket stumps and bike chains—were the only splash of apparent grandeur in the landscape.

The week before the 1949 election, muscular boys ran round the playground at St Pat's, by the toilets and changing rooms which were known as the Stockade, asking, 'Who are your parents going to vote for?'

You needed to say, 'Menzies', if you wanted to avoid a cuff or a Chinese burn or an arm twist. It was obvious that for the first time their parents had crossed the divide and were going to vote Liberal.

Chiff had done what no other Labor prime minister would have wanted to do—called in the troops as strike breakers. But it would not save him at the polls. He too would soon enough join Curtin in the netherworld. They must make two unquiet ghosts there.

In any case, my parents remained members of the 'Poor-Mr-Chifley-victimised-by-the-Reds' school, believers still in Chifley's Light on the Hill and his regard for *Rerum Novarum*, the quite swinging Papal Bull on social change (a rarity amongst Papal Bulls). And of course bouyed up by the fact that Old Mick knew Chiff and rightly swore by his calibre.

The idea put forward by Senator Bronwyn Bishop and others that Australians of Irish derivation are all automatically and monolithically Republican, or anything else for that matter, became a nonsense early in the Menzies era. The Irish ceased to be a tribe in the early 1950s. They saw the world about to be engulfed by satanic atheism. Joe Stalin's demi-Asiatic visage carried the smile of the cat who had already swallowed the free world's canary. The Christian Brothers' doctrine that Catholics should outbreed, outmanoeuvre and—with the use of books of arguments, such as Bishop Sheahan's *Apologetics* and Doctor Rumble's *Answers*—out-argue the less enlightened, and capture even more government departments and even a larger slab of the professions, had worked all too well. It became normal now for the Irish Australian working class to have children studying medicine, law and engineering. The propositions of tribalism were breaking down as they never had in Ulster. The last thing on the mind of the new Catholic middle class were the anti-British twitches of their grandparents or of some of the residual Irish nuns or brothers, who had tried to enrage them in primary school with tales about the Penal Laws in the auld sod.

And in contrast to Joe Stalin's smiling, rapacious features, there were the drawn but pleasant face of the ageing George VI, reinforced by his young heir, Elizabeth, who had been given a considerable visibility by her father.

She began making her own Empire-wide broadcast speeches—no doubt highly vetted by the platitude-mongers of the Palace staff—from the age of fourteen. This was a pattern she would not, when Monarch, repeat with her own children. Her first broadcast went out in 1940. 'When peace comes, remember it will be for us, the children of today, to make the world of tomorrow a better and happier place.'

In the early 1950s, in a period of post World War II optimism and with the hope of a new Elizabethan age dawning, her firm young face and unambiguous eyes looked like a far better bet than Mao or Molotov or Stalin. Even as I went off into the seminary at Springwood—named after Saint Columba or Columbkille, a Donegal-born literary and monastic hero of the Irish Dark Ages—I and most of my fellow seminarians seemed willing to go along with the majority enthusiasm for the young Monarch.

Not that many of her emblems were visible yet, for the old Irish guard who remembered the Penal Laws and the religious persecution as a personal affront had not yet died, any more than the most fervent Empire Loyalists had.

St Columba's was set in an immense acreage in the Australian bush, a Demilitarized Zone where only Catholic dogma prevailed. But secular and hedonist Australia were not far off. The seminary lay in the same sector of bush where Norman Lindsay was still painting his fleshy, Juno-esque nudes.

There was a Shakespearian tradition at the Springwood Seminary. A seminarian named Mulcahy from the North Coast had produced such a definitive *Hamlet* that everyone honoured him with the nickname. But Hamlet Mulcahy had gone on to the major seminary at Manly now. It became my duty to pick up his dropped sword, and since I'd been very impressed during the holidays by the movie production of *Julius Caesar* which starred John Gielgud, Marlon Brando and James Mason, I decided to produce a *Julius Caesar* definitive at least amongst the clergy.

I suppose I was at that stage of my life in a state of manic pietism rather like sectaries such as the Moonies or Charismatics these days. Just the same I was sane enough really to want to play Mark Antony, because of the resonating oratory his character was permitted to speak. But I felt that it would be an act of immodesty and arrogance to cast myself in that role. So I gave it to another sensitive soul, who after some six weeks of rehearsals found he didn't have a vocation for the priesthood and therefore left.

Good sense and art both cried that I step into the breach, which I did with a joyful speed.

I was dimly aware that away through the bush of St Columba's Seminary there was a new Australia a-forming, and that allegiances were shifting, and I submitted, in the order of events which had to be put before the Rector for approval, the

idea that *Julius Caesar* should be preceded, as were most Australian events, by 'God Save the Queen'. I was primitively
aware, I suppose, that the priesthood should make concessions to the pluralist majority.

This was partly due to the influence of a worldly seminarian
called Ed Campion who'd turned up that year at Springwood.
He had written for *Honi Soit*, the Sydney University magazine
and the Sydney *Sun*, and he'd brought in with him copies of
The Power and the Glory and *The Heart of the Matter*, and even
books by lapsed Catholic Communists. Campion used terms
like 'pluralist majority' all the time. He has gone on in his later
life to enchant and give great joy to that same majority. Then
as now, I don't think the hierarchy knew what to do with him.
They confiscated his Graham Greene books. But we all thought
he was marvellous, and he had a lasting impact upon all of
us, particularly on my somewhat neurotic self and on Brian
Johns, who would ultimately head Penguin and then SBS.

Anyhow it was as a contradictory concession to Campion's
pluralist majority (even though Campion himself identified
strongly with Irish history) that I proposed a verse of 'God
Save the Queen' to open the Shakespearian splendours.

The Rector always struck me as a fairly humourless man,
though it has to be said that later, when he escaped the seminary and became a parish priest, his parishioners seemed to
have a considerable affection for him. If he was miserable as
Rector of Saint Columba's, he certainly passed the misery on.
I remember one boy from the bush who was a day late getting
back from his brother's funeral. The Rector told the tardy
seminarian, 'Let the dead bury their dead.' It was a verse
which might resonate in the New Testament, but which
horrified and offended the seminarian.

But then in a sense the Rector—whose name was Monsig-
nor Charlie Dunne—knew of what he spoke. He knew that
beyond the gates of the seminary lay the beast called secularism. The term 'secularism'—devised I believe by Pius IX—
covered everything from sex to the pursuit of affluence to pop
music to films—even to such relatively staid entertainments
as the editorial pages of the *Sydney Morning Herald* and the
classical programs on the ABC. And secularism also included

an admiration for the Monarchy. Charlie Dunne vetoed 'God Save the Queen'. He told me that we were to have instead a hymn to the Virgin Mary called 'Hail Queen of Heaven'.

Charlie Dunne's decision does not seem as astounding as it might on first sight. In the 1960s Max Harris argued that it was the values which the Monarchy and the viceregal system represented for the women in the homestead that was a dominant force in the retention and popularity of the Monarchy, despite the egalitarian tenor of male society.

But it could also surely be true that *this* Monarch served as a substitute female deity of Australian Protestantism. Religion *does* tend to run to female deities, willy nilly. And here was a female deity suitable for the withering ennui of Australian life in the 1950s. The Madonna with the nice hairdo and the Hartnell hats, dressed in fine fabric which had been studiously worked down to resemble what any honest Australian matron would wear on a big occasion—her son's or daughter's wedding. The tough cabinet prefect, Menzies, who went breathless and throbbing over nothing, felt it was the right thing to go breathless and throbbing over the Queen in the early 1960s—in effect to worship her—when he said in the words of the 'old poet' that he did but see her passing by yet he would love her till he died. And so he did. No one could have been a more intense candleburner at the shrine than Sir Robert. For love of the Monarchy was a splash of excess which transcended the grim pragmatism of Australian political life or the staidness of the Low Church Protestant tradition in Australia. It was not a rational thing. The Queen was Bob Menzies' white goddess, and the white goddess of Australia in the 1950s and the early 1960s.

At the base of a lot of opposition to the Republic could be a profound filial panic at the idea of losing a female deity.

The major seminary at Manly, above the Pacific, was a fine architectural instance of transplanted Europeans not quite knowing where they were, and building a Gothic pile more suitable for an English or Irish moor than for a headland above one of the world's finest beaches, in one of the world's finest climates. Here we had to take a class called Ethics, conducted by a man called Father John Ford. Ford really used the subject as a hook for his passionate interest in the history of the Labor Party. He knew a great deal about Cardinal Moran's connection with the maritime strike of 1890 and with the Labor Leagues. The maritime strike was really a general strike involving seamen, wharvies, miners and shearers.

I suppose this was the new beginning of my very secular fascination with politics and Republicanism. For John Ford was writing a book on the development of the Labor Party from the Labor Leagues, and he set a group of us on to combing old copies of the *Freeman's Journal* of the 1890s looking for information on these protean events and on what the Catholic community thought of it all. I was politically and nationalistically stimulated by the traces I found in the old newsprint of this extraordinary workers' initiative. I was excited too by the idea that Cardinal Moran had supported the strikers in 1890. His cardinal's biretta and stole were encased in a glass fronted cavity by the chapel. The relics struck me as heroic, champion-of-the-people stuff. In many ways Moran was that. In some ways he was the usual closed-minded sectarian of his day. But I liked his bravery in 1890.

In any case, after I left the seminary a few weeks before ordination, in a state of what was called in those days 'nervous exhaustion', I was an Australian who could not understand or subscribe to the monarchical connection, its validity or its appeal, and my reasons were somewhat broader than those of Old Mick, though barely less primitive. When I served for a time in a CMF artillery unit, I appalled the Regimental Sergeant Major by asking if I could take an oath to Australia instead of the Queen. He told me to shut up and not be such a silly bastard.

I still did not know where my politics lay. I was still worried about Reds in the Labor Party, and yet I did not feel any emotional attachment at all to the witheringly inane civic pieties of Sir Robert Menzies. I remember at that stage going with a number of CMF officers to a dinner at the Combined Services Club, and raising the question of whether we ought to be able to take an oath to serve Australia, and whether the

Queen was relevant, etc etc. The officers thought it was a non-issue. When you challenged people then as now, this was what they said. It was a non-issue. They never let you know whether they were *really* attached to the Monarchy or not. Except of course for Bob Menzies, the most effusive Monarchist of Australian history, and perhaps the last great one.

As I began to write fiction in the early 1960s, I saw that the Australian government was in a new fix as regards their connection to the Monarch. They were sending troops to Vietnam, the first time we had attended a war not sanctioned by British participation. Australian servicemen who had taken an oath to the Queen were going to fight in battles the Queen of Great Britain and her government were not committed to. Donald Horne, the Australian journalist, author, academic and Republican, wrote, 'The Lord Warden (Menzies) could not pretend that he sent troops to Vietnam for the Queen's sake.'

This question itself did not seem to disturb many people at first. And its significance would soon justifiably be obscured by the napalm savagery of the war. Just the same, I wondered why other Australians did not reflect, by the napalm light of Vietnam, on the ironies of Australia's monarchical connection.

*

CHAPTER THREE

THE QUEER WAYS OF AUSTRALIA

DONALD HORNE WAS putting together a book on the Republic, and asked me to write a piece on the Australian contradiction: that we are a society who values equality as much as anyone on earth, and yet that we have had an attachment, a chronic addiction, to the great monarchical cherry which sits atop the very pyramid of British class privilege we despise, often at full throat.

So, with one voice, the ferocious bashing of British pretension:

I hope every lah de dah Pommy like you
Gets the trots when he swallows the plum.

And then, with the residue of the same breath, 'You couldn't possibly have an *Australian* as Head of State!'

I am not the first one who has tried to write about the Australian equality-vs-British Monarchy enigma. Max Harris, Australian poet and commentator, published an interesting essay on it in 1966. He quoted Joseph Furphy: 'temper democratic: bias offensively Australian'. Max argued that in the mid-Sixties, the truth of Australia was: 'temper monarchist, bias offensively British'.

And one of the reasons, says Max Harris, why this had always puzzled thoughtful observers was that Australia seemed to display a serious set of factors you would have believed would be certain to produce 'an irresistible Republican movement'.

First of these factors was that Australia began as a penal station and included on its books not only the primitively disaffected but also the most interesting of political prisoners— amongst others, Michael O'Dwyer and General Joseph Holt, Dr Margarot and the Scottish Martyrs, the Tolpuddle Martyrs and the Canadian Republicans (in whose honour Canadian Bay on the Parramatta River is named) and the leaders of the Young Ireland Movement. Secondly, Britain would not be likely to trample on separatism here as it had in colonial America. And geographic distance and the difficulties of getting an answer from Westminster should at first sight have been a spur to 'Republican movements [which] would have sprung up out of imperative social necessity if not out of psychological compunctions'. Thirdly, says Harris, there was—and still is—the democratic character of many of the people.

> But if the tenuous connexion of British government on the one hand, and the kind of people who came to Australia on the other, were not sufficient as factors in making Australia a dissentient component of British imperialism, then the psychological terms imposed by the Australian environment should have produced an Australian character and an Australian disposition hostile to the monarchy and the colonial system.

For even a bit of a Sydney gent and Boer War journalist like Banjo Paterson could write (fairly self-flatteringly):

The narrow ways of English folk
Are not for such as we;
They bear the long-accustomed yoke
Of staid conservancy:
But all our roads are new and strange,
And through our blood there runs
The vagabonding love of change
That drove us westward of the range
And westwards of the suns.

Harris then—reaching for an explanation of Australia's undefeated dependence on the Monarchy of Great Britain—rightly or wrongly puts the blame for the persistence of the Monarchy on the women in the homestead, particularly the squatters' homesteads, who saw the occasional invitation to meet the viceroy at Government House as the apogee of a life of rural struggle. He tends to blame Menzies's furious Monarchism on Menzies's mother.

'Slowly but surely it became bred into the generations of Australian men that they were at one and the same time complete egalitarians outside the homestead, country gentlemen at another time, self-centred rural politicians in the most immediate sense, and true-blue Queen's men in a larger sense.'

All this, Harris concludes, is 'no justification for sustaining a fabricated set of class distinctions that serve no purpose whatsoever in the organic culture of the community'.

Harris's explanation may be forced, although poll figures in the 1990s show that women are more attached to the Monarchy than men—perhaps they feel a sisterly solidarity with the mother of the unruly and self-absorbed brood of Windsors, given that they too often have unruly and self-centred broods. And it is true that the largest rearguard against the Republic are women who can remember the world of which Harris is writing—women now fifty-five years and older.

All that said, the puzzle remains.

As I claimed in the piece I wrote for Donald Horne, trying to argue about how equal Australia is is like arguing about the length of a piece of string. Whenever you say that Australia has the character of being an equal society, you are likely to be attacked by someone who has a tale of Australian inequity to prove his point. And how many of those tales there are in an age where compassion is considered to be a naive emotion and where economic rationalism, a sneer on its face, lays about itself, hacking Australia's fabric without anaesthetic and assuring the screaming patient that at the end of the slashing he'll be grateful!

What can be recognised about the country though is that

the *myths* of equality are still important here. Few who fail to observe them can expect popular or electoral success. As the myth of class dominates British matters, the rituals of equality are prescriptive in Australia. And both the British and we subscribe to our dominant myths, sometimes self-consciously, but mostly automatically, not aware of what we are doing, demonstrating in each case our own particular innocence.

A few years ago, while I was on a book tour in England, there was a driver from my publisher, Hodder & Stoughton, whose job was to tote me round the normal traps for pushing books, from the BBC at Portland Place to Bush House in the Strand to London Broadcasting out on the Cromwell Road, to Sky Television and to Shepherd's Bush Television Centre. On a Friday, I asked him whether he would take us down the next day to a wedding in Beaulieu Abbey in Hampshire. The wedding was that of the daughter of a British judge we had known since he was a young barrister. His kids had played with our kids, etc etc.

The reception was held in an enormous marquee in my friend's garden above the Solent.

We stayed overnight, and on Sunday, halfway through lunch, the driver turned up to take us back to London. I mentioned to someone else that it might be a good idea to get him in for some food from the leftovers of the marriage feast—there was so much of it, and Judy and I would be another three-quarters of an hour, and it was an utterly informal buffet in the dining room of the country house. Everyone seemed to approve of the idea, and I went outside to ask the driver inside. He was a Cockney, a limo owner, a king in his own borough. But he was tentative following me in the front door. I met my friend, the judge, just as we came through.

'Yes?' my old friend asked me, or more accurately, the driver.

'Oh,' I said. 'I just got Mick in for a bit of lunch, since we won't be leaving yet.'

'Of course, of course,' my friend said with a formal warmth. He led the driver up a corridor, skirting the dining room where the buffet lunch was being served. I followed. We emerged by a roundabout way into the kitchen, where my

friend the judge and knight of the realm told the cook to find
my other friend, Mick, some food. Mick was sat down at the
kitchen bench, my friend saying, 'So, you're all right then, old
chap?'

Mick said he was and thanked my friend. Indeed, Mick was
now at his ease, and everyone knew where they were. The
myth of class had been maintained. How important it was,
too, to a driver and a judge. I had unselfconsciously made my
antipodean mistake, and they without self-consciousness or
rancour or questioning or asking themselves any questions at
all, had amended it. They were simply being as English as I
had been Australian. I had astounded them with my way of
doing things. They certainly astounded me. An Australian
upbringing prepares you badly for knowing the long way to
the kitchen.

As Charles Thatcher, the nineteenth century Australian
poet wrote:

> So if you ever take a run
> To England for a bit of fun
> You're safe to astonish everyone
> With the queer ways of Australia.

There had, of course, been for a long time in Australia a
tension between equality as perceived by my friend the judge
and by Mick, and the raw equality which is a fundamental,
national impulse. My friend is certainly a better man than I
am, a more generous and ceremonious man. But I could not
help but compare his behaviour with the Australian norm:
Whitlam's and Hawke's cabinet ministers riding in the front
seat of their ministerial limos; the use of 'mate' instead of 'sir'
as a code word in Australian relationships, so that one will
find it used as easily by a prime minister to a man in the mall;
by a cabinet member to members of caucus; by a tycoon to an
executive; by a sporting commentator to an athlete; by all of us
generally to all of us generally, all of us 'mates'. Generations
of male migrants have struggled and yearned to achieve that
rough, democratic title, to be included in the egalitarian, battling, fraternal, woman-beset, heterosexual, honest-bastard
knighthood the word 'mate' implies. And in the years before

the Queensland government brought the system of knighthood into such bad odour, we got used to television interviews in which newly appointed Australian knights assured us that they would still be 'Fred', or 'Cecil' or 'Billy' to their mates.

Class certainly matters in Australia, but despite egregious examples like that of the Packers, it rarely sticks, becomes perpetual, or preoccupies the population.

My parents tell me nonetheless, and I half remember, how a kind of class, a cut-rate sense of an aristocracy worked in country towns. The aristocrats then were bank tellers, chemists, above all the country doctor, and the big cattle people from upriver. At some bush dances in Kempsey, New South Wales, a circle was drawn in the middle of the dance hall, and inside it the bush gentry danced, and outside it less preferred people. Dame Mary Gilmore records this same bush convention in *Old Days: Old Ways*. The superiority of those inside the circle was however very fragile, often only one lifetime or one good season deep. A drought or unwise investments, and they might not be able to show their faces at next year's dance, or might need to sell their place and submerge their shame by a move to the city.

And the heroes of the night were the boys from outside the circle who dragged their girls into it in greater and greater numbers, perhaps making it unworkable. Ordinary people counted amongst the most important virtues a lack of 'bush flashness' and 'piss-elegance'. It was the people who showed they clearly knew that their elegance was only skin deep, and based on a minuscule economic elevation over the rest, who were most honoured in towns like Kempsey.

It cannot be denied either that whether or not they are equal socially and economically with others, ordinary Australians have an impulse, almost a social obligation, to conduct themselves as if they were equal. This is the tradition that Nino Culotta celebrated to excess in *They're a Weird Mob*. The tradition is still cherished. 'There's no better way of life on earth than that of the Australian. I firmly believe this. The grumbling, growling, cursing, profane, laughing, beer-drinking, abusive, loyal-to-his-mates Australian is one of the few free men left on this earth. He fears no one, crawls to no one, bludges on no one and acknowledges no master. Learn his way. Learn his language . . .'

In fact, Culotta turned out to be an Irish Australian named O'Grady, so that now this passage could be seen as a robust, not perhaps entirely honest attempt to impose the myth of Australian equality on newly arriving immigrants, and to stroke it in the breasts of old Australians too.

There was a ferocious enthusiasm for *They're a Weird Mob* amongst Australians anxious for a mirror of themselves, and grateful to get one from Culotta. But this man (and woman) who 'fears no one, crawls to no one, bludges on no one and acknowledges no master,' was living under the patrician governance of Bob Menzies, the great Anglomane of modern Australia, the greatest champion and frankest admirer of British society and its hierarchical structures. And when that glorious being who is described by Culotta took public office of any kind, or entered the police force or the army, he acknowledged his fealty to the Monarch of Great Britain, one of the most abject means left in the post-feudal world of acknowledging a loyalty.

You could call Australia's passion for equality a myth not just because it sometimes stands more for what people believe instead of what they actually do; but also because the equality that exists in Australia survives with scarcely any constitutional underpinning. It is not enshrined in any Australian bill of rights.

In the late 1980s I was appointed by the Federal Attorney-General to a committee of the group of citizens named the Constitution Commission. Our committee was headed by the Sydney lawyer, Terry Purcell, and the Commission was under the overall presidency of Sir Maurice Byers and included former politicians such as Rupert Hamer, a former Liberal premier of Victoria, and Gough Whitlam, a former prime minister of Australia. Our committee had somehow managed to be appointed without a single woman member. Terry Purcell worked to have Rhonda Galbally, an executive from the Commission For the Future, an eloquent woman who needed to use a walking stick but seemed barely hampered by the damage inflicted by childhood polio, to be appointed. A commit-tee considering individual rights would have seemed pretty silly without her, and should have had other women too to show that it meant business.

I found that all my colleagues believed that Australian lib-erties were massively under-guaranteed in the Australian Constitution. In fact the Constitution of the most egalitarian race on earth went to some trouble to exclude wide-ranging rights. One of the reasons the Founding Fathers decided to reject a bill of rights for the Australian Constitution was that it could be used to overturn factory and mining legislation that discriminated against Asian and coloured workers. The unions were amongst those most vocal on this point.

And then Aborigines were expressly excluded from the Constitution. Section 41 of the Australian Constitution said that anyone who had acquired the right to vote for 'the more numerous House of a Parliament of a State' could not be pre-vented from voting for either House of the Commonwealth parliament. This would be used as the basis of giving women the vote at the Federal level, and excluding Aborigines from it. Generally Aborigines did not have the right to vote for State lower houses. The Commonwealth government, led by the charming and conciliatory Edmund Barton, decided in 1902 to extend the franchise to women. Even a conservative like Sir William Lyne said that you could hardly cast doubt on the capacity of women to vote when Australians had been happy 'to sit under the domination of Queens who had ruled well and ably'.

Manning Clark, in his *History of Australia* gives a chilling summary though of the debate on the franchise for Aborigines, conducted by largely decent men within the mental idiom of their times. Isaac Isaacs argued that

> until such time as Aborigines were thought worthy to vote for state parliaments members of the Commonwealth should not consider them worthy to vote in a federal election. No one de-murred. Chris Watson, advocate of the brotherhood of man, said he did not care how it was done, as long as those savages and slaves in the northern and western portions of Australia were not allowed to run the electorates in which they resided. No one was

tormented by the past, or about the assumption of superiority, or the right to discriminate. They were subduers ... King O'Malley declared there was no scientific evidence that the Aborigine was a human being at all. Edward Braddon remarked that if anything tended to make the concession of female suffrage worse it would be the giving of it to any of the numerous gins of the blackfellows. Only the Reverend Ronald warned them not to slide into the position of saying that because a man was black he therefore was not able to understand the principles of civilization.

The exclusion of all Aborigines from the franchise was not amended until 1967, when the Australian people voted at referendum to allow Aborigines to be counted in the Census and for the Commonwealth to make laws regarding them.

For Australians, the fragments of guarantees of freedom which exist in the Constitution apply only to the Federal government anyhow and generally do not bind the States. For example, in Section 116, the Constitution tells us that the Federal government will not pass any act to promote or prescribe a particular religion. Section 51 requires the Federal government but not the States to provide compensation on 'just terms' for any State or person whose land is compulsorily acquired. We are told in Section 80 that anyone indicted under Commonwealth law—that is, accused of a Federal crime—will have the right to trial by jury. But a coast-to-coast right to due process under State jurisdiction does not get a mention in the Australian Constitution.

Section 92 guarantees free trade between States, and is binding at Federal and State level.

Section 117 does have some bearing for the States. It tells us that a subject of the Queen, resident in any State, shall not be subject in any other State to any disability or discrimination which would not equally apply to him 'if he were a subject of the Queen resident in such other State'. That is, you can't be discriminated against in say Queensland just because you're a Victorian.

A similar scattering of guarantees exists in the Common Law—judge-made case law and precedent.

When our committee went on the road to hold hearings into the question of whether there should be some minimum liberties guaranteed in the Constitution, we found that Australians generally mistrusted systems of guarantees like the US Bill of Rights. Rightly or wrongly, Australia got a frisson out of operating in freedom without a set of written and enacted guarantees. As if somehow we had made equality up for ourselves, person-to-person. At every town meeting we had, we ran up against the belief that the Common Law, so spotty by nature, since it is made up of the decisions of judges in specific cases, is a total system of guaranteed liberties, covering every reasonable case, and far more sensible, humane and moral than the American Bill of Rights.

There is no denying that the reason this misconception goes unchallenged is partly because Australia has been a successful society, in which most citizens feel they are getting justice. Only those who have fallen through the gaps understand what the problems are.

At the time the ill-fated, much-lied-about Constitutional Commission was making inquiries and publishing its report in the late 1980s, these gaps were fairly obvious. Ombudsmen and the Administrative Appeals Tribunal gave citizens some recourse against the inequitable decisions of ministers and bureaucrats. But it was, for example, possible for a Queensland farmer, who presented a complaint to the Commission, to find his land used by the Queensland government for a canal, a pipeline, and a route for high tension wires, all without any right of appeal, and without proper compensation.

The principle of 'one vote, one value', though respected by Federal law which says electorates cannot vary in population by more than 10 percent, and though guaranteed by the laws of some States, had been regularly violated by other ones, particularly Queensland and Western Australia. In Western Australia in the late 1980s, a vote in a rural area could be worth four times an urban vote. All manner of chicanery and boundary rigging existed at the local government level too.

There is evidence that many of the Founding Fathers intended trial by jury in serious offences to be guaranteed—the commentators Quick and Garran, who knew the framers of the Constitution, imply as much. According to the original constitutional draft, the Commonwealth of Australia Bill, 'The trial of all indictable offences cognizable by any Court established under this Act shall be by jury'. But the High Court again interpreted the section as narrowly as possible, particularly quibbling over what was and was not an 'indictable offence'.

We know from the recent enquiry into Black Deaths in Custody that cruel and unusual punishment exists in our jails, but no one can invoke the Constitution as a recourse against it, though there are other laws which are meant to give protection. That right though, to recourse against the cruel and unusual, would seem to be *so* fundamental as to deserve a place in the Constitution.

Without constitutional protection then, prisoners are not permitted to vote or take civil proceedings for damages. All this is fine if you want not simply to punish but deny civil identity to prisoners. It is ironic too, in that the first civil case brought in Australia was by a convict named Henry Kable who successfully sued the captain of his convict transport for not returning a sum of money Kable had entrusted to him at the start of the voyage. Kable would probably not be able to do that now.

Without civil guarantees, heinous things happened. Under an old Northern Territory statute ultimately abolished in 1961, people charged with serious crimes could be summarily tried, or in some cases detained in psychiatric hospitals without trial 'at Her Majesty's pleasure'.

I remember while the Constitutional Commission was in progress, an egg farmer on the outskirts of Sydney, in rebellion against the State Egg Board and selling his produce outside the controls set down by the board, had his property entered by officers of the board, who smashed eggs and hutches, confiscated equipment and left a desolation behind them. Footage of their rampage appeared on the evening news. Their justification was: Other farmers obeyed the law. Why not this joker?

But was this an excuse for inhuman and undemocratic mayhem?

What the egg Brownshirts were doing was called 'discretionary power under the Act', and Australians of all stripe suffer from it regularly. We can complain about it post-factum to the Ombudsmen and—at the Federal level—the Administrative Appeals Tribunal. We have no upfront protection against it. Mate!

These are but a few examples of the limits of free and equal Australia. It is partially true just the same that the equality myth is itself a little like an unwritten constitution, one which will not protect us for ever but which has been a robust influence, so potent that Australians never question that they live in a free society—a sure sign that by-and-large they do. The cry, 'It's a free country, isn't it?' is a staple of daily conversation. The springs of equality are fed by what is still, at the time of writing, a genuine but sadly receding flexibility in our society. And of course, equality is celebrated everywhere. As the ennui of a static feudal society is the barely hidden message of *The Cherry Orchard*, 'Waltzing Matilda' celebrates the equal right of every Australian man and woman to make his own vigorous—if foredoomed—proletarian gesture.

But the fascinating question is, what sort of equality do Australians see themselves as having? And—as Max Harris asks and tries to answer—how does it come about that the Monarchy has sat so long, so comfortably with this Australian tradition? How does it fit, for example, with the fact that early in our history, our society accepted rehabilitated convicts into the highest offices; that in the 1830s, what Manning Clark calls 'the rude, egalitarian, noisy, vulgar, but magnificently alive society of Sydney' rejected the seriously proposed idea of Bishop Broughton and the Tories of an aristocracy, the extension of the British arrangement of squire and parson and tenant farmer to the Australian bush, a cry later taken up by W. C. Wentworth? How does it fit with the fact that we extended male suffrage and then female franchise earlier than nearly any other nation? And that we told the squatter to open his own bloody gate?

With such a tradition, how have we been happy with more than two centuries of dependence upon the constitutional Monarchy?

To be fair to the Monarchy and to the British tradition in Australia, it has to be said that in some crucial ways the British did not stand in the way of Australian progress. They did not impede Home Rule as they did in Ireland—New South Wales had some nascent form of self-government from the 1830s onwards, certainly enough to keep the Jeffersons and Washingtons of New South Wales pursuing constitutional means. In fact during the ferment in 1836 over the formation of a New South Wales Legislative Assembly, the *Sydney Morning Herald* took Sir Francis Forbes, the departing British-appointed Chief Justice, to task for being too democratic, for being 'cheered by convict clamour and a host of transported Jews' and for 'being an apologist for the unwashed in the corridors of power in London'. And Governor Bourke was pleased to pass on a petition by six thousand colonists to the Colonial Office with the note that the majority of colonists wanted the establishment of trial by jury and 'a legislature either wholly or in part representative'. This petition was opposed by one from four hundred worthies put together by the *Sydney Morning Herald*.

Such an experience of at least partially progressive viceroys battling the local conservative press on behalf of the unwashed colonials was totally the reverse of the Irish and the American colonial experience. (Though we will see later that John Dunmore Lang, clergyman, commentator and Republican, saw Governor FitzRoy as typical of the oppressive British governors of colonial North America.) As well, no Imperial taxes were levied as in colonial America, no trade inhibited. Progressive ideas: Chartism, Republicanism, unionism, land reform, were vigorously expressed, and none of the barriers to them which had existed in other colonies—again Ireland and America—were put in place with anything like Imperial energy. Far from inhibiting trade, the great woollen mills of the north of England, the shipyards of Tyneside and Glasgow, the food markets of southeast England, consumed just about everything we could produce. The Monarch became the symbol not only of shared values, but of shared economic interests.

So there could be seen to have once been some validity in the Monarchist cry that the constitutional Monarchy served Australia well. Even if so, though, where were the grounds for the almost religious tendency to attribute all Australian bounties and benefits to the Monarch, the Empire's mother-goddess?

The truth was that the Monarchy was a passive player in the whole business of Australian progress. It was transplanted democratic ideas from various parts of the British Isles and Ireland and elsewhere, as well as the energy of progressive Australians, which produced the results. But the concept of the Monarch as Great Guarantor, and as the symbol of the horn of plenty, has been promoted for more than two hundred years.

Tending to believe therefore that the balance of all our benefits derives from the Monarchy, Australian Monarchists claim that foreigners are not confused by the contrast between roughly egalitarian Australia and by our attachment to the House of Windsor. No, foreigners, we are asked to believe, are impressed and envious. In radio, television and press debates following the emergence of the Australian Republican Movement, John Howard, Senator Bronwyn Bishop and others always made this claim—that we were *respected* in Asia, Europe and America for retaining both the constitutional Monarch and the liberties which so palpably flowed and were—in their minds—dependent on the constitutional Monarchy.

They must have met different foreigners than I have. In my experience, foreigners are bewildered by the contrast between the unbuttoned fraternal tolerance which has been, up to now, part of the Australian national habit, and then the apparent servitorship inherent in the monarchical connection. When I first went to New York University as a visitor in 1988, teaching in the graduate writing program, I found that eventually, throughout the course of the semester, every single member of the English Department and a number of other departments as well, and every member of my class would raise with me the nature of Australian government. Yes, I would say, we're virtually a sovereign nation. But then why do you have the Queen of England? they'd ask.

It has to be remembered that when Americans think of the Monarchy they think of the frog-faced George III as depicted in the American propaganda of the War of Independence and as still depicted in their high school history books. Whereas what Australians of a certain age remember are the gentle features of George VI as he walked amidst the ruins of blitzed

London, and the wholesomeness of the young Queen Elizabeth II. The why-the-British-Monarchy question has nonetheless been raised to me by American writers like John Irving, E. L. Doctorow, Sharon Olds, by deconstructionists like Hillis Miller, Harold Bloom and Jacques Derrida. It has been raised by Israelis and Arabs, and by rebels in bunkers in Eritrea during the late 1980s. None of these were unsubtle minds, yet they thought our arrangement crazy. It is only to the blithest and most conditioned Monarchist that it seems normal—as the crazy always does if you're exposed to it long enough. Gough Whitlam's decision to style the Queen as Queen of Australia, designed specifically to deal with the world's mystification, still did not give us an explanation foreigners could follow, not even foreigners who had domestic Monarchs of their own. They persist in seeing us as at best a crypto-colony with yearnings for the continuance of the Empire. And again they always wonder why such knockabout people as us are so subservient.

Entrepreneurs like Malcolm Turnbull, the famous *Spycatcher* lawyer and merchant banker; like Franco Belgiorno-Nettis, whose company Transfield was involved in the building of the Sydney Harbour tunnel as well as in large ship building projects; and Jenny Kee, the couturier—all of them argue that doing business internationally is at least delayed if not inhibited by our needing to deal with foreigners who can't understand the meaning of our arrangement, and who presume we are—as in the early 1900s—a European-leaning, white supremacist colony.

It is my argument that we have clung to the Monarchy, against the increasing volume of contrary data the world sends us, specifically because we have a different concept of equality than the Americans. In 1987, reviewing Robert Hughes' *The Fatal Shore* for the *New York Times Book Review*, I contrasted America's first Europeans with Australia's. I argued that America's first Europeans *saw* themselves as the redeemed, whereas the first European Australians saw themselves as the damned.

This generated some letters from experts who argued that before the American War of Independence the American colonies, particularly Virginia, Georgia and the Carolinas, received great numbers of British convicts as indentured labourers. That is the case. In fact, there were members of the First Fleet, including the child-convict John Hudson, and Australia's first theatrical entrepreneur, the convict James Sideway, who were ultimately sent to New South Wales because they had earlier escaped a transport bound for the Americas. I argued in a short letter in response that American convictism had not however entered the American self-perception. Whereas for good or ill, it was central to Australian self-perception, and —if recent British attacks on the Australian character can be believed—is central to the British definition of all of us, the offspring of both bond and free, the respectable and the crass, the Monarchist and the Republican alike.

American self-perception grew out of Calvinist dissent. So did the American concept of equality. It was an equality of redeemed and elevated souls. The progress of American colonial history both encouraged and was fuelled by this self-image. The Puritan settlement of New England still feeds into the American sense of the individual, of social responsibility, of civil rights, of virtue and sin, of damnation and redemption. It also feeds the American urgency to impose redemption by American culture upon the world. This is its less admirable face, as is the tendency also to focus on the private rather than the civic virtues of candidates for office, and an ability on the part of many Americans to write off millions of homeless as— in virtual terms—the 'unredeemable'.

In the same way, our origins, colonial and penal, mark us. I believe despite the cries that Australia has grown up and has certainly long outgrown convictism, that that remarkable institution remains with us. To take up the point I made in an earlier chapter about Uncle Johnny and World War I, there was a tendency in the history text books of the 1950s and 1960s to say with a grateful sigh that transportation to New South Wales ended in 1840. It was as if from that point on, all convicts immediately stopped breathing and breeding, that they became gothic phantoms, and their substance and their input to our society was immediately cancelled and taken up by robust gold miners and land seekers. Tasmanians seemed particularly grateful to think in these terms. There transportation, and therefore the transportees, apparently became ghosts after 1855 and left no offspring.

It is highly significant that no specific attention was ever paid to who the last transportee was? We didn't want to know. In America, enormous civic energy went into keeping track of and honouring the last Confederate or Union soldier of the Civil War to die in the twentieth century. I hope some Australian energy goes into honouring the last World War I nurse, the last Gallipoli veteran.

Transportation to Western Australia did not end until 1867. Admittedly, the bulk of the last convict ship, *Hougoumont* were criminals. But who so hardened, that by the 1940s and 1950s, his passing should not have been noted with some interest or even fascination by Australians?

The truth is that by the time the last transportee had died, Australian society had not recovered from what it said it had recovered from: the obscure shame of convictism. It was not ready yet to celebrate its origins.

1980 was the hundredth anniversary of the death by hanging of Ned Kelly, Australian criminal or social bandit depending on your point of view. Ned was also, according to Sir Sidney Nolan, who did much to augment Ned's aura and to fix it in place in Australian art, a reincarnation of the Celtic god Cuchulain. In the anniversary year I went to visit East Greta, and the ruins of the cottage where Ellen Kelly and her husband, an Irish convict who had done his time in Tasmania, tried to raise their family on less than ninety acres of hard pasture land. The unremarked remains of the Kelly homestead lie on land which now belongs to descendants and in-laws of the Kelly family, the Griffiths.

As a young woman, Mrs Griffith had known and looked after Ned Kelly's brother, Jim, who had been in jail in Wagga (on what some say was a trumped up charge of horse stealing) at the time of the Kelly outbreak. Jim, son of a convict, brother of the bushrangers Ned and Dan, had been a gentle old man, said Mrs Griffith. He had lived alone, and led an orderly life. After suppression of the Kelly outbreak and the reform of the Victoria Police, he never came to the attention of the authorities again.

Mrs Griffith told me about the opening of Woolworth's in Benalla in 1938. Jim had taken some of his savings to town. It was a big event in Northeast Victoria, this opening. Old Jim went along a counter, having laid down a ten shilling note, a small fortune in the Depression years, and issued his orders. 'I'll take a dozen of those, half-a-dozen of those, etc., etc.' Mrs Griffith says she warned him against leaving his money around like that. People might cheat him.

It is easy to take a facile amusement in the idea of the young Mrs Griffith warning the brother of Australia's legendary bank robber against the malice and dishonesty of others. But what is most fascinating is that Jim did not die until 1942, when the Australians were fighting for survival on the Kokoda Trail in New Guinea and at El Alamein in the Western Desert of Egypt.

It is quite likely that far from all disappearing from our national life in 1840, 1855 or 1867, they and their children remained. Veteran convicts of Port Arthur, some of them men capable of living on into the twentieth century, were photographed in 1874. Some children of convicts may have lived on into the age of television, or even in an occasional freakish case, up until the 1970s or 1980s.

I say this not to attribute convict ancestry to everyone—that would be ridiculous. But I say it to reassert the reality of convictism. Orthodox Australian history used to imply that the gold rushes, the settlement of the land, the work of the European explorers, and the blood sacrifice of World War I, all redeemed us from convictism. I would simply like to argue with the authority of most serious commentators, including Russel Ward, Robert Hughes and Manning Clark, that convictism has never gone away. 'There is no monument of any kind,' writes Hughes in *The Fatal Shore* 'to the men and women of the First Fleet, and none appears to be planned ... Yet despite neglect, amnesia and a thousand unconscious acts of censorship, the System did continue to flourish in popular memory.'

The Australian European Adam and Eve, as distinct from the perceived American Adams and Eves of the *Mayflower*, wore not redemption on their foreheads, but the mark of their crimes. They were for example the young thieves, Henry Kable and Susannah Holmes. Kable, with his father and another man, had been condemned to death in Norwich for house breaking. According to Kable family tradition, Henry was pardoned on the scaffold in view of his youth—he was nineteen at the time of his sentencing. In Norwich prison he met the adolescent Susannah, whose crimes were more modest and who would not have been transported if kindly jail visitors hadn't decided it would be the best thing for her, given that she was carrying Henry's child.

Their lives would exemplify the ambiguities of Australian transportation and the redemptive capacity of Australia itself. But on the Sunday after Susannah was landed, and the Reverend Johnson married them in the Rocks, yes, they were detritus. They were robust detritus—Henry would bring the captain of the ship to court for not returning to him fifteen pounds raised by subscription from charitable Norwich people. He won Australia's first civil case before Judge-Advocate David Collins. He and Susannah served their time, raised ten children, went into partnership with another convict, James Underwood, in sealing ships, held the first brewing licence in New South Wales, etc., etc. Model convicts and model ex-convicts, though they had liquidity problems in mid life. Susannah lived until 1825 and Henry till 1846. Their descendants were distinguished Australians, hundreds of whom celebrated the bicentennial of Henry's arrival at Kable's Restaurant in the Regent Hotel in Sydney in 1988.

For most of Australia's history, though such people would have been considered in the light of having redeemed themselves, they carried what the young Sir William Molesworth, chairman of the Select Committee on Transportation, called in 1838 'the stain of convictism'. William Charles Wentworth, whose mother was a convict called Crowley, would know all about the stain also. His hopes of a British baronetcy were blocked during his 1854–5 visit to London by the gossips of Whitehall who 'were talking behind his back about whether he looked like other ticket-of-leave men'.

It is my argument that—particularly given the unconfronted and subliminal phantoms of Australia's own Peculiar Institution of convictism—Australians still tend to see the robust equality they share as the equality of the fallen, the spiritually defeated, the venal. Our penal origins, our cultural conditioning as what A. D. Hope called 'second class Europeans' who 'pullulate timidly on the edge of alien shores' and as people who got into further trouble trying to find European parallels on a continent which was the Anti-Europe—all this has made us cry too easily *Who amongst us is worthy?* Our dependence on and belief in Britain would have been explicable purely in the reasonable terms of our being a colony and looking like all colonies to the Centre. But it was accentuated by a profound sense of being associated with fallen people, and by a sometimes saving, sometimes perilous cynicism about our civic instincts and about the probity of all public officials.

This rugged self-mistrust has saved Australia from demagoguery and political excess. But it has also induced in us a near mystical belief that we need an outside source to provide a holiness and authority for our institutions. We seek a transglobal light to shine on us from another hemisphere, from across the Equator, and endow the irremediable squalor of our institutions with some meaning, validity and solemnity. The equality, therefore, which Australians see as uniting them tends to be an equality of fly intent and mean motivation. Our atavism tells us that only the closest thing to heaven, a Monarch by the grace of God, could save our sordid little parliaments and institutions from themselves.

In fact, the idea still pushed by Monarchists is that our institutions developed only as a result of the Crown's benign influence. It is well expressed in an essay by the modern Monarchist (if the term isn't an oxymoron) and political scientist J. B. Paul. Paul writes in *Quadrant*, 'Those who would argue that a link with the Crown symbolizes a continuing colonial dependency ignore the fact that Australia's emergence as a fully independent nation, was fostered under the

Crown which is a no less fitting symbol of that development.'
While this is a technically coherent view, it is not one which
would appeal to nationalists, for it seems to give the merit
for what has happened to Australia, to an institution whose
physical representatives have been, as the occupiers of high
office, particularly hereditary high office, a string of Anglo-
Teuton nobility of great stamina and marked enthusiasms—
whether the enthusiasms be for horse flesh as in the case
of George V and Elizabeth II, for Lily Langtry in the case of
Edward VII, or for the condition of Welsh miners and grand
passion as in the case of unhappy Edward VIII, the only one to
abdicate the throne, and with it his sovereignty over Australia.

And it is to this institution and its sometimes lacklustre
occupants that the merit for Australian success has been
attributed. The very argument is naive. It could even be
argued that it shows ignorance of British history, during
which democratic institutions wrested their power from the
hands of unwilling Monarchs. The only thing British kings
and queens could be credited with in Australia would seem to
be the passive virtue of not attempting through their own
influence to inhibit Australian impulses.

But even to say that is not quite the truth. In 1931, the
Australian government of James Scullin wanted to appoint the
Australian jurist Isaac Isaacs as the new Governor-General.
George V did not want to appoint him. He asked for a list of
names from which he could, as had been the practice up to
now, make a choice. He wanted solid British men, or at least
an Australian who could be admitted to the Melbourne Club,
from which, because of his Jewishness, Isaacs was barred.
The British Prime Minister Ramsay Macdonald asked Scullin
to back off until the thing could be resolved face-to-face at the
Imperial Conference in London, the one which would produce
the Statute of Westminster. Scullin would not wait. He was
attacked by the Opposition, who flayed him for his 'strident
and narrow Australian jingoism'. Manning Clark writes, 'The
conservatives, as ever, were "not now" or "some other time"
men.'

Isaacs was appointed, and knighted. The King deliberately
altered the Proclamation posted at Australia House, changing, 'His Majesty George V is graciously pleased to appoint' to

'His Majesty George V appoints'. But an Australian precedent was set.

The most astounding aspect of Paul's argument—the usual 'we are a crowned republic' argument generally uttered with a straight face by Monarchists—is that it tells us that the supreme and only viable symbol of our independence as a nation is a symbol of dependence and of subjecthood! We are independent because we are dependent! We are citizens because we are subjects! Our allegiance to Australia operates only because we have allegiance to the Monarchy.

So whether it be parliaments, professional groups, hospitals or golf clubs, the Monarch is seen as somehow essential to either their status, their seriousness, or their viability.

It has to be concluded, therefore, that to the nation of rough equality, to be a subject has seemed a more valid destiny than being a citizen. Until recently, most of the public documents of our lives—passports, service enlistment papers, etc.—said so. At the time of writing, we are in a sort of limbo and the question is still fudged. Our passports shy clear of giving us explicitly the decent title of citizen.

For the allegiance our institutions and their members owe is—according to the oaths which officials of all kinds take in Australia—to the Monarch.

During a hearing of the Constitutional Commission in Perth, a young American immigrant to Western Australia appeared to say that he was appalled at the way officials, elected and appointed, refer to Australian citizens as 'members of the public'. He said he saw it as placing Australians in limbo between citizenship and subject-hood. 'Members of the public' was the safest, but far from exalting description of our condition.

It would be naive to argue that the coming of a Republic would prevent all misuse of official power. But an excellent start on upgrading the position of all Australians would be to make certain that Australians cease to be 'members of the public' and become, beyond any doubt, citizens.

CHAPTER FOUR

*

THE FELLOWSHIP OF FOLIAGE

THROUGHOUT THE WORLD, in a number of centres from Houston to Besançon, from the Nouvelle Sorbonne to Aarhus in Denmark, there exists departments of Commonwealth Literature. One of the premises on which these departments are based—apart from the reasonable ambition and generous intent of the academics who teach in them—is that there is a continuity between the experiences of, say, Patrick White of Australia, Wole Soyinka of Nigeria, and V. S. Naipaul of Trinidad. White and Naipaul, unlike Soyinka, never spent time in prison, though White, in particular, saw himself as something of a prisoner in another sense.

One of the aspects of continuity between all Commonwealth writers up to this point of history is that they were raised with a sense that they were on the periphery, and that there was a Centre where everything was done essentially better than they could do it, whether it be a matter of dining, of vowels, or of cultural sensibility.

This dream of the Centre, and of the inappropriateness of

one's colonial location, is unlikely to go on providing a basis for comparing Commonwealth writers in the future. Australian writers younger than, say, Peter Porter or Clive James, have lost that old sense of the Centre. The Centre is now, for an increasing number, Asia or Sydney or New York, or even better, where they are themselves at the moment. David Williamson's play *Emerald City* dealt with the viability of Sydney over Melbourne as if they were the earth's only two golden cities.

As you will see, I will not argue that Australians are utterly secure in their own culture. That's why we have Commonwealth literature. Our identity is astray. Our public symbols have little to do with the reality of our souls. As Les Murray wrote in *Republican Australia* in 1977, we have 'a vernacular culture'.

> We're not flag people. We express our identity much more in images of drovers and bush eccentrics, surfers and skindivers, diggers and mining ventures, and big wins on the TAB. We are a vernacular culture, and the yarns, and the accent they're told in, are our flag. I do not say, though, that the vernacular elements are enough in themselves ... without a genuine national symbolism and without a declaredly independent form of national government, they will remain incomplete, as it were stunted and robbed of their creative potential. They will be a sort of museum culture preserved for sentimental reasons.

This is, I confess, not an original thought, but I see the European history of Australia, up to this point, as a long struggle by the European sensibility to find a purchase, a spiritual home in Australia's wantonly anti-European strangeness. Australia was not really the Anti-Europe either, though people saw it that way. The most disconcerting thing was that it was itself, and it didn't give a damn for Europe.

Sometimes, finding no handhold, no European template, people gave up in disgust. The first Lieutenant Governor of New South Wales, who was also Commandant of the Marines on the First Fleet, a Scot named Major Robert Ross, comes up, in the midst of a moaning letter back home to Undersecretary Nepean, with a remarkable and passionate perception: 'I do not scruple to pronounce, that in the whole world there is not a worse country than what we have yet seen of this; all that is contiguous to us is so very barren and forbidding that it may with truth be said—here nature is reversed, or if not so, she is nearly worn out . . .'

Robbie didn't know what the Australian situation was. He needed to give Nepean alternative choices. And you can almost feel that, struggling for expression in his tent, he still can't get at how weird the damn place is. And yet—on the other hand —he is in Sydney Harbour, tourist dream of the late twentieth century!

An early defeated observer, Barron Field, trying to get a purchase on the place, wrote of a visit to the Blue Mountains:

> The King's Tableland is as anarchical and untabular as any His Majesty possesses . . . Jamison Valley we found by no means a happy one. Blackheath is a wretched misnomer. Not to mention its awful contrast to the beautiful place of that name in England, heath it is none. Black it may be when the shrubs are burnt, as they often are.

In other words, despite the brave Imperial names attached to geographic features, Australia gave offence to many from the start. To quote Field again, 'The common consent and immemorial custom of European poetry has made the change of the seasons, and its effect upon vegetation, a part, as it were, of our very nature. I can therefore hold no fellowship with Australian foliage.'

Only a firm connection to the British order of things through labelling could half-redeem the Australian landscape from its offensive self-ness.

Barron Field's best known utterance of abhorrence and exasperation is found in his book of verse, the first published in Australia. That is, the country's first verse-work declares verse impossible.

> Kangaroo, kangaroo!
> Thou spirit of Australia,
> That redeems from utter failure,
> From perfect desolation,
> And warrants the creation
> Of this fifth part of the Earth.

And then, more serious than mere abuse, Field wonders whether Australia has the same theological standing as the rest of Creation:

> Which should seem an after-birth,
> Not conceived in the Beginning
> (For God bless'd His work at first,
> And saw that it was good),
> But emerg'd at the first sinning,
> When the ground was therefore curst;—
> And hence this barren wood!

This is a very serious denial of legitimacy, and denial of legitimacy has been one of the habitual Australian mental games, the belief that we are not legitimate enough to have our own Head of State being only one manifestation of it.

The tone of this passionate alienation has a more loving and more recent echo in A. D. Hope's famous 1938 poem, 'Australia'.

> They call her a young country, but they lie:
> She is the last of lands, the emptiest,
> A woman beyond her change of life, a breast
> Still tender but within the wound is dry.
>
> Without songs, architecture, history:
> The emotions and superstitions of older lands . . .
>
> And her five cities, like five teeming sores,
> Each drains her: a vast parasite robberstate
> Where second-hand Europeans pullulate
> Timidly on the edge of alien shores.

Yet after the despairing imagery—as much to do with women and ruination as was Lawrence's, and not far in sentiment from Robbie Ross's statement of alienation—Hope ends with the defiant prospect that from this 'Arabian desert of the human mind' perhaps 'the prophets come'.

The best hope therefore is for a cultural Moses or Mohammed, since the ambience still seems to be inappropriate for the European soul.

A. D. Hope's perception accorded with that of D. H. Lawrence, during his visit to Australia in 1922. In *Kangaroo*, you can find the same denials, the same sense of failing to get an answer, as in Barron Field.

'Como,' said the station sign. And they ran on bridges over two arms of water from the sea ... a bit like Lake Como, but oh, so unlike. That curious sombreness of Australia, the sense of oldness, with the forms all worn down low and blunt, squat. The squat-seeming earth. And then they ran at last into real country, rather rocky, dark old rocks, and sombre bush with its different pale-stemmed dull-leaved gum trees standing graceful ... It was virgin bush, and as if unvisited, lost, sombre, with plenty of space, yet spreading grace for miles and miles, in a hollow towards the west. Far in the west, the sky having suddenly cleared, they saw the magical range of the Blue Mountains, and all this hoary space of bush between. The strange, as it were, *invisible* beauty of Australia, which is undeniably there, but which seems to lurk just beyond the range of our white vision. You feel you can't *see*—as if your eyes hadn't the vision in them to correspond with the outside landscape. For the landscape is so unimpressive, like a face with little or no features, a dark face. It is so aboriginal, out of our ken, and it hangs back so aloof. Somers always felt he looked at it through a cleft in the atmosphere; as one looks at the ugly-faced, distorted aborigine with his wonderful dark eyes that have such an incomprehensible ancient shine in them, across gulfs of unbridged centuries. And yet, when you don't have the feeling of ugliness or monotony in landscape or in nigger, you get a sense of subtle, remote *formless* beauty more poignant than anything ever experienced before.

'Your wonderful Australia!' said Harriet to Jack. 'I can't tell how it moves me. It feels as if no one had ever loved it. You know what I mean? England and Germany and Italy and Egypt and India— they've all been loved so passionately. But Australia feels as if it had never been loved, and never come out into the open. As if man had never loved it, and made it a happy country, a bride country—or a mother country.'

When Harriet asserts that she would love it if she were an Australian, Jack replies,

'I'm afraid most Australians come to hate the Australian earth a good bit before they're done with it. If you call the land a bride, she's the sort of bride not many of us are willing to tackle. She drinks your sweat and your blood, and then as often as not lets you down, does you in . . . They (Australians) treat the country more like a woman they pick up on the streets than a bride, to my thinking.'

Whenever texts like this are read in public, Australians rise with a slightly suspect indignation and say they never felt like this. Good for them. But one wonders how many immigrants and visitors have felt like Somers and Harriet and Jack. And even if no one feels like that any more, what does it say of our ability to find ourselves, locate ourselves, identify ourselves in this continent?

It is not only the writers, native and visiting, who have cast doubt on Australia's legitimacy—to grab D. H. Lawrence's terms—as 'a mother land', 'a bride'. In 1988 Patrick Mc-Caughey, Australian curator of the Hartford Atheneum, gave a lecture at Yale in which he argued that Sidney Nolan and Russell Drysdale painted Australians, often solitary males, as if they were Orpheus descended into the Underworld. That sense of descent into Hades is there in Nolan's Burke and Wills paintings as vividly as it is in Patrick White's *Voss*. These two great Australian artists, whatever their animosities towards each other, had that in common.

McCaughey argued that by 1988 such a conception of the European Australian was out of date, however triumphantly realised it had been in Nolan's paintings. Rightly or wrongly, McCaughey had attributed Sidney Nolan's persistence in looking upon Australia as Hades as a result of his living so long out of the country. I do not quite accept that—McCaughey is an expatriate, but that in no way disqualifies him from commenting on the society in which he developed.

But I believe it is just to say that by 1988 the young had moved on from the Hope-Nolan-White view of Australia as of its essence a venue of exile and alienation. Writers of the 1960s such as Thea Astley, Randolph Stowe and myself, were probably the last to subscribe utterly to the idea of Australia as a purgatory for sensitive souls. We had our reasons: we were massively influenced by Patrick White anyhow. But then, as other Australians of our generation, we had heard our elders speak of the Northern Hemisphere as home, our teachers speak of the centre of Australia as the Dead Heart; and we had seen many of our peers flee the country pleading its essential cultural desolation. 'The Arabia Deserta of the human soul.'

In the era of Vietnam, social realists, writers who praised the proletarian virtues of Australians battlers, were out of fashion. The profoundly exiled Voss, doomed explorer, and the Jewish refugee Himmelfarb of White's *Riders in the Chariot*, the Barrenugli (Parramatta) suburban human sacrifice as Voss had been the Central Australian Christ, were the model of the Australian soul. As the Australian Jack said in D. H. Lawrence's train in *Kangaroo*, some sort of price, some destruction of the soul, was inevitable in Australia.

At the same session at which McCaughey spoke, an Australian writer-academic attacked Patrick White for exalting such figures and portraying Australians as a *massa damnata* (damned mass) of spiritual *untermenchen*. The simple truth is I think kinder: that Nolan and White were the supreme interpreters of the Age of Exile in Australia, and that you have to get through the Age of Exile before you reach the happier celebrations. The younger McCaughey and younger writer-academic were members of the party of celebration and could point to such painters as Margaret Preston (who was a celebrator before it was the dominant fashion), Fred Williams, Brett Whiteley, and to such writers as Judith Wright, Les Murray, Eric Rolls. Other writers still—David Malouf, Elizabeth Jolley, Frank Moorhouse —did not even address the question of whether Australia was heaven or hell, home or exile. They had grown beyond it. The question did not apply.

But back to Commonwealth literature, which apparently exists, since there are regular lectures at the Commonwealth Institute in Kensington High Street in London as in other centres.

In the childhoods of Commonwealth writers, literature was mediated to the colonies and Dominions along the normal lines of communication and supply of the British Empire and

Commonwealth. Under that old beast the Cringe—as it then was, and as distinct from how it now is—we barely considered ourselves to possess a native literature: or fundamentally, most of us considered the question of a national literature not to be on the national agenda. Other things were. No Australian may have written *Paradise Lost*, but Bradman had run up a score of 300 six times in a stellar career. That sort of thing was our metier.

While the literature we were presented with in our age of antipodean exile was perfectly sublime literature, it did not in any respect touch upon my own life, nor could I find myself establishing an intimate, as distinct from a fantastical, parallel between the lives of the people in the books and my own experience of a country town in New South Wales and the western suburbs of Sydney. I kept trying to *think* myself into seasons of mists and mellow fruitfulness, but Australia remained maliciously bright. I tried to see *La Belle Dame Sans Merci* in various local girls, but they told me to cut it out and stop being a drongo. We had a Prime Minister whose advice was pretty much to stick at what we were good at: cricket, fine wool, and game self-sacrifice in foreign wars.

At a stage when *Ulysses* was still obtainable only for bona fide university study, in an Australia which was girding its loins to ban *The Catcher in the Rye*, I happened to find—or was led to by a teacher—Joyce's *A Portrait of the Artist as a Young Man*. In all other literature I had read—ripping yarns by Rolf Boldrewood, Marcus Clarke, Louis Becke, Rider Haggard or Captain W. E. Johns (creator of Biggles), the colonial youth was as fervent about the Imperial Centre, about being brave for its sake, about replicating its values, as the Briton ever could be. But Stephen Dedalus wasn't like them, and the fact he wasn't came to me as a thunderclap in Homebush, NSW in 1952. Stephen's soul did not work by specific Imperial values. It found a *modus vivendi* for itself between the absolutism of the Church and the civic values laid down by the official Empire.

Observing Stephen do that, I felt the sharp but imponderable joy of identification. I, too—like Stephen—had grown up in a colony, albeit a younger and in many ways more liberal one than Joyce's Ireland. My ambiguity about nation, about being Australian, was exactly replicated by Stephen's ambiguity about being Irish, about what he owned under that title, and therefore what he could accept from the occupying culture, and what was unacceptable.

But when I re-read *Portrait* in 1991, under the terror of having to give that paper in Dublin, I saw that it went into a further aspect of the colonial soul. If you are a colonial you can never tell where the gaps between the Imperial-colonial model and the nationalist one begin and end. You can never tell what you own and what you do not.

I remember having a conversation with an Australian critic about what terms and idioms were really Australian, and what were imported. We had an argument over some items of idiom which he claimed were purely Australian. (For example, the bush practice of calling 'dinner' 'tea'.) I argued that this was a British and Irish working-class usage, though he seemed convinced that it had somehow arisen spontaneously from the Australian gift of cutting away all pretension. The very fact, of course, that we were having such a discussion in the late twentieth century, showed that we were both still afflicted by the uncertainties which had first befallen us in the classrooms of our childhoods.

And there is a similar argument in *Portrait*. It occurs in an upstairs room in St Stephen's Green, where the university Dedalus and Joyce attended, University College Dublin, operated in a series of roomy townhouses on the western side of the Green. Stephen Dedalus, the undergraduate, is talking to an English Jesuit, the Dean of the college, who is lighting a fire in the very same lecture hall where the Joyce Summer School is now held. He is engaged in a smart alec Thomistic conversation about whether you can be an aesthete and at the same time avoid heresy and 'save your soul'. This used to be a favourite subject of young Jesuit-educated ethereal lads.

In the middle of all the talk, flashy Stephen invokes the light of Aristotle and Thomas Aquinas. And the Dean in return invokes a banal image.

—To return to the lamp, he said, the feeding of it is also a nice problem. You must choose the pure oil and you must be careful when you pour it in not to overflow it, not to pour more in than the funnel can hold.

—What funnel? asked Stephen.

—The funnel through which you pour the oil into your lamp.

—That? said Stephen. Is that called a funnel? Is it not a tundish?

—What is a tundish?

—That. The . . . the funnel.

—Is that called a tundish in Ireland? asked the Dean. I never heard the word in my life.

The incident causes Stephen to think,

The language in which we are speaking is his before it is mine. How different are the words *home*, *Christ*, *ale*, *master*, on his lips and on mine! I cannot speak or write these words without unrest of spirit. His language, so familiar and so foreign, will always be for me an acquired speech. I have not made or accepted its words. My voice holds them at bay. My soul treads in the shadow of his language.

Like Stephen—and this again was until recently the binding and communal factor of so called Commonwealth literature—the colonial is uncertain about the sense in which the language belongs to him, and whether it belongs at all.

Later, again, of course, Stephen consults a dictionary and finds that 'tundish' is after all an English word, brought from England in an earlier century and ending up stranded there.

It is the nature of colonised people not quite to know where the border lies between the words they own and the words owned by the centre. Mark O'Connor the Australian poet speaks in terms like those of James Joyce when he describes the English language as one which has a name for every minute flower in an English hedgerow and yet brought one blanket word for the entire diversity of Australian vegetation—'bush'. The English language has undergone a transmutation here as Australians came mentally to adjust themselves to the continent. And the more the language was adjusted to Australian reality, the less Australian writers and Australian English speakers could be covered by the blanket term: Commonwealth literature. We were making a fellowship with the foliage, and it was an experience unique to us.

'O gentle, gentle land,' wrote the farmer-poet David Campbell,

Where the green ear shall grow,
Now you are edged with light:
The moon has crisped the fallow,
The furrows run with night.

This is the season's hour;
While couples are in bed,
I sow the paddocks late,
Scatter like sparks the seed
And see the dark ignite.

O gentle land, I sow
The heart's living grain.
Stars draw their harrows over,
Dews send their melting rain:
I meet you as a lover.

David Campbell, at least, was at home. He had fellowship with the foliage.

★

CHAPTER FIVE

A Sunday with Neville

THIS IS AN account of how the most recent phase of Australian Republicanism, the Australian Republican Movement, began. I first heard the proposition of founding such a body from the lips of Neville Wran.

To say that figures like Neville Wran and his partner and fellow-Republican Malcolm Turnbull are controversial is a little like saying that Barry Humphries is mildly amusing. But I cannot satisfy those who want to hear the prominent maligned. I can write about such men only as I know them.

In my experience it was typical that Wran should have been concerned about the current constitutional arrangement by which the Queen of Great Britain (or according to the Styles and Titles Act, the Queen of Australia) is automatically Head of State of Australia. This was, he said, 'bloody disgraceful'. (I believe that Franca Arena had been urging him to propose a Republican committee for the previous few years.)

There were of course people who said *he* was bloody disgraceful, although they were generally people who didn't know him. If he had a fault it seemed to be that he placed prodigious weight on old-fashioned mateship. His creation of the Lionel Murphy Foundation to honour his late friend and provide in Murphy's name scholarships to young Australian lawyers seemed to me to bespeak Wran's fundamental seriousness when it comes to the defence of a friend's name and stature.

To begin, I suppose my main connection with Neville Wran derived from the fact that his wife, Jill Hickson, was my literary agent. I had approached her to see if she was willing to negotiate fees for any articles the Australian press asked me to do. Often the editors in question were friends—the red-headed, Croatian-derived buccaneer Max Suich of the *National Times*, the *Sydney Morning Herald* and then the *Independent*, or states-manlike Chris Anderson, editor in chief of the *Herald* in the years before it became star-crossed, or June McCallum, editor of *Vogue Australia*. I was not game to ask them for the fees I considered just. Now Jill did it for me. She was an energetic agent and a first class negotiator.

She and Neville Wran made a remarkable couple. Given his reputation for parliamentary toughness, I found the ardent regard he had for her touching. 'Jillie,' he would warmly intone in his politics-wrecked voice.

Potent mythologies attached to the Wran-Hickson menage. Where I lived, in the electorate of Pittwater, everyone seemed certain Wran was involved in unnameable and baroque ploys too subtle to be caught in the net of the Street Royal Commission, which had exonerated him of charges of trying to influence a magistrate in a matter involving the disgraced head of the Rugby League, Kevin Humphreys. You would hear in Sydney too tales told of both Wran and Hickson, tales to do with their relationship, with their network of friends and influence, which in my consistent experience were disproved by acquaintance with them.

Wran is as contradictory as the nation itself. As a member of the New South Wales Right of the Labor Party, a faction which was Australia's answer to Tammany Hall, he was the inventor of blowtorch-to-the-belly politics, and possessor of the fly nickname Nifty. He nonetheless transformed Sydney during his ten year premiership, leaving it an immensely more urbane place, a city of accessible events and of public art. The great open air performances of the Sydney Festival began in the Wran era. And though Wran did typify Balmain larrikinism and the larrikin end of the Sydney Bar, he had sophisticated interests.

I remember an elegant speech he gave at the Holdsworth Gallery on a Sunday in 1987 about his enthusiasm for Judy Cassab's abstracts. That afternoon, I met him again at the Balmain—Canterbury Rugby League Grand Final, where he made another competent speech to the League constituency. For his tenth anniversary as Premier, he asked the number-crunchers of the New South Wales Labor Party to give him a Lloyd Rees landscape of Sydney Harbour. It hangs in his house at Woollahra, with the Nolans and Blackmans and Hermans he and Jill have collected.

I suppose one of the things I am trying to say was that there was more than a provincial vision in Wran. He saw Australia not so much as an item in the British Commonwealth but as a nation with its way to make in the world. He had established a special relationship with the government of the Chinese province of Guangdong. Since I was a Sydney member of the Australia–China Council appointed by Andrew Peacock, I was sometimes present in the State Office Block high above Sydney Harbour when New South Wales entertained Guangdong officials, and Chinese interpreters bravely tried to translate Neville's robust English into Cantonese for the good of commercial, technical and cultural exchange.

There were also Neville Wran's annual Premier's Literary Awards, the first of their kind in the nation, thorough-going bashes where writers from all the States were honoured. Neville always attended and spoke at them with his characteristic pungency. It was a matter of fierce literary pride to be invited.

I have spent a little time on this sketch of Neville Wran because it was not a surprise to hear from him the idea that a committee of prominent Republican citizens be formed who could not be written off as—to quote the usual cant—'fringe ratbags'.

The day I first heard the idea of such a committee expressed by Neville Wran was one of those lotus-eating spring Sydney Sundays in late September of 1989. Jill Hickson had asked my wife and me to come to lunch at the Hickson-Wran household in Woollahra. The other guests were Edmund Capon, the director of the New South Wales Art Gallery, and his wife Joanna, who in her own right was an expert on Chinese art. Hence interest in Asia, in Australia's relationship to it, was to be pretty high at that lunch table. Edmund Capon was, of course, sated with paintings, but I always begin every visit to the Wran's house with a sweep of the art. There are plenty of similar collections in plush Woollahra, but I came from the Northern Beaches where, excepting Morris West's place, the intramural art of houses was more modest, all the art being external—the dazzle of Pittwater, or else the variations of surf on grand beaches like Whale and Bilgola.

Wran's conversation at the lunch which followed my reconnaissance of the art was first of all about Guangdong. The Prime Minister, Bob Hawke, had wept at a recent parliamentary memorial service for the dead of Tiananmen Square, and though Wran thought that the gesture was decent and justified, he wondered why Australian parliamentary tears had been so sparse over the depredations of the Indonesians in Timor.

I had recently seen events as frightful as the Chinese massacre, since I had four months before come back from Eritrea where Africa's greatest and most ignored war had been in progress: Mengistu of Ethiopia attempting to crush the Eritreans with Africa's biggest army and air force. This war was the engine which produced the cyclical famines of the region, but went almost totally unreported and unnoticed. (It has to be said in fairness though that Bob Hawke's government had been generous with efficiently distributed aid to Eritrea, without which the situation would have been utterly unspeakable. Hawke also began towards the end of the 1980s to put some diplomatic pressure on the Soviets to stop supplying arms to Mengistu.)

It was no use getting into the business of comparative atrocities anyhow, especially not over a full table in an as yet still more or less lucky country. But I was very passionate about

Eritrea. No one except Jimmy Carter was making much of an attempt to get a settlement in this terrible business. As admirable and right as it was to weep for the dead of Beijing, I asked who wept for the three thousand Ethiopian conscripts whose corpses Judy and I had seen littering the trenches above Keren the previous May? Who wept for these dead boys' family photographs fluttering up and down the front trench on a dry wind, and their sun-dried rictus of anguish appalling at each turning of the trench? Who wept for the nameless Eritrean young who had perished, or for the Eritrean innocents, women and children who died by massacre and *induced* famine?

But the conversation of course returned to China, to how in the 1980s Australians had looked to China for unrealistic returns. The Chinese had adequately warned us not to expect too much: *Let Foreign Things Serve China*, read half their banners. We had expected free-wheeling cultural and scholarly exchanges. Often we got instead a situation where a modern Australian writer had to eat dinner and converse with an aged cadre playwright whose work included such sure-fire doctrinaire favourites as *Brother, You Have Taken the Wrong Path*. We became aware too that a great deal of the salary and allowances paid to Chinese exchange students and academics was collected up by the so-called 'Education Attache' at the Chinese embassy in Canberra. We had expected a trade bonanza too: joint ventures. We had gone brashly and with hope into the thickets of China's stupefying bureaucracy.

At table, Neville Wran croaked, 'I've eaten bloody snake for the New South Wales–Guangdong relationship and I'm not going to abandon it too easily.'

I remember telling at that lunch table a story about Justice Murphy in China. Lionel Murphy and his wife had shared a dinner with members of the Australia China Council at Chiang Kai-shek's summer residence in Shanghai. Our hosts were officials of the Chinese Tourist Association. Justice Murphy had learned a trick whereby, through a mathematical calculation, if you told him what the date of your birth was, he could tell you what day of the week you had been born. His willingness to impress the Chinese officials was probably heightened by Mai Tai and Chinese wine, for Murphy was an enthusiastic drinker. He worked through the formula for a number of the Chinese, and they were politely astounded when he came up with the result, crying, 'Tuesday!' or 'Saturday!'

A feature of Chinese banquets and perhaps an index of the cultural gulf was that whenever the chief Chinese official rose to go, all his juniors rose as nearly as simultaneously as they could and the party exited as a group. Whereas when Australian delegation leaders rose and left, their junior colleagues stayed and continued to apply themselves to what was left in their glasses, and in the bottles scattered around the table.

Justice Murphy had a middling official in mid-calculation when the head of the Shanghai Tourist Association rose to go. The entire balance of Chinese rose to leave except the man Murphy had determined hold of by the wrist. 'No, no,' Murphy was urging, 'multiply it by nine.'

This was Murphy of the enormous Irish hooter, former Attorney-General in the Whitlam government; general—during his time in cabinet—of the famous dawn raid on ASIO; at the end of his life accused in court of doing too many official favours for 'his little mate', the Sydney solicitor Morgan Ryan; accomplished jurist and writer of High Court judgments utterly accessible to layfolk. Possessor of at least one major party trick. Like Wran himself a typical Sydney man, evading at every turn Sydney's tendencies to low church respectability and demonstrating at most turns Sydney's other and contradictory urge to wryness, cleverness out of the corner of the mouth, hearty boozing, and the tribal exercise of power. A man of course, like Wran, whose whole history seemed rightly or wrongly at odds with the Britannic solemnities of the law.

In one of Roy Slavin and H. G. Nelson's little books about Australian sport, I am described as a novelist who rabbits on about Celtic deities round about Grand Final time. It is meant to be a joke, but there's some truth to it, in that I do tend to look upon certain humans, and particularly politicians, as revenants, standard figures from somebody's pantheon. Only in a fairly stable nation like Australia, in which politics makes inroads and may destroy through neglect and misinformation but not by direct intent, can such a temperamental tendency hope to be justifiably indulged. One would be too busy suffering and trying to resist under Stalin, Pol Pot, Mengistu or Omar Bashir of the Sudan, to justify such fancies.

I believed that men like Wran and his late friend Justice Lionel Murphy tended towards the benign end of the pantheon. Flawed as they both might have sometimes appeared in their public life, they were the sorts of men who worried about questions to do with defining Australian identity, with stopping to be a tributary people—changing our arrangements not for the sake of jingoism but so that a certain degree of promise, inherent in the Australian character, could be explored. Such questions did not seem to concern many of their less flamboyant peers in the legal community. But Wran and Murphy were people of fairly muscular ideas.

(If the idea of 'a certain degree of promise inherent in the Australian character' seems a little vague here, it will certainly be explained more fully later in this account.)

The lunch at Jill Hickson's and Neville Wran's table had now reached the point where nearly all the fish they bought the day before at the Sydney Fish Markets had been eaten. In a manner all too typical of generous Sunday lunches in Sydney, a number of bottles of Hunter Valley Chardonnay had also been drained. Neville Wran leaned over the table and said, 'The other thing I want to see happen before I bloody well die is an Australian Republic. And there will have to be something done about the reserve powers of the Crown, and the Senate's power of veto.'

Both the latter, as most Australian lay people know, had a bearing on the dismissal of Gough Whitlam, but Wran's concerns, and mine ran wider than that one incident. People like to speak as if the dismissal of Gough Whitlam was a one-off event which would never occur again. Sir John Kerr's actions and the justice of his exercise of the reserve powers was validated, some said, by a subsequent election, one which showed that the majority of the Australian people at that stage of history wanted Malcolm Fraser's conservative care-taker government confirmed in office.

Some Australians speak too as if the constitutional crisis ended in late 1975 with the election, as if that was the end too of the constitutional question itself. It was considered bad taste and tired old stuff somehow to point out that the mechanisms still lay about in the Constitution, in Section 61 and 64, for example, dazzling implements—that was certainly how Sir John Kerr himself saw them—available, whilever the Constitution went unchanged, to subvert the popular will even more drastically than in the Whitlam case, and to override Australian democracy.

A Republic might provide an opportunity to examine such problems, and the question of the powers of the Senate too. In a Republic, some of the reserve powers might be suitable for transfer to the new office of President, and others may be seen as too dangerous to be left available to a non-executive Head of State. And in what sense is the Governor-General Commander-in-Chief of the defence force? Can he call Duntroon and bring out the cadets with their Armalites?

Neville Wran was always an instinctive practitioner of *Realpolitik*, whereas I—like most private citizens—had never had to be. During his long premiership of New South Wales I had therefore often found myself refusing invitations to attend State levees in honour of visiting Royals. But it was not politically viable in the late 1970s, early 1980s, for an Australian politician to go Republican. Elsewhere in this tale I include an account of twentieth century politicians who were destroyed and barred from their legislatures for uttering Republican sentiments, particularly Republican sentiments which were seen to bear on the Irish question. Even in the early 1980s, Republicanism had seemed the property of a few stubborn Whitlamites, unregenerate Irishmen such as Dinny O'Hearn, and discontented immigrants like Franca Arena, who were told they just had to settle down and accept the fact that the Queen was an essentially Australian institution. Otherwise, they could go back to ... etc., etc.

But I did notice there had been enough Republican sentiment to change some things. At one Premier's Literary Awards
dinner, an official had proposed the loyal toast, and a number
of literary figures, including of course Donald Horne, sat tight,
would not rise, did not drink, even if the majority did so either
through habit or their own version of politeness or because
they believed devoutly in it. From that point on, loyal toasts
were abandoned at the Literary Awards.

The idea Neville Wran proposed then was the one mentioned earlier: to put together a small committee of visible and
markedly Australian people who would enunciate the Republican credo. Their repute would need to be such that as a body,
whatever anyone had against them as individuals, they could
not be written off in any of the three ways I indicated before.

I reacted to the idea with tremendous enthusiasm. While it
may be naive to believe that a Republic would solve all national
questions, it was also likely that we would go on delaying to
act on many of them until after we became a Republic. The
fallacy of the Crown, I believed, gave us a sort of mental
reservation which covered a mass of sloppy arrangements
and unanswered questions, amongst them the besetting matter of Aboriginal sovereignty before and after European settlement. I was always certain—some would say naively—that
the establishment of a Republic would act as a great catalyst
for the sort of mature analysis we needed. The institution of
the Crown gave us a feeling that even our crimes were not our
own. We sometimes indulged ourselves by describing the deci-
mation of indigenous Australia as a British crime.

So that I saw the question as one much broader than the
symbolic, or I should say, even broader than the symbolic;
for symbolism influences everything, since it affects the self-
definition and is the equation under which all practical problems, including art and commerce and foreign policy, are
managed.

The Australian poet Les Murray, that intense, brilliant and
enormous human being, believed this proposition too. He had
written in 1977:

'Under our present absentee monarchical system, what I
call the mercantile protectorate, energies are held down and

made abortive. If we get the Republic right, there ought to be a surge of creative energy and good innovation comparable with that in the 1890s when the creation of the Commonwealth was preceded and accompanied by all sorts of valuable and pioneering pieces of social legislation and a surge in several of the arts.'

Les Murray says that out of respect for another country's symbolism, he hesitates to compare the Crown, as multifariously depicted on everything from government drivers' caps to legal documents, to a lesion caused by a disease of dependence.

'I am afraid, though, that the connection with the English Royal Family which this object symbolises is just such a disease. I never thought of it as a harmless survival of traditional pageantry, as many did in Australia before Sir John Kerr's usurpation. I have too much respect for the real power of symbolism to have made that mistake. The Crown remains what it has always been, a psychic weapon held in benign reserve against our growing up and finding ourselves.'

Next, in that long vinous September afternoon which I was beginning to enjoy very much, Neville Wran asked me about taking the chair in such an organisation. I was easily scared by such an idea and begged off that. I am, as friends and enemies will no doubt tell you, terrified of taking the chair in anything. There are men and women who seem to savour the rules that govern the management of committees, who know exactly the order of debate when an amendment has been moved to an amendment of a motion, and who can deal with the most arcane point of order with a few samurai swipes of procedure.

I had spent three turbulent and not very contented years in the chair of the Australian Society of Authors, with an energetic but controversial Queensland writer, Ken Methold, as the deputy chair. I had been recruited by Barbara Jefferis and by Ken Methold himself. Duty had been invoked and the need to bring in a greater number of members, perhaps reaching two thousand published members. One of Ken's main preoccupations was that the Literature Board, the chief source of patronage for writers in Australia, favoured fiction over other genres, and above all handed out grants to their mates on a cyclical basis. By doing so, according to Ken, they thereby ignored a great accessible Australian literary voice, perhaps in the tradition of Lawson, which went neglected and unsupported by the high-culture membership of the Literature Board.

Having served on the Literature Board myself, I believed that with a few inevitable quibbles, the Literature Board was serving Australian writers from its offices in Walker Street, North Sydney, as well and certainly as honourably as it could with its diminishing funds. Its dilemma, apart from making sure it was fair to applicants from all States in the Commonwealth, was the split of funds between supporting the old, established writers, who in a more populous nation would have been able to live off their books or the lecture circuit, and then encouraging new writers. In defending it, I argued I was speaking purely from my own experience of fair operation within the board. I was not a client of the Literature Board. So I had no motivation anyhow to stand up for the Literature Board if I felt it was corrupt or fraudulent. I still argued that the writers the Literature Board supported were often magnificent Australian practitioners and almost always deserved it.

That is another aspect of writing and government patronage I used to hammer with Ken and, indeed, with the press. Grant money helped generate wealth. It produced books which helped enrich and employ editors, booksellers, academics, teachers and librarians. Often it produced in the end foreign currency from overseas editions and film versions. The author paid taxes on grant money and royalties, as did everyone else in the chain of production and distribution. So, apart from the immeasurable cultural benefits of a native literature, there was also an economic rationale. Patronage was not an economic black hole.

When the assessments of the manuscripts were made, a large team of critics, writers, publishers and booksellers were brought in from all over Australia for a long weekend to make a panel. The purpose was to insure as much as possible that regional, gender, and genre bias should not prevail. In my experience, the great populist voice Ken Methold of the Australian Society of Authors spoke of was not there in the submissions, not in the sense he meant it anyhow.

As to genre, science fiction and mystery writers, romance,

tales of the outback, etc., etc., all came to the Literature Board in great number. The only projects of quality which sometimes were rejected were ones which were in fact so promising that there wasn't any question the author of the project would be able to find a commission from a publisher. The author would be advised on how to do just that.

In any case, towards the end of my chairmanship, Ken Methold read at an authors' meeting a fictional 'Letter from Mt Isa' supposedly written by an immigrant who was trying to work out why Sydney and in particular, Balmain, did so well in the Literature Board grants.

This brought a ferocious response from the executive officer of the Literature Board, Tom Shapcott, a poet and novelist whose small body of assistants ran the secretariat of the Board. The press took up the controversy between Shapcott and Methold, with the Society of Authors stuck in the middle, and a sizeable number of our membership siding with Methold against Shapcott.

Shapcott then hit on a ploy which was enthusiastically backed by Frank Moorhouse, a frequent recipient of grants from the Literature Board and therefore one of Methold's *bêtes noires*, and by Donald Horne, author, and chair of the Australia Council. Shapcott put forward a motion for the Australian Society of Authors' annual general meeting that Methold be expelled from the Society.

The office manager of the Society, Gail Cork, and I spent weeks liaising with all parties. I could not approve of Shapcott's lobby since I believed that any attempt to expel and thus silence a writer within the Society, was against the spirit of the profession, particularly in a year when the Ayatollah had tried to choke off Salman Rushdie with a death threat.

With great press attention, the annual general meeting came on at the Royal Automobile Club in Macquarie Street. Speakers had to compete with the rush of traffic outside the window on the Cahill Expressway. I made a speech as long and undramatic as I could get away with, in the hope that both parties sitting in the room would be denied the chance to speak in haste. I urged members to look at the Methold affair in the light of what had befallen Salman Rushdie and thus to put it into proportion. I remember saying also that the press had come to see mud-wrestling between authors, and they should at all costs be denied that spectacle. I also spoke of a possible schism in the Society if Methold was expelled.

At lunchtime a deal was forged. Shapcott and his supporters would not move a motion of expulsion if Ken Methold would remove his name from the ballot for deputy chair. He agreed to that. But after the AGM, he would continue his campaign in the management committee for some time before resigning, and—according to what he then proposed—going off to form his own broad-based, equitable, populist writers' organisation.

I was ecstatic to leave the remarkable Blanche d'Alpuget in the chair when my three years at the ASA were up.

So all my fears about chairing things had been confirmed by the ASA experience. On that basis and because of the demands of time it would make, I would reject, in the year following the lunch at Neville Wran's, an approach from the Minister for the Arts, David Simmons, to become chairman of the Australia Council. The prospect of following Donald Horne had scared off a series of potential chairs, including the genial playwright David Williamson and the novelist Morris West. When the film and stage actress Noni Hazelhurst was offered the job, she asked for a $100,000 stipend to compensate for the impossibility of acting in a film while chairing the Australia Council. I thought something adequate should be paid her, since she was not an academic with an assured salary and acting was her main income. Donald Horne took me to task for saying so in a press interview. He said you could do it all in two days a week. Donald's two days though are like the days of creation. I wondered how an ordinary human could manage the diverse voices, the artform complexities of an art community as complicated as Australia's at less than fulltime commitment.

Eventually—from the short list—the novelist Rodney Hall accepted the chair, and seems to be handling things with a competence I would certainly be unlikely to match.

But although I had said no to Neville Wran in the matter of the Republican committee, I wanted to be a member. There were now however a few persuasive calls from Neville. He said the sorts of things people always say when co-opting a chair: 'It'll only be three or four meetings a year, and Donald could be deputy chair and take over meetings you were away for.'

I had heard the 'only four meetings a year' cry from others. And the idea of chairing a committee which included Wran and Horne was an awesome one in itself. I said that my only organisational capacity was that of being a spokesman. 'That's exactly what we want,' said Neville in his inveigling, gravelled voice.

I gave in. And indeed there was little work at first. We intended to go public on 26 January 1991, just under ten years from the stated target date of 1 January 2001.

The first meeting was in December 1990, in Neville Wran's offices in Turnbull & Partners in Chifley Square. Malcolm Turnbull had defended Peter Wright in the *Spycatcher* trials in Australia and England, and the room we met in was called Spycatcher Room. This small conference venue was decorated with court artist's sketches of the trials Maggie Thatcher brought on in an attempt to suppress the publication of Peter Wright's book in Britain and Australia. Turnbull, himself, was represented, square-chested with lifted chin in scathing mid-question. Former Rhodes scholar, journalist, friend of Kerry Packer, and presently lawyer, merchant banker, rugged player in the events surrounding the collapse of the Fairfax Group and in other media deals, Turnbull was not present at this meeting. But he was a passionate Republican and would be a great benefactor of the infant Republican Movement.

Present for the first meeting were Geoffrey Dutton, Neville Wran, Franca Arena and myself. Franca would tell me that she had first proposed the concept to Neville Wran at his retirement and had then frequently urged him to pursue it.

Geoffrey, for a larger part of his life, had been an important literary figure in national terms, but he had until recently been heavily identified with South Australia. In his early days he had always been considered as the child of 'a leading South Australian family'. This sort of term is rarely heard in Sydney, in which Geoffrey had been settled for some years at the time of the first ARM meeting. You might at first sight think that the founding Duttons of South Australia would have been appalled to know that their scion would one day feel it necessary to plan the end of the Monarchy for Australia with two working class louts like Neville and myself, and with an Italian immigrant.

But not so. Geoffrey had had a great-uncle who had been premier of South Australia *and* a Republican. Geoffrey indicated that on special days, this Adelaide grandee would ride on horseback through North Adelaide bearing a Republican flag of his own devising.

Geoffrey's own huge contribution to the long, glacial flow of the Republican debate will be detailed in another part of this book.

The great Australian modernist, Patrick White, had fallen out with Geoffrey after years of friendship because he attended, in White's opinion, too many seminars, and was too busy with literary committee work. Patrick White might have approved of his involvement in this movement though, since amongst a list of White's unfulfilled desires, reproduced in David Marr's biography of White, is the wish for an Australian Republic. White, ever an absolutist, both in his writing and his friendships, had ended a friendship with Kate Fitzpatrick over her attending one of the Royal cocktail parties of the Wran years. His fears for Geoffrey, that he dispersed his talents with too much literary politics, might have been assuaged in part by the validity of this cause, though I am sure White would have chosen someone other than Wran for Geoffrey to share this founding occasion with and I doubt he would have thought much of me as chair, either.

Franca Arena was a Genoese, and had immigrated to Australia in her youth. She had always been a tremendous networker and a vigorous delegate for the Italian community. She owned a quite prodigious reserve of energy. One night in the early 1980s I had seen her bravely standing up for Republicanism in a televised debate in the ABC studios at Gore Hill. The event had been heavily attended by robust Monarchists, members of various loyalists societies, the badges shining on their lapels as symbols of their devotion.

I remember that when Franca pungently explained her reluctance to accept a Commonwealth where you were expected to frame the terms of your loyalty to Australia in terms of the

British Monarchy, Senator Bronwyn Bishop told her that the Monarchy was essential to Australian identity, and that if she didn't like that she had the option of returning to Republican Italy. Being here, Franca replied, being an Australian citizen, I am entitled to work for the Australia I want, wherever I come from. Franca told Senator Bishop that she spoke as if her own dynasty had been in Australia for ten thousand years instead of two hundred. We were all immigrants, argued Franca, all European Australians, and one immigrant didn't have the right to deny a place to another, or coerce approval for absolutely *every* aspect of Australian society as a test of migrant suitability.

Of course, Franca's forthrightness was sometimes thought to be too much. She was not always tactful. People flinched at her tigerishness. But she had ferocious energy, she was a tremendous letter writer, and to counteract the Crown which appeared on parliamentary stationery, she always ruggedly signed each letter, 'For Australia—Franca Arena'.

She was obviously going to be secretary of the committee. A woman called Denise Darlow, a migrant from England in her childhood, would serve in her own time as the committee's adviser. She was a Canterbury-Bankstown girl, forthright, no-nonsense, a calming voice. Since she was used to working with Neville Wran, she had plenty of practice making her advice known to people with firmly held convictions.

We had already approached a number of possible members, impressing on them the need for confidentiality. I had approached for example David Williamson, Bryan Brown the actor, and Fred Schepisi the film director. Others I approached gave me a knock back. Franca had recruited for our committee Franco Belgiorno-Nettis, diminutive engineering tycoon and art patron, and also Claudio Alcorso, the Tasmanian entrepreneur, who undertook to recruit prominent people in that State. She was already writing to retired political figures all over the Commonwealth who had shown a progressive attitude in constitutional reform, either as members of the Constitutional Commission or of the earlier, parliamentary Constitutional Conventions. She wrote as well to lawyers, artists, performers and entrepreneurs of all stripes.

When people said no, they did so for three expressed reasons —apart of course from the fact that a few declared themselves to be Monarchists. (An esteemed jurist, for example, who was of Northern Ireland Loyalist descent, felt for the sake of his heritage that he could not join the movement. Later he would join a Monarchist committee.) But back to the three reasons given by those who *were* Republican but wouldn't join. One was typified by the Midnight Oil's lead singer, Peter Garrett. He believed that he must commit himself more urgently to other matters, including the environment. He did not agree with my position that a Republic could have a positive influence on all areas of Australian life. Others agreed in principle with Republicanism, but believed that an overt Republican movement would divide the community. It seemed that Australians should be permitted to argue about anything except this shibboleth. Others said that though Republican in sentiment, they did not want to declare themselves because it would affect their standing either social or commercial. A well known actress said that a large part of her audience were Monarchists, and like most Australian artists, she needed to keep her audience, given how marginal the theatre was in Australia. Many of this third group said, reasonably enough, look, the prospect of a Republic was not a practical one, so why put themselves in the Republican camp to no good purpose?

In the space of two years, these fears would be proved baseless, but I felt them myself at the time. Having just gone into partnership with my wife, Iain Finlay, Trish Sheppard and other friends in a guesthouse in the Blue Mountains, I did worry about the impact of my Republicanism upon business at the place and upon the book sales and other writing which would be needed to support it. If the guesthouse went sour, it had the power to destroy the partners, jointly and severally.

I also anticipated, as did we all, threats of physical violence, and so was concerned about my family.

The truth is that we, as much as other Australians, were taken in by the idea we had grown up with, that the institution of the Monarchy had primal power. You didn't mess around with it. *Nil me Impune Lacessit—No one hurts me with impunity* was written on that area of our subconscious labelled

Monarchy. This again was an extraordinary piece of psychic baggage for a supposedly free and equal people to carry around.

But on the day of the first meeting, on the edge of summer in 1990, all of us, like all Australians, were still enthralled and in some fear of it. It would only be proven in the next two or three years what a chimera it all was. It would be proved that it was not actually bad for your health to envisage a Republic. Your ears did not fall off. Your friends did not abandon you. You were not accursed in the land. Such was the mysterium of the institution though, that we ourselves did not know that in 1990.

We were disappointed by the number of Victorians, former politicians, and other community leaders, who refused to be involved. Anyone looking at the history of Australia is aware that nothing which neglects Victoria and Melbourne can hope to succeed. There is potential uneasiness in Melburnians over any Sydney-based institution which, because it serves Sydney or has wide support there, therefore claims to represent the nation.

Henry Lawson himself complained about this tendency in Sydneysiders. During my time on the Literature Board, Melbourne artists and writers, including notably amongst the writers Jack Hibberd and Peter Mathers, complained that because the Australia Council secretariats, including that of the Literature Board, were based in Sydney, the grants were subject to a kind of Sydney crony-ism. Victorian artists were excluded, Sydney alliances were favoured. (Another version of the Methold proposition.) This ignored the fact that both on the Literature Board itself, and on the adjudicating panels, the representation of Victorians was always high. The Australia Council, aware of Melbourne's reasonable enough demand to be taken seriously, went to pains to ensure it was always well-represented. Just the same, the figures for grants, bluntly stated, did perversely favour the Melbourne view, or if you liked, the Melbourne paranoia. For a time in the 1980s Victoria was under-represented in Literature Board grants. That, I heard certain blithe Sydneysiders say, was because a lot of the talented had moved to Sydney anyway—David Williamson, Barry Oakley, Helen Garner, various painters and performers. Even the ultimate Melburnian, Phillip Adams, had become a devout New South Welsh person.

All these unreasonable and provincial arguments did very little to appease anyone. Even the then soon to be discredited Premier of Victoria, John Cain, took up the cry at a Victorian Premier's Literary Awards Dinner in Melbourne. Perhaps the crony-ism which characterised some of his colleagues in the right wing of the Labor Party of New South Wales had deceived him into believing that that was the way every Sydney setup worked.

Because of the history of the two cities therefore and, because of the mutual rivalries, paranoias and arrogances which characterised and afflicted their relationship, we hoped to involve as large a number of Victorians as we could. The Victorians had been the front runners in Federation and were needed in this movement. They had been the bulk of the Australian Natives Association, the citizens' body which had forced the pace with Federation. But they were fairly unwilling to join our infant movement.

Again, a lot of the refusals came because people didn't believe that this was a viable movement, that the forces against the proposition were too entrenched, and that like many other groups of similar objective in the past, we would soon be written off as a clutch of fringe people engaged in the mutual self-massage of each other's sensibilities.

So we would be obliged to go public with unequal numbers of New South Wales and Victorian people, and this was regrettable. We were working to a timetable, however, and had to seek whatever reasonable support we could.

We had a base document to work on at that meeting too. It was a statement about the Monarchy and the envisaged Republic which had been drawn up by Graham Freudenberg who had written speeches for Whitlam and for Wran.

Of course, the invocation of those names, Whitlam, Wran, Arena, Freudenberg, is itself an indication of the peril that we would be dismissed as stooges of the Labor Party.

We were in no way acting for any party, nor were we pursuing any party's political advantage. For that reason we did not ask Gough Whitlam, who would have been many people's first choice for membership, to join the List of One Hundred we were trying to recruit. It was important to show that we were a group who would have arisen ultimately *irrespective* of 1975. It was inevitable though, that a large part of our early support should come from people with Labor voting backgrounds, since it was in that part of Australian society that people didn't feel inhibited in declaring themselves Republicans. In the conservative parties, Republicans—of whom it would prove there were a substantial number—kept their counsel, concentrated on practical politics, and waited for what everyone thought would be a glacial creep of public opinion. Nonetheless, it had to be acknowledged that Malcolm Turnbull had once tried for Liberal pre-selection, and we would *need* to have support from people of no political affiliation, or of conservative ideas.

Graham Freudenberg's draft had reached Franca and Neville in November 1990, and was signed by Geoffrey Dutton and the late Professor Manning Clark.

Manning's signature was appropriate. He was now aged and failing, and was in many quarters among the most loved men in Australia, in a few amongst the most condemned. At his funeral one autumn day in 1991, attended by half the Federal cabinet, as well as by a vast number of writers and scholars, one of his sons, a master at Melbourne Grammar, told how on a drive to Williamstown a little time before, his father had uttered the desire to see Australia become a Republic. So, at his death, Clark's wish list like White's included this shining item.

Graham Freudenberg's declaration was three pages long, and everyone who was presented with it had a different, reasonable suggestion about copyediting. For example, there was a sentence in Graham Freudenberg's eloquent draft which referred to Australian sovereignty as deriving not from the Monarch but from the 'uniquely diverse' Australian people. I wondered about introducing the question of Australia's ethnic diversity right at the heart of the declaration. It seemed dangerous to introduce upfront any questions on which a simple consensus was not possible. Not that this aspect didn't fascinate me, or that it wasn't a source of pride or strength within Australia. But I doubted that the Australian people were in a literal sense 'uniquely diverse'. America was at least as culturally diverse. And as we shall see, early Republicans, moved by the same questions of identity which moved us, did not see ethnic diversity as the base of Australia's claim to sovereignty. It was our ultimate ethnic diversity which made modern Republicanism outgrow the narrowness of the earlier model proposed by William Lane and Lawson, but it was not in itself the basic cause of the call for a Republic. Even if we had somehow restricted our immigration mainly to people from the British Isles, Republicanism would still have eventually become the dominant opinion.

Amongst the names we were putting together, you would have found substantial agreement on a lot of questions, and a desire to work for justice and good sense in a range of areas. But as an organisation the Australian Republican Movement should have a very simple goal.

None of the more than one hundred prominent Australians we were recruiting in confidence seems to have had any trouble with the simple formula, based on Graham Freudenberg's draft, that we came up with.

Freudenberg's prose was already quite eloquent by anyone's standards. I was worried about the opening, 'We, as Australians . . .' I didn't think the 'as' was necessary. I wasn't even sure if it was grammatically advisable.

But good sense told me anyhow to go with the amended Freudenberg version. I had enough to be getting on with. At the time I was writing many drafts of a screenplay of a novel called *Towards Asmara*, set in Eritrea. The work was fuelled by a certain urgency, since the the war between Eritrea and Ethiopia was still in progress and tens of thousands of young Ethiopians and Eritreans—more Ethiopians *than* Eritreans at that stage since the Eritreans were in the total military ascendent—were perishing in a conflict they did not understand and which the world knew nothing of. I was writing many drafts too of a novel that would ultimately be called *Flying Hero Class*. On top of that I was writing a travel book on the American Southwest, based on a two month journey I made there in early 1990. It was an idea put to me by the travel writer, Jan Morris. The travel had been a delight. It was the writing which of course—as always—was hard and time consuming. Finally, I was writing a book on an Irish journey—*Now and in Time to Be*. I was certainly overcommitted and all the imagery in my head belonged to other projects. Freudenberg's Republican Declaration, as tinkered with by a small committee, was— I am happy now to say—exempt from my literary ambitions. Two years later I still read it without regret.

> We, as Australians, united in one indissoluble Commonwealth, affirm our allegiance to the nation and people of Australia. We assert that the freedom and unity of Australia must derive its strength from the will of the people.
>
> We believe that the harmonious development of the Australian community demands that the allegiance of Australians must be fixed wholly within and upon Australia and Australian institutions.
>
> We therefore propose as a great national goal for Australia:
>
> THAT BY FIRST OF JANUARY, 2001—THE FIRST DAY OF THE TWENTY-FIRST CENTURY AND THE CENTENARY OF THE PROCLAMATION OF THE FEDERATION—AUSTRALIA SHALL BECOME AN INDEPENDENT REPUBLIC.

CHAPTER SIX

*

MEMOIRS FROM A YOUNG REPUBLIC I

THE IDEA WAS that we should go public on Australia Day, 1991. Until then, we were to do everything possible to prevent ourselves from becoming a small mention in a gossip column, a two or three day wonder. We were to continue to recruit, to build up the list of names we could publish as foundation members of the movement. After the launch, we were to settle in for the long haul: liaising with pollsters, reasoning with the press and public, talking with politicians on both sides of politics. Though we had set 1 January 2001 as the target date, the task seemed so prodigious, so like the digging up of a pyramid, that some of us thought the timetable fanciful.

We had registered the name, Australian Republican Movement, for fear that it might be captured by other groups, and Lucy Turnbull, Malcolm's wife, was advising us on how to incorporate ourselves.

We wondered what should happen on the day itself: an advertisement in the *Australian* perhaps, with the names of all our foundation members appended. We looked at the cost of that. Though we were meeting in a merchant bank, the move-ment itself had few funds at the moment, and the cost was not quite justified. In the end we hoped that the novelty and forthright good sense of our Australia Day declaration would interest the press enough so that they would do our work for us.

We were aware of all the perils. If we concentrated on the names only of the elite, how could we appeal to the egalitar-ian Australian people? But if we did not have the elite, citizens known to the community and unable to be dismissed as a group, how could we manage to be taken seriously? And could we become a popular movement?

And where would the secretariat come from to handle mem-bership, produce newsletters, sell badges? Perhaps we would advertise after the launch, inviting membership. But Franca raised a problem that if we opened the movement to everyone in Australia, what was to prevent it being hijacked to serve other purposes? Taken over by an ethnic group, for example, or even God forbid—by Monarchists?

At that stage, above all, we had no idea of the strength of our possible numbers, the numbers of Australians who agreed with us.

There was also at that time a perception that the idea of a Republic would be easily dismissed if it was put forward in a time of public crisis. The possibility of a Gulf War hung over the world. I couldn't believe it would occur however. The divisive peril of another long-running Vietnam alarmed me, and I believed it should worry America and its Allies. I apolo-gise to the reader again for mentioning the Eritrean case, but it did demonstrate how fiercely people will fight for a place which others might well consider a desolation.

I was uneasy, too, that in the Gulf conflict, no one was talking about the history of the boundaries. At the height of Imperial power post World War I, the British had drawn the boundaries between Kuwait and Iraq for their own conveni-ence, giving small Kuwait a long coastline and big Iraq a short one. On the other hand, in favour of an attack against Iraq, were the civil and international crimes of Saddam Hussein—his crimes against the Kurds, his use of lethal gas in assaults during his war with Iran. But then there was the question, was Kuwait, a rich, illiberal little enclave, worth the young blood of Americans or Australians?

That Christmas, just after the meeting in the offices of Turnbull and Partners, I went with my wife and one of my daughters to meet my other daughter for Christmas in New York. My New York child wrote copy in New York for the Australian Overseas Information Service at the Consulate General at Rockefeller Centre. During Christmas, we stayed in a loft in Tribeca, Manhattan, the home of Gordon Elliot, a wild Australian television journalist who worked for Murdoch's network Fox Five. Gordon is Liverpool-Irish. He was a supporter of the Republic, but I made sure that he knew the news was embargoed.

David Williamson and his wife Kristin were in New York for Christmas too—they had swapped their house in Balmain for the playwright Israel Horowitz's brownstone on Eleventh Street, in the heart of the racy region known as the West Village. Williamson had signed on as a member of our committee and his friends Peter Carey and Alison Summers agreed to subscribe as foundation members when I approached them. Peter was writing novels and teaching writing at NYU. He loved New York passionately, a man who had found the two finest English-speaking cities on earth, Sydney and New York, and he had what I believe was a thoroughly reasonable ambition to get to know American publishers and to penetrate the American market even further than he already had. I admired his professionalism, and could never see why the Australian literary community could sometimes carp at it.

All of us had a wonderful long Christmas lunch in the Rainbow Room at the Rockefeller Centre. The staff treated us kindly not because of Carey's or Williamson's stellar reputations, but because Gordon had made a show with the Rainbow Room sommelier on morning television.

It was interesting to see Carey trying to persuade Williamson of New York's turbulent charms. Williamson was very insistent for such a gentle man in his belief of what constituted a tolerable city. Sydney Harbour, the commute from Balmain to town and back, was clearly the centre of Williamson's liveable universe. Kristin Williamson seemed to like berserkly racy New York a lot though.

There was no denying either the breathtaking pool of talent in New York, and we all attended a reading of *Siren*, Williamson's play, directed by Alison Summers, which impressed Williamson enormously.

But transcending all other questions now, hanging over even the Christmas lunch, was the question of the Gulf. The United Nations gave Saddam an ultimatum, which President Bush was anxious to interpret to the very letter. And Saddam made no concessions.

Recession America and recession Australia were going to spend prodigious money and perhaps spill prodigious blood, and at the end of the process still be stuck with the same social problems. Again I thought of Mengistu squandering the wealth of his poor nation on massive armaments, and killing off his farmers and herders in a conscript army, all to no good purpose.

One afternoon in a bunker in Eritrea in 1987, while an Ethiopian shelling was in progress, the shells—thank God—falling in most cases a kilometre or two up the road, an Eritrean veteran I was with told me the calibres of the shells we could hear landing, and filled me in on the approximate price of each in US dollars. $275 for a 72 millimetre shell, $400 for a 122 millimetre. And a bombing raid, in fuel, logistical costs, armaments and mechanical wear and tear, cost a nation $40,000. Most of it dead money—if the pun can be forgiven—unproductive; not producing wealth for the Ethiopians, who had to buy their planes and parts from the then Soviets, using their scarce reserves of foreign capital from the commodity crops they produced and sold overseas even at the height of the Ethiopian famines.

In any case, I could not see this war doing the West or the Persian Gulf much good, even though the economic equation was somewhat different from the Ethiopian case. (And indeed, the ultimate fallout from the war, as far as it is apparent in international relations and upon America, would look more and more ambiguous as time passed and as the problems of the Gulf region remained.)

I came back to Australia earlier than the rest of my family, just after New Year, and the plane was full of young American reservists and National Guardsmen flying to California—San Diego Naval Base, Camp Pendleton, Tustin Marine Base—for final training before the conflict. They sounded very normal, non-militaristic boys; they didn't speak of nuking anyone, and they didn't disparage Arabs. There is still, after two hundred and twenty years of complicated presidential politics, a civic piety in Americans. If the President calls on them, there is a tendency to swallow private reservations and answer the call. Admittedly this civic response was not as notable during the Vietnam era, but it is apparent in the youth of America in the 1990s. Despite all the doubts people have about Congress, the party system, the lobbyists who blight the Capitol with their money-hurling presence, the mechanisms of the White House —the Presidency still *does* possess a residual holiness.

In Australia, that holiness had always been perceived as residing in the Queen. We had never had the grounds nor the confidence to imbue any of our internal institutions with sacredness.

The experience on the plane convinced me that the war was afoot, and it could be massive and tragic, and in its context our issue of Australian national identity might well appear, or be made to appear minute. In world terms it was.

The beautiful Australian Republican Movement banner, designed by our committee member, the renowned architect Harry Seidler, would need to stay furled in a closet in Chifley Square for the duration.

Back in Sydney, the first sun-struck two weeks of January passed briskly. Impossible to believe on the dazzling beach at Bilgola that a great conflict of wills was perhaps about to consume the youth of the West or of the Arab nations. We were of course sending only three naval vessels—as in Vietnam, it was the gesture that was most appreciated, and by and large our personnel would be fairly well protected throughout the conflict. But one could not predict the centripetal force of this engagement, its capacity to suck in greater and greater forces, more and more young men and women.

By now we were speaking to a publicist, Libby Greig, a woman highly committed to the idea of the Republic and willing to work on it for a pittance. She had already planned a press launch for 26 January. Ted Wright, the American manager of the Regent Hotel in Sydney, was lending a function room, and we were lashing out and ordering a morning tea for the press and whatever members of the founding committee and membership could turn up. Libby Greig was planning for a few days furious attention to the media, and after that thought we would really have to work to keep the debate going. So did all of us.

She too was certain—when the Gulf deadline expired, the rockets began to fire, and the fighter bombers took off—that we would have no choice but to cancel. We knew that this would create problems of maintaining the movement's confidentiality. A journalist, perhaps an acquaintance of one of our discreet membership, might hear of the group, write the story prematurely, and thus dismiss it. A number of us undertook to speak personally to those members we had recruited, most of whom had already given us their membership donation and were therefore expecting to see it used at the earliest possible date.

The bulk of the contacting, and the exhortations to continue in confidentiality, was carried out by the unsinkable Franca Arena.

The deadline expired without any withdrawal from Kuwait by obdurate Saddam. The huge air war that was fought in the Gulf continued, principally over Iraq. Saddam's forces unleashed SCUD missiles at Israel. There was a lot of talk of smart weapons, and most people seemed to accept that the Allies were successfully and surgically destroying Iraq's military infrastructure with barely any damage to the citizenry. It was feared that there would be great losses on amphibious landings the Allies seemed to be planning, but that expectation was in fact part of a contrived feint the military were using the press to disseminate. When the land battle came, it was a case of the Allies rolling up the Iraqi flank from the west. One hundred and fifty thousand or more young Iraqis seemed to have perished, but the West did not shed even a token tear for them. There *was* some largely ineffectual concern for the Kurds, who had marched back into their homeland in Iraq from the north and who would be left high and dry by the war's quick conclusion.

We now planned to go public in April. The delay was an opportunity that would bring new experts into the committee. The genial Mark Day, former talk-back radio host, owner of *Truth* and of a number of radio stations, and unlike most of his breed, one who didn't feel it necessary to play the troglodyte for the sake of ratings, came in at—as far as I remember —Libby Greig's advice. He had an enormous number of contacts in the Australian media, including talk-back radio. There was a chance he might influence some of his colleagues to consider the Republican proposition not as heresy but as a reasonable idea.

With Donald Horne, Mark formed an excellent media and polling subcommittee. Polls were seen as crucial. As long as the defenders of the Monarchy were able to claim that a majority of Australians opposed a Republic, then the more convincingly we could be portrayed as a gratuitous nuisance group. Both Mark and Donald believed that in many cases the polls did not represent the true position, since for comparison purposes, pollsters were asking them questions irrelevant to the Australian situation. Australians had frequently been asked by pollsters to choose between a Monarchy and an elected presidency. The *kind* of elected presidency was not specified, and so people tended to imagine an American style presidency, with the division between the President's executive powers and the Congress's legislative powers which that brought with it. They were being asked therefore, in effect, to choose between the Australian version of Westminster, which they tended to believe in as tried and true, and a totally new and untried set of political institutions.

In confusing circumstances, therefore, they had voted the way Australians had always voted, against change unless it has been adequately presented and argued for.

The problem was that the only reasonable poll question was a simplified version of this:

Would you prefer that the Monarch of Great Britain continue to be Head of State of Australia, or that we have a directly or indirectly elected Head of State whose loyalty would be purely Australian and powers would in practice be largely ceremonial? No self-respecting pollster would of course ask a question as ramified and adjectival as that, but we had to encourage them—directly or indirectly—to ask questions which reflected real Australian possibilities, and which were therefore not fantastical.

The pollster Irving Saulwick was at that stage, without our knowing it, taking a fairly reliable poll which would show on the eve of our ultimately going public that 52 percent of Australians favoured a Republic. Since, however, other polls showed a much lower percentage, and since one figure from an ANU poll—according to the academics themselves who actually took the poll—was taken out of context and showed the Republican proposition didn't have a chance in Australia, we knew that we would have to listen for a time to Monarchists claiming that most Australians still wanted to cleave to the Crown.

We now had a committee strong in the media. Geraldine Doogue had already joined us. She had made an excellent television series on Catholics, and another on old Australian Reds—the latter earned the ire of conservatives in the last days of the Cold War for seeming to make these old apostles of failed Stalinism cuddly.

Geraldine was in a way typical of Irish-Australian talent, the kind whose concern for a sane nationalism was always written off to their Irishness and so dismissed. On the Indian Ocean coast of Australia, in a convent in Perth, she had been coded by Irish nuns with that sense of Irish history which lies at the base of, but also belies and confuses, many Australians' search for Australian identity. She had survived that. She had recovered from or outgrown the Ned Kelly virus. She was on to Australian identity now.

I loved the way that as a native Western Australian, Geraldine would raise her heroic chin in committee meetings and chide us for the besetting Sydney sin of forgetting other States. She knew we were in peril if we forgot our responsibility to Victoria and other States.

David Hill, Managing Director of the Australian Broadcasting Corporation, had also brought his expertise to the committee. He, too, a Dr Barnardo boy shipped to Australia from England, gave off that same sense of motors humming beneath the surface that you got from Neville Wran and Franca Arena. David was also involved in the administration of a professional Rugby League team, North Sydney. I could not help but hope that his arrival amongst us would have the same dramatic, sudden and positive impact upon our cause as did his arrival at North Sydney. He had played the game at a professional level in his youth, and I remember a former Norths forward had commented to me that if David had concentrated on the game instead of buggering off overseas in search of a post-graduate degree, he could have gone right to the top and played first grade for Norths.

A less turbulent committee member than the rest of us was Faith Bandler, an author who was of Torres Strait Islander descent. She was a gentle woman who would nonetheless sometimes fume at white Australian folly. She was passionate on the subject as well as on the environment and Aboriginal sovereignty, an issue which must still be adequately addressed by Australians. She resented the fact that 26 January, the anniversary of British settlement and of the claiming of British sovereignty over most of the land mass of the continent, should be celebrated as Australia Day. The implications, she said, were too divisive.

I remember telling her that I had an unfashionably perverse pride on that day, specifically because the European Adam and Eve of Australia had been rejected humans, an underclass. And yet from that fact there derived somehow a complicated society some of whose values were—particularly in relative world terms—a matter of celebration. I argued that it was too late now to deny all legitimacy to European occupation.

I argued that those first condemned were characteristic of later waves of immigration, the poor of the British Isles, the victims of World War II and of Lebanon, Vietnam, Kampuchea. Of course, what vitiates all white Australia's celebrations is the ghost of Aboriginal sovereignty past and present. Until it is given body and acknowledged, we cannot hope to be content. If I might mix metaphors a little, it is the basis of our own internal Ulster. As little as Loyalists understand Nationalists in Ulster, so little does white Australia seek to understand the Aboriginal world and the prodigious significance land plays.

In fact the comparison to Ulster is valid, for not only has the culture of Aboriginal Australia gone unexplained and devalued in white minds, but some demonstrate contempt for the idea that there is anything there at all—in Aboriginal tradition—to be learned.

I didn't really win the argument with Faith, and I won't be secure in my civic Australian identity until this question of sovereignty is resolved. I do, however, still believe that it is perilous, and perhaps, self-indulgent to despise the Australian past; that it is an inverse form of the desire to shine, to make a mark. We are the *most* racist, the most *sexist*. It is not enough to be merely deplorable in our own terms, and particularly deplorable in the light of our declared values. We must be Olympic status.

Another member of the group was the painter of magnificent three-dimensional abstracts, Colin Lanceley. I had first met him through his friendship with Robert Hughes, who stayed with him in Paddington, in the Lanceleys' fine terrace house across from the Sydney Cricket Ground. At the stage Colin got involved with the Republican Movement he was getting ready for an exhibition of his work at the Chicago Fine Arts Museum, the magnificent art museum, richly endowed, on the shore of Lake Michigan. It seemed true to me as a lay appreciator of Australian art that—despite Lanceley's increasing international repute—he was a quieter operator than many members of the Australian art establishment, and than most of our committee for that matter. A calm counsellor, and in no sense a self-promoter.

Harry Seidler's office had already produced a fine three-coloured banner, and a young designer named Joe Bolen from Franco Belgiorno-Nettis's office had now designed a logo, a single star on a blue field trailing away dynamically into threads and streams which may have gone to represent the diversity of Australia. Stickers were manufactured in the same successful design.

We had a second launch date planned now for April. But Nick Greiner, the Liberal Premier of New South Wales, called a sudden State election. We were concerned that we would somehow get embroiled in the election. There could be a double tarring with the same brushes, the Republican Movement being used to discredit Bob Carr, the Labor leader, and more dismally for us, Bob Carr being used to discredit us.

Greiner I had always found a personable man. He was of Hungarian descent and had been educated by the worldly Jesuits. That he was a Liberal leader indicated how thoroughly the Hungarians had succeeded in Australia and how little sectarianism counted for any more. But we were utterly sure his strategists would have exploited us, glibly labelled us, reduced our credibility and diminished our purpose.

So Franca Arena patiently wrote to all the growing list of foundation members, some of them located in foreign parts (Roger Woodward, for example, and Robert Hughes), and explained why their membership dues were yet again not ready to be constructively deployed.

The State election of 1991 proved to be a close run thing. Against all the indicators, Bob Carr's Labor Party came to within a seat of winning—and even that seat, on the Central Coast, was subject to a legal challenge over the counting method. Franca was returned to the Legislative Council. Elsewhere, throughout the world's democracies, a high independent vote figured in elections, giving the traditional political parties an infallible sign that they should mend their Byzantine structures and deceits or pay the price. (At the time of writing, Ross Perot, not necessarily himself a candidate anyone would trust, was nonetheless performing the same service in a badly frayed American democracy.)

At last we were free to plan a day. The first Sunday of July, the seventh. The speech I had put in my word processor in the small computing room above a beach in the conservative electorate of Mackellar, I now refurbished, taking out the most obvious references to Australia Day. Franca spoke again to Ted Wright at the Regent, and she and Denise Darlow, our unofficial executive secretary, decided that we had enough in kitty to provide morning tea and coffee to those who would attend the event. Is this the Boston tea-and-coffee party? someone asked.

After a committee meeting one dull afternoon, a group of us began assembling Libby Greig's press kits on the marble table of Turnbull and Partners' conference room.

There was one matter which preoccupied me at this stage. As improbable as it might sound to many reasonable Australian academics, I was being headhunted by the University of California system, and had been politely refusing to go there since 1989. Now they offered me an ample research grant and other terms which it had become folly to refuse. I needed to raise and discuss the matter with the ARM committee.

The fact was that in the University of California at Irvine, in Orange County south of Los Angeles, there existed a Graduate Writing Program which was said variously to be 'the best graduate writing program west of the Mississippi', or else, in the words of the *Los Angeles Times*, 'the best writing program in the United States'. Its chief rival was the Iowa Graduate Writing Program. In July 1992 *Newsweek* would call the UCI program—for what these sorts of endorsements are worth— 'the hottest writing program in the country'.

The program consisted of poetry and fiction workshops, twelve writers in each. Each year six fiction writers and poets graduated, having in some cases already placed with a publisher the novel or book of verse they had written, or going on to do so—some of them filling in the time before their fiction was ready for publication with journalism and teaching.

The fiction section had been run until early 1991 by two American writers. The first was Oakley Hall, a writer of very stylish Western and other fiction (his novel *Warlock* was short-listed for the Pulitzer) a precursor of Larry MacMurtry and a former screen writer; and Don Heiney, who as MacDonald Harris wrote some of America's most original modern fiction.

Each year the fiction and poetry programs had a visiting fiction writer and a visiting poet. These people were also required to teach some undergraduate fiction writing. I went there in 1985 as visiting fiction writer.

I found that Orange County seemed a bit staid. It is to Los Angeles what Canberra is to Sydney. It is full of wealthy communities which remind you of Canberra, both for their well-planned air, and the way the architecture seems a statement against anarchy, eccentricity and quirkiness. If there is too much saving berserkness in New York and Los Angeles, there is too little of it in Orange County. It had a massive and complicated Latino community though, and was one of the centres of concentration of the old and new American Asian communities of Southern California. Little Saigon was located just a short way up Highway 405. In 1991, Asian undergraduate enrolments at UCI were 50 percent of the total, a figure which —given that there are so few problems between Asians and whites in Southern California, the Latinos and blacks figuring more strongly in interracial conflict with other Californians —casts more than a doubt across the paranoia of the Australian debate on Asian immigration.

It was specifically my experience at UCI in 1985, of seeing a massive and full-fledged 'Asian community' (a phrase which somehow always seems to imply that all Asians are in cahoots), that caused me to write a respectfully dissenting open letter to Geoffrey Blainey at the time he predicted massive conflict in Australia from a far more modest level of immigration than was found in Southern California.

In 1985 the writing students I was meant to teach were highly talented. Many of them were well on the way to ultimate and in some cases spectacular levels of publication—Michael Chabon of *The Mysteries of Pittsburgh* would become a major figure and Marti Liembach would soon be writing in class there a novel called *Dying Young*, which Nan Talese of Doubleday would publish for an advance of half a million dollars. A young woman named Whitney Otto was similarly writing in class *How to Make an American Quilt*, which would be much praised and much purchased.

After 1985, I particularly maintained friendships, or more accurately they generously maintained them with me, with two young novelists named Jim Brown and Michelle Latiolais. Jim was a little like Tim Winton: he had published his first novel at the age of eighteen years. It was a tough guy novel about car theft in Los Angeles. It was called *Hot Wire*. Michelle had ultimately finished her novel *Even Now*, and it had won the California Gold Medal for Literature.

Such were the patterns of patronage of young writers in the United States: very different from the largely government-based patronage found in Australia, and with strengths and weaknesses very different from the patronage near-vacuum in which young Australians have to work.

From 1989 onwards, the University of California had been asking me to come and take the retiring Oakley Hall's place at the head of the Fiction Writing Program. I didn't want to, to a passionate degree. It was that fear of the chair again. First of all, I couldn't imagine leaving Australia for a long period, especially now that after fifty years or more of experience of it I believed that I had learned something of it which I wanted to exploit in my writing. I also had a reasonable enough fear of taking over administering a program which had produced so many published novelists. By 1989–90, the American publishing industry was, like the Australian and British publishing industries, in recession. It was going to be harder now for the program to achieve as visible a success as it did in its glory days under Oakley.

The University of California kept writing me letters, though not as much as Oakley himself, who was well into his seventies and was now anxious to retire. The university said they would structure an arrangement by which I would be able to spend a great part of the year in Australia. They would employ what they dismissively called 'a young two-book novelist' to do all the administrative work. I would give one workshop a week for three quarters of the year one year, and one a week for two quarters of the second year, and so on. If I wanted to teach two classes in one quarter, it meant I could be back in Australia six months of the year. These were outrageously non-onerous terms. I would have a secretary and a research grant which would pay for any bona fide expenses associated with writing my books, including travel. I would have the most shamefully flash title of Distinguished Professor, a nomenclature impossible to utter in Australia, and especially while looking in a mirror, with a straight face.

I frankly admitted I had never graduated from an Australian secular university. Oh, from seminary days I had my Bachelor of Theology from the College for the Propagation of the Faith in Rome. Honourable enough in itself, and enough in 1960 to get me a job teaching in the Catholic school system for a few years. But no great basis for a job in an increasingly pluralist and complicated Australia.

I had begun studying Solicitor's Admission Board law, but that had been short circuited by my writing a first novel in the Christmas holidays of 1962–3, and when it was accepted by the English publishers Cassell, I was innocent enough to think, 'Tom, this is your future: publication will bind you to a literary career'. So, although I had been deep in constitutional law, Windeyer's legal history, the law of contracts, etc., I now poured everything into writing another novel. I had a naive belief that writing would support me, which in fact is not a bad conviction for a young writer to have.

In any case, I told the University of California and its President Frank Gardner that I lived in a degree-less condition. Not even an honorary degree to bless myself with. They didn't seemed fussed though.

When Neville had approached me about the job of chair of the Republican Movement, I had told him that any arrangement the Americans were making with me might require my absence for four to six months at a time. He told me absences wouldn't matter, but I was uneasy about them. The great problem would prove to be that we were making decisions in ignorance of how the Republican idea would catch on in Australia, of how large and continuous press attention would be.

I told UCI then about the Republican Movement, how it might develop only as a small lobby group but how it might become something larger. I was told by Oakley Hall that if necessary I could take leave without pay for as long as I needed, returning to the Writing Program whenever I was free to.

Assured by this, I accepted the UCI post in 1991.

I was to start there in October 1991. According to our original timetable this gave me the major part of the year to work on the ARM after it became a visible organisation. First the Gulf War and now the State election had so diminished the time available that I felt I had to put the problem to the committee and ask them what they thought I ought to do. I would be in Australia for barely three months after the launch of the movement. I said that of course I could return for special events, and in my free quarter for a few months at a time, and then I would be back in Australia as well from early June to early October the following year. But in view of the time absent, I offered to withdraw from the chair.

Donald Horne and the others could see no reason for me to do so, and I pledged that if it became necessary, I would simply give up the job.

Unknown to us as we approached the launch, gangling, boyish-faced Senator Chris Schacht of South Australia was working on a resolution to put to the Australian Labor Party's National Conference in Hobart in late June. The resolution read: 'This conference calls upon the government to embark upon a public education campaign, culminating in a referendum which would effect reform of the Australian Constitution and other political institutions to enable Australia to become an independent Republic on 1 January 2001.'

The motion was presented unexpectedly—at least from an observer's point of view—on the floor of the conference and was unanimously passed. Franca had let Schacht know previously about the existence of our movement, and now she felt he had used the news for his own political benefit at the Hobart Conference. But I believe that in this as in so many other matters, Schacht was something more than a practical politician and was ahead of general Australian opinion. He knew there was room in the question for a number of bodies, and his later behaviour would show that he wished the general success of the proposition in the broad community nothing but good.

The press gave his motion lots of attention, as did letter writers. Even so, by the Wednesday after the conference, the issue was starting to die. The Monarchist letter writers returned to their daily business, sure that the point had been made. Never before had Republicanism experienced such a run in the press—it was generally a one-headline wonder—but even so the enemies of constitutional Monarchy had been promptly picked off and chastised, just as had always seemed to happen in the past.

We were convinced that what little thunder we had had been stolen. We thought we were reduced to a citizen's debating club, and politically suspect at that.

To add to our bemusement, the Saturday before the launch, Leo Schofield, the food columnist who writes a more comprehensive column in the weekend *Sydney Morning Herald*, mentioned as his lead piece who we were, and when and where we were to meet. Schofield was a supporter of the republic, but he was here simply unleashing his boyish enthusiasm and his need of copy. He had no doubt heard from one of our members.

In any case, the small thunder left to us seemed half used up now. We foresaw a week of making 'No comments' to the press, persuading people to wait for the press kits by Friday. 'Meet the Press', a news interview program on SBS, wanted me to do a quasi-debate on the issue, but we couldn't arrange it so that whatever confidentiality still existed could be retained.

July seventh was one of the duller Sydney winter days. Not grim, but a plain Sunday morning. I had a final read over of my speech in the little computer room at the top of the stairs. My life then, as always, was lived at what I found a berserk pace, and I hadn't had time really to rehearse the thing. I knew it wouldn't satisfy most parties either. The Monarchists would think it the voice of the anti-Christ. Leftists and Brit-baiters would think it too mild. It took a less than iconoclastic line on the Monarchy and on the British past, but that seemed to me and other members of the committee the only sane and fraternal line to take. I had never been a lover of the Monarchy and I had never thought that attachment to it was part of the definition of an Australian. And yet I knew various Australians who still did, and for that reason, for the reason of the affections of other Australians rather than for the Woman of Windsor herself, we believed that the past was worth acknowledging.

The speech would dissatisfy some because it did not buy into other passionately debated issues either—justice for Aborigines, the unemployment of the young, the lack of guaranteed rights in the Constitution, and so on. Again, we were convinced that too big a portmanteau of issues would sink us, and we even believed that there was hope for all Australians and all their concerns implicit in the drive towards a Republic.

The Australian Monarchy had been throughout my childhood and youth such a hedged-about subject, such an institution above uttered reproach, that many of us had a sense that

Sunday that by the afternoon we would be looked upon in a different light by our communities. We would be pariahs. Solid citizens would shun us.

My community was a markedly conservative one. It was the tip of Sydney's Pittwater-Palm Beach Peninsula, and the conservative primary vote had rarely been much less that 60 percent. A younger generation had thrown support into independents, including the former world surfing champion and environmentalist, Nat Young. By and large, however, the Peninsula was safe ground for the Liberal Party. The Federal member Jim Carlton was an urbane man, indeed an old friend, but 'a dry' economically—to suit the temper of his electorate. He was at least a genuine political thinker, not just a kneejerk conservative.

I wondered what it would be like coming home to Jim Carlton's electorate of MacKellar having made the statement I was about to make. I was thinking as most normal human beings do of my strained finances too. Though I had been a very fortunate writer in earning my own living (a fact which I find sadly—in the view of some of Australia's literary wowsers—means your work can't be serious), I was, like most artists, or primary producers for that matter, sometimes stretched.

Again, a guesthouse named Echoes was high on my mental agenda. Judy and I had gone into partnership with various friends in a beautiful but cash-absorbent little guesthouse near Echo Point at Katoomba. It was a grotesque thing to do, and we did it of our own volition, in part enchanted with the great Jamison Valley escarpment and with the vision of banding together skills to produce something beautiful there. There were remarkable omens, it seemed to me: just one, the builder was an Italian who had grown up entirely in Asmara up to the time the war started in Eritrea. (This sadly is characteristic of the basis on which I have generally made decisions, sometimes very fortunate ones.)

When Echoes began business on St Patrick's Day 1991, bringing in some hundreds of visitors and press, Nick Greiner kindly came up officially to open it. Immediately it began taking guests, the locals—as is the normal custom of country towns—began predicting its demise. It was, to use the nifty term, 'highly geared'. It was slow, as these places are, to work up a clientele. By July, we were hoping we could refinance to satisfy various creditors.

In a sense, it was for me a bad time to be driving good Monarchists away from my books *and* our shared guesthouse. As long as they didn't break the windows of the place. We didn't want to add the cost of glazing to our other expenses.

Going to town from the north over the Bridge is always a genuine journey. Sydney and the Harbour seem to deliver themselves to you. But this Sunday had settled in to leadenness. It was not the sort of dazzling humid day on which Arthur Phillip, a complex, talented, but small-beer official with nonetheless enormous powers to claim-on-behalf-of, converted through the utterance of a few words two million square miles of Australia into Crown Land. This didn't look like a day for transmuting anything.

At the Regent, a small reception room upstairs had been prepared. Foundation members and the press had been invited, but the crowd was sparse when I arrived, and Libby hoped that some television and some of the dailies would yet be there.

We were worried that Monarchists might try to break up the meeting. Franca, whose connections were manifold, had got Superintendent Ireland of the Special Branch to provide two men for the door. The strange and sad thing was that the only people they turned away were Republicans, who had read about us in Schofield and were excited by the prospect of something happening at last. It wasn't the first time we misjudged our public, or out of fear for the integrity of our message, failed to meet the wants of potential supporters.

The primal spell of the Monarchy—which had hung over Australia all this time, an extraordinary survival, an amalgam of magic and atavism and dependence and a relic of our obvious but decreasing Britishness—still seemed so strong. Though it was about to be diminished in a most significant way, that was not the way the modest press event felt to me.

At last a number of press, radio and television people turned up, as well as more foundation members. I could see in the audience, for example, Alison Broinowski, author and diplomat; Ian Chappell, the test cricket captain; Bruce Petty, the cartoonist; John Bell, the actor; and the naturalist, Vincent Serventy.

All the members of our committee arrived and sat at a long

table under Harry Seidler's colourful banner, and the rostrum at the centre carried the logo designed by Joe Bolen.

I made a simple three and a half page statement. It was in some of its parts a much more cajoling document than should have been necessary so late in history. But the old problem was there: in the irrational Australian habits of debate on this question, attachment to Britain was somehow enlightened internationalism, but to claim purely Australian identity was both jingoistic and—most scandalous of all—a denial of the past and an insult to the Monarchy.

'Here in the Rocks,' I said,

> we are close to where, on that humid day in 1788, Captain Phillip acknowledged the supremacy of the House of Hanover over two-thirds of this astounding continent. Since that day this country has had a special connection with and affection for the Monarchy. Special institutional relationships have existed between Australia and the Monarchy of Great Britain. Acknowledging and respecting that fact, we nonetheless propose that on 1 January 2001, etc. etc.

I argued that a Republic was not a denial of Australian identity but a confirmation of it.

> Ever since that January day two hundred and three years ago, we have harboured a suspicion that store ships, bounties, kindnesses would be sent on their way to us from a more benign hemisphere than our own. We came to feel we possessed both an inherent worthiness which would assure that others—our betters—would look after us; and an inherent inferiority which convinced us we were not worthy to manage ourselves or speak with an utterly independent voice. Both these suspicions are delusions and have damaged us and have kept and will continue to keep us a stunted nation ... If we cannot find loyalty, sanity and human decency amongst ourselves, then we are finished. If we wish to be a genuine nation, we cannot indulge for much longer our lust for dependence on others.

At this stage we proposed that the ultimate form of the Republic would be decided by public debate. Ultimately though we would find questioners wanted us to put up a basic model, which we would do.

I mentioned all the oaths we took to the Crown, and said it was time to cease that.

> It is time we did ourselves the honour of finding from within our own resources and from amongst ourselves a Head of State whose identity is entirely Australian and does not depend for its legitimacy on anyone other than us and anything other than our institutions.
> It is time we ceased to divide our soul . . .

I distanced the ARM from the Labor Party resolution of Hobart. 'The Labor Party passed a similar motion in 1986 and has done nothing to advance the debate on the question. It is the duty of citizens to advance the debate . . .'

At one point, I felt instinctively that I should say, 'Three cheers for the Monarchy, four cheers for the people of Australia'. I suppose it was a means of making the point, but the three cheers did not come from the pit of the soul, since I thought the Monarchy, again through little fault of the Monarch, was a disaster for Australia. I suppose that I was acknowledging the mystical and visceral place the Monarchy occupied in the world plan of many fellow Australians, particularly ones my age.

When I had finished, the floor was open to questions. The first question was from Vin Serventy. Vin was a renowned naturalist of Hungarian descent, a much-honoured campaigner for endangered species. His work had been internationally recognised, as it has been at home by an Order of Australia. He was a tireless writer too, enormously prolific. I had a prejudice in favour of people who wrote strenuously and copiously. He was a champion of Aboriginal rights, too. He said now he wanted to ask Faith Bandler on the committee whether she thought the ARM should also add to its objectives the abolition of the present Australia Day, insulting as it was to native Australians.

Whether wisely or not, I explained that the movement wanted to campaign on this one issue, given that it was one from which a consensus could be easily derived. But the climate of Australian thinking would be transformed by the Republic, and it was unlikely that a Republic would continue to celebrate as its national day the anniversary of what was an event in the Imperial settlement of Australia. I said therefore we were not a committee formed to deal with the Australia Day controversy and ruled the question out of order for that reason. Vin said with a Hungarian intensity, 'You've made the biggest mistake of your life.'

Fortunately, other members of the committee, Donald Horne and Faith herself, were then asked questions. And then we all did separate interviews, television and radio, in sundry corners of the room, and Franca introduced me to the Special Branch men, whom I thanked, one of them saying, 'I think it'll be a long wait for it to happen.' And then an imaginative press photographer took us all down to Circular Quay so that, standing in a long line, our picture could be taken holding Harry Seidler's multi-coloured banner.

We were public now. Our declarations were on tape and in the can. Some of us went to a Chinese meal with Malcolm Turnbull at the Imperial Peking in Campbell's Warehouses. We cracked some bottles of Chardonnay in a mood of tentative exhilaration. I still had to face the possible scorn of Brookvale Oval. I had an arrangement to be there every time Manly-Warringah played. Though Rugby League was a proletarian game, Brookvale nonetheless stood in the midst of a fairly conservative electorate represented by Malcolm Fraser's former Immigration and Health Minister, Michael MacKellar.

The day's light was still grim and un-exultant. On the car journey out to the ground, the launch was headline news, and various excerpts from my speech were run. I was impressed that most of the reports concentrated on the main issue and avoided taking statements out of context. The speech had been crafted so that very little in it could be taken in isolation from the chief message, but just the same, this early radio response—and radio is prodigiously important in Australia—seemed open-minded, and concerned with doing some justice to the issue.

I reached the ground just before kick-off. As I moved behind the stand on the way to my seat, I was detained by the highly muscular hand of a man called Gordon Willoughby. Willoughby was a Manly committee man and had played on the wing against France in great test matches of the 1950s. In the club history there is a fine press photograph of handsome Gordon at his height, wearing a ferocious grimace as he breaks a French tackle.

Now Gordon said, 'I've got a bone to pick with you on this Republican business. You reckon you want to say good-bye to them with a kiss. I don't agree with that. I think they're a pack of bludgers. Tell 'em to go to buggery.'

In the stand, I sat in front of Doug Daley, the club's chief executive, and other committeemen and their wives. Apart from a fairly jovial passing reference, none of them seemed to think some great blasphemy had been committed. Everyone was full of the characteristic, cathartic tension of pre-whistle time, waiting for the great Wallaby and Kangaroo centre Michael O'Connor and the boys. The semi-finals were only seven or so games away.

Could—after all—the austere magic of the House of Windsor have such a poor grasp on these genial, middle class Australian men? Even the committee wives did not seem to treat me like a pariah. One of them, a generous and gentle woman I have known for some years, put her hand on my elbow and said, 'I'm so pleased you said that we'd leave with a kiss. I think that's the right way.' I did not bother her with Gordon Willoughby's more pungent suggestions.

Even by that evening, it was apparent that Australian Republicanism would have an impact not only on Australians, but would generate interest in other nations as well. The BBC World Service found me at home, and an interviewer, perhaps not up to the general intellectual strength of that fine organisation, said, 'You know, if you become a Republic, you won't get the BBC World Service anymore.'

I said that that would certainly give us reason to pause. 'But India gets the BBC World Service, doesn't it?'

'India's not a Republic,' he asserted.

'I believe you'll find it's been one since 1950.'

'Really?'

The next day when the radio and television interviewer Michael Parkinson called from London, having been a man consistently interested in Australia and one who had a no-nonsense Yorkshire proletarian upbringing, I confessed to him that sometimes I did not know with super-Brits whether they were being very dumb or very subtle. Parkinson said, 'I think you can't go wrong presuming they're dumb.'

The New Zealand Broadcasting Commission quickly reached me at home. I had got to know many of the New Zealand press the year before, when I had fronted a documentary in New Zealand about the destiny of the two nations. New Zealanders are appalled by the prospect of the ultimate union which is in progress through CER (Closer Economic Relations), under which the two countries enjoy free trade, and their highest courts have the power to convene in the other country in matters to do with free passage of goods. Many New Zealanders of course reasonably enough dread involving themselves in the mish mash of powers shared by Federal and State authorities. They would never want to buy into that mess as just a separate province. Their history, their view of themselves, and their national stature make it an impossibility that they would do so, so that when and if the day comes, it will call forth some form of super-federation between the two nations. We will have to make our sacrifices too. Christchurch would probably need to be a likely site for the new suprafederal capital.

The New Zealand interviewers seemed startled by our very ordinary move in a way the Australian press didn't. One of the New Zealand radio people told me that a Republic was considered a pretty sacrilegious thing to suggest in New Zealand, but that now those New Zealanders who saw its inevitability knew that our success or failure would have a large bearing on them.

'We'll wait the week out and see if it's still sacrilegious here,' I told them.

Later in the week I had to go to Ireland—it was a long-arranged commitment. I had agreed to give a paper on *The Portrait of the Artist as a Young Man* at the Joyce Summer School in St Stephen's Green in Dublin. It was a chance to see my daughter, who had gone to Dublin as a young journalist because the Australian media had been decimated by the speculations of the 1980s. I was due to leave on Thursday afternoon, since Libby Greig had guessed that there was no way the press furore would last much more than three days.

In fact, the interest was massive and continuous. On the Monday, we did between us thirty-three press, radio and television interviews within Australia, and at least seven or eight international interviews. I remember appearing on 'Good Morning Australia' and encountering the Monarchist starch of Kerry Ann Kennerley. Later in the week I engaged in debate on the '7:30 Report' with Lloyd Waddy, QC. Malcolm took on Senator Bronwyn Bishop on 'A Current Affair'. The good Senator took so irrational a position on a Republic, predicting that we would have tanks in the streets and would become a neo-Bulgaria, that Malcolm ended up making a strong recommendation to all of us that we should not debate the issues, given that at that stage it seemed that the strategy of our opponents would be primitive alarmism.

In both Bronwyn Bishop's and Lloyd Waddy's case, there was a tendency to lay all the credit for Australian institutions upon the Crown, or else purely on Britishness-under-the-Crown. Lloyd Waddy made much of the fact that the trading partners we wanted to get on with—Thailand, Japan—had royal families. Yes, I said, but the Japanese royal family *is* Japanese, and the Thai royal family *is* Thai.

There were from some occasional dismissive references to the Irish too, but we had the advantage that it was very difficult to cast Franco Belgiorno-Nettis or Jenny Kee as Fenians.

As well as the interviews, there was writing: Malcolm Turnbull had been commissioned to do an article on Australian Republicanism for the *Daily Mail*, and I had been asked to do one for the editorial page of the London *Daily Telegraph*, and pieces for the *Australian* and the *Age* as well.

It was obvious within a few days that the ARM's concentration on basics—that we were not talking about an American system of presidency; that we were not talking of denial of the

British colonial past so precious to some and precious in its way to us too, but that we were talking of celebration of Australian maturity—began to bring about extraordinary results. the *Telegraph Mirror*, for example, the sort of newspaper which up till now had been associated with affectionate support of the Monarchy, ran an editorial commending the debate to Australians.

I was concerned about possible threats against members of my extended family. I had had a silent number for some years, since in the late 1970s I received a number of death threats from anonymous callers who claimed to be upset about something I was researching at the time. I did not want to have parents, siblings, and cousins bearing that disorienting initial panic which goes along with someone threatening to kill you by sunset. On the Sunday night of the launch, when I called at my parents to let them know they should contact me in the event of unpleasant phone calls, a woman *did* call the number and abrade me fairly gently for the position I had taken. She was charitable enough to argue that someone had got at me, was using me, because she knew from my writing that I was not really that *type of person*.

All the other calls relatives received were from people who wanted to get in contact with the ARM. That was the other thing—the passionate response of many Australians. I remember waiting to go on the ABC program called 'AM' one grim morning that week when a young man who had taken the trouble to call from Victoria, called the station and told me how pleased he was that this had happened, how bemused he had been on joining the Air Force to find that he had to take an oath to the Monarch of Great Britain.

I suppose you can gather from this mish mash of impressions that the interviews and the debates ran right up to plane-catching time on Thursday. I was going to do further work in Ireland—write the piece for the *Telegraph*, do some interviews with British radio from the studios of Radio Telefis Eireann at Donnybrook on the south side of Dublin. One of the broadcasts I had agreed to was to be a debate with an Australian Monarchist on BBC Scotland. For the Scots too were interested in the ARM, given their own strong sense of identity, their Republican streak, and their desire for at least internal self-government.

I work a lot on planes—I was working on a novel called *Woman of the Inner Sea* as my wife and I flew to London to catch the Aer Lingus commuter plane over the Irish Sea. *Woman of the Inner Sea* was an utter fable. Unlike the books which preceded it, *Towards Asmara*, which was concerned with the enormous war Ethiopia was waging on the Eritreans, and the way that war, with its waste of lives and resources, was the engine of the cyclical famines of the Horn of Africa, and *Flying Hero Class*, which was about Palestinians and Aborigines, *Woman of the Inner Sea* was purely a fable. It was the tale of a wealthy young Australian woman named Kate who loses her two children and undertakes a redemptive journey into the interior of Australia, changing herself into a more ancient kind of Australian woman, travelling with archetypal figures—a battler named Gus, a kangaroo named Chifley, an emu named Menzies. An apparently utterly unpolitical book. And not politically correct either, since I, an ageing Australian male, was daring to break the edict which said that men, particularly patriarchal Australian men, should not write from within the consciousness of a woman.

During that long night's journey to England, I worked a little on the Kate book and at last fell asleep.

I have never become mentally adjusted to intercontinental travel. In World War II in Australia, when passenger trains were constantly side-railed to let troop trains through, it could take us as long to get from Sydney to Brisbane as it now takes to get from Sydney to London. Sometimes I wonder if 'they' —the masters of the whole stunt of flying—are not running a film outside your window and simulating your destination for you when the film runs out.

But the London papers and the accents, combined with the pre-dawn gloom of an average English summer day, brings its own conviction. The Sunday before, the *Times* had run a long, basically genial, sceptical feature on the ARM. They seemed to find Malcolm Turnbull the sort of sharp-minded larrikin they most wanted to dampen with half-amused but sometimes steely contempt. On the morning we landed, there were two letters in the *Times* about the Australian Republican Movement. I read them on the way from Terminal One to Terminal Three. One was from the Australian Trade Commissioner in London, who argued reasonably enough that whatever the rights and wrongs of the Republican debate, it had to be recognised that Britain had made trade arrangements to its advantage from which Australia had been excluded.

The second letter was from a Western Australian couple holidaying in the United Kingdom who wanted to assure the readers of the *Times* that not all Australians harboured the same ungracious sentiments as Tom Keneally and the ALP displayed. This showed in one sense that the Labor Party resolution still hung over us and seemed to compromise us in a way we had not chosen. But the tenor of the letter was in some ways pitiable when it wasn't amusing. Most Australians, this couple asserted, treasured British institutions and Australia's British past. Therefore their attachment to the Monarchy was four-square.

Not only was there the old depressing gulf of logic here, in that it is possible to believe in the heritage as at least a mixed blessing, yet still not to believe in unending dependence. But the text of the letter spoke all too clearly of the servile desire of Dominion people to prove their respectability to the inhabitants of the mother country.

As we crossed North Wales on the way to Dublin, I wondered what would be in the Dublin papers. I hoped that it would be nothing one way or another, since any approval from that direction would be a sure sign to folk like Peter King and Senator Bronwyn Bishop that we were somehow stooges of the Irish. Not that the *Irish Times*, for which my daughter wrote features, and did occasional sub-editing, had ever been a Republican paper. It had always been the Anglo newspaper of the grand, small city of Dublin, whose character was in any case an inextricable amalgam of British and Irish. In fact the press of the Republic of Eire would always show less interest in the

Republican movement in Australia than the British press did.

When, having given my talk at the Joyce Summer School, I went to Radio Telefios Eireann to do the hook-up to Scotland for the debate, sitting in the usual comfortless radio booth from which these matters are always arranged, I found that my opponent would be Bronwyn Bishop. Senator Bishop was the most notorious pusher of the idea that Australian Republicanism was Irish and therefore dismissible—when it wasn't Stalinist and deadly dangerous.

I have to confess that Bronwyn was, for whatever reasons, a good tactical champion of the Monarchy, but never a good strategic one. She was formidable not intellectually, but in the business of the tricks she could play. She was one of those practical politicians whose chief talent consists of scaring the electorate away from honest, visionary options by means of what could most kindly be described as over-exaggeration. Her electorate was the electorate of fear. Over coming months, her idea that an end to the Monarchy would mean bloodshed and flame-throwers would obviously fail to impress most Australians. But she did not know that the morning we had our debate.

In my little closed booth I heard the hook-up occur, the commentator in Scotland speaking to Australian journalist Murray Hedgecock in London and Bronwyn Bishop in Sydney. Senator Bishop's opening statement indicated a belief that my presence in Dublin bore out certain suspicions she had always held. 'I think it's very interesting that Tom is speaking to us from Dublin. Of course I don't know what he's doing there. Probably visiting some relatives' (with a heavy emphasis on 'relatives') 'or other.'

I confess that her tone made me very volatile. I took the option of questioning her Australian identity, and calling her the Senator for South Britain. I said that I didn't know which to attack first, her racial slander or her lies that only a minute and raucous minority wanted an Australian Republic. This latter claim was the argument which would be used in nearly every debate on the issue over the next year, before the tide of polls made it no longer tenable.

The question of who Australian Monarchists represent and

are speaking for is a valid one, despite the Royal Styles and Titles Act of 1973 which calls the Monarch Queen of Australia (a title with no constitutional force), but as I say elsewhere in this memoir, as valid as it is to put the question in terms of national identity, it has not been valid in the past to question the Australian nationalism of those who support the Monarchy. For the whole matter was a far more complicated one earlier in this century than it is now. The present William Charles Wentworth, former Menzies minister, wrote about the dilemma of the post-Empire Australian Monarchist in the late 1970s,

> To most of us the Queen is still primarily Queen of the United Kingdom. Her technical title of Queen of Australia seems secondary. The doctrine of two separate offices being held by the same person does not seem to have made its impact ... The Monarchy has thus tended to lose its old significance because the United Kingdom means less to us than it once did.

In 1984, the *Australian* ran an editorial pointing up the same problems:

> It is not absurdly pedantic to suggest that this (Britain and Australia sharing the Queen) could lead to difficulties. It is unlikely that most of the world's inhabitants fully appreciate the intricacies of our constitutional monarchy and some of them may assume that, when the Queen of Australia, in the course of her travels, says something to which they take exception, she is speaking on our behalf.

Professor Michael Pryles told the Constitutional Commission in 1988, 'If the British government continues to use the Queen in this way' (when pretending to be Queen of a number of countries including Australia she speaks only for Britain) 'the conclusion must be that it is intolerable to have the same person as Head of State of two independent countries.'

Indeed, though none of this seems to trouble them in their Monarchist stupor, modern Monarchists (that oxymoron again) have less grounds to claim Australian identity than they used to, since the shifts of world power and trade have made the Australian Monarchy a more baseless, inconvenient and grotesque attachment than it even was before.

Bronwyn Bishop's Monarchism was of this order.

In any case, I had the calm left to fall back on the question of our membership, and what ethnic groups they stood for. As in a debate at Sydney University with John Howard nearly a year later, I raised the question of whether Franco Belgiorno-Nettis could credibly be considered a crypto-Fenian. I wondered if Jenny Kee could be considered to have been infected with Derry Republicanism? I wondered if David Hill, Dr Barnardo Boy, could have been swayed by Irish history in the dressing room at North Sydney? Were Donald Horne or Malcolm Turnbull motivated by the grief of Irish Famine and dispossession?

For the first time in that year but not for the last I was delighted that only two of our committee, myself and Geraldine Doogue, were of overtly Irish derivation.

Up to the time of this visit to Ireland, I had hoped to be going to Eritrea in August with Fred Hollows, the brave, pragmatic and honest-hewn Australian eye surgeon. Fred, despite his failing health, had been travelling to Eritrea for a number of years, operating on cataract, trachoma and glaucoma cases. The war added savage eye trauma to the Dhalak blindness caused by the pitiless glare of the land and the Red Sea.

It was never an easy journey into Eritrea. It involved travelling through the turbulent and increasingly disordered Sudan to Port Sudan, and then by truck into what the Eritreans called 'the Field', the tragic zone in which they fought for survival for thirty years, first against the Emperor Haile Selassie, next against the vicious and prodigal Mengistu.

Typically, Fred's commitment to the Eritreans had begun when he had treated one of them in his Sydney surgery. He was *par excellence* the sort of man who *was* ruled by his reaction to specific cases, who *did* react with vigorous and thorough-going generosity, whether it was ill-advised from a personal point of view or not.

So Fred was prepared to travel into Eritrea by truck, journeying at night to avoid bombers, even while suffering from a potentially terminal cancer. He had also worked with and taught the chief Eritrean eye surgeon, Desbele, in Sydney, and the Eritrean reunions between the dawn-arriving Fred and Desbele, who had just finished a night of operations, were a fascinating image of the kinship between Australians and the Eritrean underdogs.

Now Fred had unapologetically used his stature as Australian of the Year to raise money for an intra-ocular lens facility for Eritrea. In their bunkers in the hills north of Asmara, to the astonishment and admiration of Fred and other visitors, the Eritreans had been for some years manufacturing their own intravenous drips. Their laminar flow sterilisation plants had been built, maintained and operated by night under the noses of the Antinovs and Migs of Mengistu's Ethiopian Air Force, the largest in Africa.

The month after the ARM was launched, Fred was going to Eritrea again to initiate the installation of the lenses facility, which would enable the Eritreans to manufacture the small plastic lens used in cataract operations, and ultimately to export them to the rest of Africa at a fraction of the $140 a piece it would take to import them from their European and North American centres of manufacture.

But when I got back to Sydney and spoke to Denise Darlow, Neville Wran's assistant and our unofficial executive secretary, it became apparent that there were too many debates to be had, too many interviews to be given, too many articles to be written, to permit me to travel in Fred's valiant shadow to an Eritrea now newly at peace.

I remember one particular debate I had on SBS television, 'Meet the Press'. The two pressmen I had to meet were David McNicoll, the veteran journalist and Packer henchman, and his son D. D. McNicoll. David McNicoll is a famous Australian curmudgeon who knows everyone, including—especially by his own report—members of the Royal family. When I debated him he had just returned from the splendid, English stars-and-Royals-graced wedding of the Packer scion in England. David McNicoll's son D.D. was a journalist for the opposition, Murdoch's News Ltd., with less of a flamboyant air than David. He insisted upon being called D.D. and in this, as in many other attitudes, one saw a lifetime of affection between them, combined though with the banked electricity of past hostilities.

Some people said about this debate that it showed the Republican issue was a little like the American Civil War, which split families. The difference was that the Republican idea did not lead to fratricidal or patricidal strife. It was no more divisive than any issue of the kind they call 'generational'.

David McNicoll uttered the one question which seems to younger Australians like a frank confession of colonial inferiority complex, even though I know it does not seem that way to those who ask it. 'Well,' (with an indulgent chuckle at the impossibility of what is being proposed) 'what Australian could you pick for such a high office?'

Again the question was recurring which is not even raised in most mature societies. *Who amongst us is worthy, Lord?*

I suggested a number of women: Ita Buttrose, Geraldine Doogue, Faith Bandler . . . The press seized on the Ita Buttrose nomination and that became the fatuous story that arose from the debate.

My colleagues were not too happy. I pleaded jet lag. But I still believe that Australia is full of appropriate talent. That many amongst us are worthy.

CHAPTER SEVEN

*

MEMOIRS FROM A YOUNG REPUBLIC II

THE MOOD OF our first committee meeting after the launch was one of jubilance mixed with awe. We had seen ourselves as Sisyphus, pushing the rock uphill which, for all the pushing, would only acquire more downhill, damaging momentum. (There are various Australian pungent versions of this myth, all to do with pushing certain substances uphill with billiard cues.) Now the boulder was at the summit and rolling down the other side with increased momentum, and our problem was to run beside it and make its path smooth. Hundreds of people were writing to ARM every day, asking for membership. All this based on occasional mention of the telephone number and the box number on radio or television.

It was apparent we would need a secretariat, and Turnbull & Partners generously offered to be the base for recruiting an executive officer and paying his or her salary. Franca Arena had worked on a number of State parliamentary committees whose administrative officer had been an efficient young man called Tony Pooley. The last such committee had been a controversial parliamentary hearing into compensation for Aids victims. Tony Pooley had not been associated with the findings of the committee. His job was purely to arrange venues, witnesses, act as an executive secretary, keep the records, etc., etc.

Franca, who was chair of the committee, had come under severe pressure. Rightly or wrongly, the committee had found in favour of compensation for those who had acquired Aids through such means as blood transfusions, and not to compensate those who had acquired it through their style of life. Reacting to the decision, the gay action group Queer Nation began to 'out' people, writing the names of supposedly homosexual politicians and notables on walls in the Eastern suburbs. They outed, as well, Franca's two sons and threatened an attack upon her with a syringe full of Aids-infected blood.

They were not the only critics of the committee's finding. Even those who would be compensated considered the compensation Franca's committee offered inadequate. Bryce Courtenay, author of *The Power of One*, appeared on television bitterly attacking the proposed compensation payments as fragmentary and an insult. His son, who has since died, was a haemophiliac who had acquired Aids through blood transfusions.

In the midst of all this attack, anguish and physical danger, Franca still had time to recommend Tony as a viable candidate for the job.

When he was appointed to run ARM's office, Tony still had a number of weeks to serve working for a further parliamentary committee, but soon he was operating from Turnbull & Partners. If and when Australia becomes a Republic, that company should have honour for providing logistical and financial backing to the movement, which in its first year of existence and even after, became the chief protector and advancer of the debate.

Fred Hollows went to Eritrea and was honoured at their September festival, the first peace time celebration of the commencement of the Eritrean resistance. In Australia, the Republican question amazed even experts like Libby Greig by simply rolling on and on. I was still trying to finish *Woman of the Inner Sea*, but it was daily a difficult business to get to it given the demand of speaking engagements, for articles from organs as different as *Australian Business Monthly*, the *Age*, the *Australian*, the *Irish Times* and the London *Daily Telegraph*. Other members of the movement, particularly Donald Horne, Malcolm Turnbull and Franca Arena, were under a similar continual pressure.

One meeting I spoke to seemed to me significant. It was a branch of the Young Liberals on the North Shore of Sydney. The meeting demonstrated the changing face and demographics of the Liberal Party. The grandchildren of the Irish, and the children of Jewish and European immigrants, who might once have been out of place in the Liberal Party, had now found a spiritual home there and were active and—as Nick Greiner had showed—even dominant.

I have a brother who says, 'Yes, but the only thing that made such liberality possible was the Labor Party!' His argument is that these people should show a little gratitude.

That aside, I had a drink after this speech with two of the young Liberals, one of them of Lebanese descent, the other with an Irish name. One of those typical Irish Australian giants, he had political ambitions. He confessed that he was a Republican in principle, but that the Liberal Party probably contained only 10 percent of Republicans at the rank and file and parliamentary level. His estimation was that there were 30 to 40 percent 'inevitablists', who believed that Australia would become a Republic one day but who, like St Augustine praying for chastity, didn't want it to happen yet.

The rest, 50 percent or more, were either passionate Monarchists or else reflex ones.

This young, lanky, political animal said that though he was a believer in the Republic, there was no way he would stand on it. As a genuine Liberal ideologue, he was willing to let the Republic look after itself while practical politics was attended to.

A year later, I met him by accident at Parliament House in Macquarie Street, and he told me that he believed that there had been a large shift by then in the Liberal Party's mix of Republicans and 'inevitablists'. The closet Republicans had grown to more than 20 percent and the 'inevitablists'—again to his estimation—to more than half the parliamentary party. There was still a group in the New South Wales Liberal Party, led by such people as Peter King and Bronwyn Bishop and numbering John Howard amongst their supporters, who were explicitly devoted to the preservation of the Monarchy in Australia. But he believed that as little as a quarter of Liberals were now passionately devoted to the survival of the Australian Monarchy.

We realised then, as we always did, that it would be when sitting members found it safe and reasonable to identify themselves as Republicans, and only then, that the matter of Australia's constitutional future should go to referendum.

Given the pace of the debate up to this point, it may not be too long before the first brave Liberal, or group of Liberals, emerges. Meanwhile, many of them have the opportunity to hide behind the argument that Republicanism is a Keating smoke-screen, or that there are far more serious matters to look at—again, as if Australia's present economic disaster does not arise anyhow from the whole culture of dependence and small thought, of which the attachment to the Monarchy is the living symbol.

In that post launch period, one of the invitations to speak came from the Australian businessman Bob Ansett, something of a hero of the boom times of the 1980s, now a businessman under siege, but still of adequate eminence to be President of the North Melbourne Football Club. Given Australian Rules football's place as the touchstone and point of intersection of Melbourne life, the city frequently rewarded its best and brightest with such club presidencies. Whereas Sydney Rugby League clubs, except in exceptional cases like that of David Hill, tended to stick with old players who sometimes, but not always, had business expertise. Presidency of a Melbourne Aussie Rules Club was a large, if honorary, commercial prize.

The North Melbourne Grand Final Breakfast was to be held

at the Hilton. I found out that the thing was televised and was the prime grand final breakfast of them all. Prime ministers and leaders of the Opposition and premiers and cabinet ministers attended, along with other notables. The primary interest of the breakfasters would be to get a nice champagne-glow on so they could take it out to cold VFL Park with them. (Because of renovations to the Melbourne Cricket Ground, VFL Park was the venue for the Grand Final in 1991.)

Yet there was always an at least demi-serious speech, often given by a politician.

I began to work hard on the speech. I knew that in some ways it was an important test for ARM's message.

In terms of AFL football, it was an historic year, in that for the first time an out-of-Victoria team, the West Coast Eagles, was playing a Melbourne team Hawthorn for what Australian Rules people called 'the flag'. In that sense, in the code whose supporters always said that it was the only truly 'national' game, it was possible for the first time to call this Grand Final a genuinely 'national' Grand Final. I was of course going to put the argument—it would frequently later be put by the new Prime Minister Keating, who was a Collingwood supporter—that if you wanted to claim a 'nationality' for Australian Rules, what was wrong with claiming a nationality for the nation?

Most famous Melbourne males I had known, and many famous females, find Aussie Rules not only their world's central game, but a sort of passionate central rite. I think of Manning Clark, Carlton supporter—I believe it was the first time I met him in 1967, when I went down to speak to his students at ANU, that I was told that. Carlton supporter; part of his definition as a human. In Volume VI of his *History of Australia*, he finds a key to the character both to Prime Minister Curtin and Prime Minister Menzies in their Melbourne team affiliations. He looks at its impact on artists too. 'As Louis Esson (the writer) told Vance Palmer later, football was "taken with high seriousness in Carlton." Any "weakening of the old Blues" was regarded as a national calamity.'

That honourable Australian craftsman and political activist Esson was appalled that Carlton supporters considered a Carlton loss more significant than a general election, but the fact didn't stop him becoming an habitue of Carlton himself. '[Football] is the most serious matter in the State.'

One day in the late 1970s, when the ABC got a number of us together for a weekend in the Dandenongs as a sort of think tank for a proposed series on the history of Australia, Manning Clark had gone walking before breakfast in the bush in his trilby and encountered a Carlton immortal called Percy Jones, who was on suspension that particular Saturday. Manning returned to our breakfast table in a state of Paulian, thunderstruck transcendence.

David Williamson the playwright had sacrificed Melbourne for hedonist Sydney, and many Melburnians never forgave him for it. But Collingwood, the traditional battler's team, still claimed him. The arts community in Sydney rarely scheduled events for David—whether they were panels of the Literature Board or Australian Writers' Guild seminars—in terms of whether Collingwood was on the television or not, or playing the Swans on the Sydney Cricket Ground. Williamson was frequently called on to make the Saturday sacrifice of not seeing the Aussie Rules game on Channel 7.

Perhaps the most intense instance of the identification of Australian rules with Australian identity is the case of Fred Schepisi, enormously talented film director and foundation member of the Republican Movement. Fred once told me that during the filming of one of his less successful pictures, *Iceman*, when, in Churchill above the Arctic Circle in Hudson's Bay, he had broken his leg and there was a morale problem amongst the actors, he had staged a special Aussie Rules night using tapes of Hawthorn's last quarters as the chief party pieces. A drinks trolley was set up in a corridor so that people could pour themselves some liquor before entering the room to behold the Hawthorn wonders. Schepisi told me that the actors, including Timothy Hutton and Lindsay Krause, were astounded by what they beheld and asked rhetorical questions about why America hadn't been blessed with a game like this?

I would later meet one of these actors, the character actor Josef Sommer, who said that the game had been incomprehensible to himself and the other actors. They had left Fred in his wheelchair, jabbing his finger towards the video screen yelling, 'Look at that!' and had congregated in the corridor.

At a party at Fred's place just after Christmas 1989, Meryl Streep—who had acted in two of Fred's films—asked me, 'Do you watch that crazy game that Fred makes all his actors watch?'

Since Aussie Rules was part of the model of Fred's universe as it was of Williamson's and Manning Clark's, Fred even wanted to make Meryl Streep and Michelle Pfeiffer privy to the fact. He boasted that that good Scots separatist Sean Connery had loved what he saw of Hawthorn!

From these exemplars, I therefore knew that if you were ever to draw a universal Australian lesson, your best chance to draw it—at least in Melbourne—was from the great national game. I would acknowledge in the speech that one thing noticed by everyone who watches Aussie Rules played, whether in Riverside Park in New York or at Hermannsburg Mission in the Northern Territory or at the Melbourne Cricket Ground; the one thing noticed by all of us foreigners of the game, both the internal strangers within Australia itself and the strangers beyond the seas; the one thing that is utterly legible to all of us, is the degree of national pride which infuses what the players are doing. Playing *their* game, *their* national code, playing *Australian* rules.

'I want to give a brotherly assurance to everyone here that all the Australian Republican Movement wants is to see that sense of identity extended to the full national sphere!'

The conditions under which speeches are given at the Australian Rules Grand Final Breakfast are somewhat awesome. The official guests and celebrities wait in a reception room until everyone is seated and the television lights are running, and then they are introduced one by one, and applauded or boo-ed on their way to the head table. This resembles the table in the Last Supper, but extended to accommodate some eighty or ninety people, State and Federal worthies who aren't going to be happy to sit with the ordinary punters.

In such company, I was pleased to go armed with recent quotations from experts like Professor George Winterton, a constitutional lawyer who wanted a Republic but understood both its broader implications and its peculiar but superable constitutional difficulties. A little over a week before, Winterton had helpfully written in the *Australian*,

> Many believe that Australia appears second rate and quasi-colonial, both to Australians themselves and to people overseas who are not versed in the intricacies of legally distinct Monarchies sharing the same person. More over, our headship of state (the Monarchy) corroborates the suspicion of our neighbours that we see ourselves as Europeans geographically displaced in southern Asia . . . We will never be seen as a truly independent nation sure of its place in the world when we patently appear (not) to be . . .

From the existence of Aussie Rules and the calm reason of George, I argued banally enough that day that the time for national identity, the time for having a Head of State whose identity was Australian, had come.

In one sense certainly the argument was made valid by the existence of Aussie Rules. In another sense it was limited by the fact that most of the old players who were amongst those who filled the ballroom thought that the game transcended ordinary life anyhow and existed in its own universe. 'Prime Minister Bob,' one of them intoned, 'Leader of the Opposition John, and *Mr Ansett, President of the North Melbourne Football Club*!'

The breakfast was as big a circus as all that!

There was some politicking to be done in the speech.

> I do not want to interpret the motives of the Prime Minister and the Leader of the Opposition, not when there are commentators at the breakfast who are actually paid for trying to do that. I would however like to congratulate both of the honourable gentlemen for standing aside a little from this particular question. For this is not a political issue in the way that the economy or taxation or health is a political issue. It is ultimately an issue for citizens. I urge both leaders to continue to have the wisdom to stand aside from the matter until, later in the century, a citizenry who have properly debated the issue, presents it to the politicians for a suitable decision by referendum . . .
>
> It will probably take another ten or so Grand Finals, another ten or so years of new champions and Brownlow Medallists, before this happier maturity occurs.

As well as that I took on the argument about there being more important things to attend to. The idea that to make a positive change in one direction would produce no positive outfall in others is a favourite argument for Australian pragmatists, the one-paddock-at-a-time attitude which marks and limits us, and which runs counter to all historic evidence and to similarities between growth in society and growth in individuals and organisms. Then I attacked the idea, also heavily promoted in the second half of 1991, that the question was divisive. I said it was certainly a matter of robust difference of opinion, but that it was lunacy to pick out this one topic as too dangerous to discuss when Australians were discussing equally inflammatory matters to do with health, immigration and the desirability of a consumption tax. Could we be such wimps as to be fit to play a supreme game like that day's, and yet on the other hand to possess a social fabric so tremulous, so fragile, that to claim our own identity would damage it?

I got through the speech—which good Monarchists like Lou Richards and Senator Kemp would later call 'boring', but which Bob Ansett said 'contributed enormously to the liveliness of the event'—in about twelve minutes, rather less time than politicians generally exploited on Grand Final Day, but then I had need of some goodwill from the largely over-forty crowd.

Then Bob Ansett rose and said that it was unfair that I should have an unchallenged forum for Republicanism. He had invited along someone who could put the opposite view.

The lights in the Hilton Ballroom were dimmed, the darkness spiked only by press and television lighting, and an heroic fanfare emerged from the sound system. If I hadn't seen the comedian Gerry Connolly so frequently in the flesh or on television, I would have thought that it was Elizabeth II Regina who now entered and made measured progress amongst the tables, distributing the Royal wave generously amongst the Grand Final breakfasters.

In his impersonation of the Queen, Gerry wore a very passable version of a Hartnell dress and a lilac coat, and of course a broad straw hat.

With the fanfare resonating, the stately being reached the dais, proceeded along the back of all the whimsically standing dignitaries, paused by me and began beating me with her handbag. The audience, of course, enjoyed this more than me. I had that weekend, in the midst of a bitter Melbourne cold front, developed tooth trouble, which was rare with me. With every blow from the Royal handbag, the filament of pain between the abscess and the brain vibrated. But I had called the tune and had to—as footballing folk put it—take it sweet and not spit the dummy.

After the assault concluded, the Monarch/Gerry Connolly gathered herself again and bore on towards the rostrum, where she told us what ungrateful sods some of us were. But without warning, the Queen's voice faded and a well-modulated male voice asserted itself.

'You all know I'm not the Queen,' said the Queen. 'It's no use pretending . . .'

Gerry swept the lilac overcoat off and tore the wig off his head. Beneath the fabric that fell away was a naval uniform, and beneath the wig the pronounced ears of a pseudo-Prince Charles.

'I'm getting on,' said Prince Charles/Connolly, 'and Mummy keeps clinging to power. She thinks I'm ineffectual, and it's so unfair. The reason I've come here is that Bob [Hawke] and John [Hewson] have managed to get rid of a number of their political predecessors without blood or fuss. And I want to ask you, Bob and John, How do I get rid of Mummy?'

After the breakfast broke up, John Hewson spoke to me. His demeanour was relaxed. He said he thought the matter should be debated, and gave standard congratulations on the speech, and by then moved on in a normal male way to discuss—a little *sotto voce*, Sydneysider to Sydneysider—the fate of his Sydney Rugby League team, St George. It was clear that he did not, in fact that therefore many Liberals did not, find the mention of a Republic obscene.

So, within a few months, Republicanism had been—to use Donald Horne's term—'normalised', turned into something that was part of the mental landscape of Australian discourse, and something so familiar now that you could joke about it. By contrast, when Gerry Connolly 'did' the Queen again five months later at a banquet for the players and officials of the

International Cricket World Cup, the England Captain Graham Gooch and the player Ian Botham both rose and took a long walk out of the banquet hall. The British tabloids approved their loyalty and denounced Aussie crassness. For the simple truth was, that what was blasphemy in Britain had now become a matter of accustomed opinion within Australia.

CHAPTER EIGHT

★

THE MONARCH'S PLEASURE

WHAT ALWAYS STRUCK me about Malcolm Turnbull was the way he combined a hardbitten Australian delivery with considerable legal-scholarly interest. He was even something of a bibliophile, particularly when it came to cabinet papers, arcane studies on the Australian Constitution, Australian-Imperial relationships, and the judgments of the High Court. No matter how busy he was he could always write a punchy speech whose assertions were backed by the most pungent quotes from constitutional authorities and historical reference.

If you added to Malcolm's historical sense the scholarship of people like Professor George Winterton and Dr Elaine Thompson, then we were well provided with people who understood intimately the process of Australia's advance from colony to sovereign nation, and who could argue cogently that the Republic would be the final and natural step in the process.

It was through leads Malcolm Turnbull laid down—for example, in a Lionel Murphy Memorial lecture that Malcolm gave in October 1991—that I became aware of such arcane matters as the Royal Styles and Titles Acts and became involved too in the details of the relationship between Australian governments and the Crown.

The first Royal Styles and Titles Act had been passed in 1953 by the government of Sir Robert Gordon Menzies, that most exuberant Monarchist. This act described the Monarch as: Elizabeth II by the Grace of God of the United Kingdom, Australia and Her Other Realms and Territories, Queen and Head of the Commonwealth, Defender of the Faith.

This was the first time that Australia was specifically mentioned in any Monarchic style, since up to that point the official title which applied to the male Monarchs of the first half of the century included Australia under the general heading 'and His Dominions Beyond the Seas'.

In the high season of his accession to the prime ministership, Gough Whitlam introduced a new Royal Styles and Titles Act in 1973, and the Queen's title for use in Australia under that Act became 'Elizabeth II By the Grace of God, Queen of Australia and Her Other Realms and Territories, Head of the Commonwealth'.

The desire of Gough Whitlam and his cabinet was no doubt to give the Crown an Australian reality to match the sense of a new Australia most of us had in the early Seventies. Our commitment in Vietnam now at an end, the whole nation was briefly of the one mind, determined to remake itself on a more mature model. But because the world would never see the Queen as Queen of Australia, because when she travelled abroad she did not travel as Queen of Australia (unless she travelled *in* Australia) it is possible to agree with Malcolm Turnbull's argument on the matter: 'By changing the label they hoped to obscure the real legal and constitutional fact that the Queen was no more an Australian Institution than the House of Lords or the College of Heralds.'

So while the proponents of the 1973 Act might have been pleased that it gave the Monarch a more nationalistic orientation, 'there was,' says Turnbull, 'a problem at the heart. And that problem was that there was no sense in which the Monarch personifies and embodies the Australian nation.'

Many constitutional lawyers chuckle indulgently and speak of convention when Australian layfolk get upset about the prerogatives and powers awarded the Monarch under the Constitution. They are massive powers though, and Turnbull always confronted that question, taking to heart the fact that the Queen has in some matters—Section 59 of our Constitution, for example (to be explained later)—more power than she does under British constitutional conventions.

It is worthwhile looking at the Monarch's powers as they are literally defined in the Constitution.

I remember getting into trouble once for saying that the Constitution is as dull a document as the Articles of Association of the Dee Why Bowling Club. Complaints immediately came from members of the Dee Why Bowling Club, who considered their Articles of Association far sexier than the Constitution. Indeed, though the Constitution influences every aspect of our lives, because it is a fairly staid document to do with power-sharing, most people are repelled by the mention of specific sections of the Constitution. I can only assure you that if you stick with me for ten minutes, you'll probably learn things about our constitutional status which will either enrage or astound you, and which will certainly change your attitude to that founding Australian document.

First, Section 58 of the Constitution gives the Governor-General the right to withhold bills of the Federal parliament for the Queen's pleasure. If he does that, the Monarch has two years to approve them. But as well, under Section 59 of the Australian Constitution the Monarch has the right to disallow legislation, approved of by the Governor-General, at any stage within twelve months of the enactment of the bill in the Australian parliament. 'This exercise of the Monarch's right shall annul the law from the day when the disallowance is so made known.'

To a layman it seems that the offer of such power to the Monarch might either have been an act of courtesy from the colonials or an act of hubris on the part of the Imperial parliament who passed our Constitution as an attached section to its own Australian Constitution Act (63 and 64 Victoria) on 9 July 1900.

How can the Australian Constitution be considered a great democratic document when such enormous powers are given to the Sovereign of Great Britain? This is what caused Manning Clark to write in 1977, 'On a literal reading there is not one section of the Constitution that is democratic. It is an autocratic Monarchic document.'

Well, in practice, say all the experts, these powers will never be used, especially not after the Statute of Westminster of 1931. They are the Constitutional equivalent of the warheads in the silo. One can't help wondering whom they were meant to deter and chasten before 1931, and why they are there now?

Sections 58, 59, 60 and 74 of the Constitution confer certain powers on the Monarch which are now clearly outmoded. 'As long ago as 1930,' writes Malcolm Turnbull, 'the Imperial Conference noted that disallowance of Dominion legislation was outmoded, and that such provisions were obsolete.' So one wonders why we leave them there? Indeed, the Australian Constitutional Convention, made up entirely of Australian politicians from all sides of politics, at its meeting in Hobart in 1976 unanimously adopted a resolution that Section 59 be repealed because 'its power is never used and it is out of step with reality'.

In 1988, the Constitutional Commission did not regard the fact that the powers thus given would not be exercised was a reason to retain them in the Constitution. 'We do not regard this as a satisfactory solution, because it seems inappropriate now that the Constitution should give the Monarch a role in the legislative process of the Commonwealth, and the retention of these provisions is, in our view, unnecessarily misleading.' They recommended a referendum to delete Sections 59 and 60, the last part of Section 58, and the reference in Section 74 to reservation of bills for the Queen's assent. That referendum has not yet been held. Though the reasons why it hasn't are probably complicated, an outsider might reasonably think it is because we wish to go on maintaining, at the heart of our founding document, the fantasy that we are a feudal people.

The constitutional commentators, Dr Quick and Mr Garran, who were so close to the processes of the Australian Constitutional Conventions of the 1890s, were eyewitnesses to the process of Federation. Their relationship to the making of the Constitution was similar to that of the famous eyewitness historian Charles Bean to the First AIF. In their 1901 commentary on the Australian Constitution, they wrote in relation to Section 59, 'There can be no doubt that the reserve power of disallowance will be wisely and sparingly exercised, in accordance with the rule long established, that Her Majesty's (Imperial) government refrains from interfering with any colonial legislation which is consistent with colonial constitutional law *except* in cases involving Imperial and international relations.'

In other words, British constitutional conventions were to govern the exercise of this fairly muscular power. Quick and Garran are influenced by their age, and by Australia's obviously and frankly admitted colonial status, to see this clause as being better than the alternative proposed by some British bureaucrats in the Colonial Office. These officials had urged that the Crown should list in the Constitution the sorts of bills which would be reserved for Royal approval. Men of their time, indeed brilliant men of their time, Quick and Garran could see nothing wrong about guaranteeing British Imperial rights smack in the middle of the Australian Constitution. 'This method (Section 59 etc.) of conserving Imperial interests is more satisfactory, and more in harmony with the larger measure of self-government granted by the Constitution, than the old system of (the Imperial parliament) instructing the Governor not to assent to certain kinds of Bills . . .'

Even while involved in the forming of a media acquisition group named Tourang in early 1991, Turnbull found time to give a lecture arguing that the Royal power to override the approval of a law by the Governor-General under Section 59 is even now a potential problem for democracy and is by no means of academic interest only. He gave an example of one particular government proposing legislation which is approved by the House of Representatives and by the Senate. A new government could be elected within a year but without control of the Senate, and the Prime Minister of *that* government could advise the Queen to exercise her power under Section 59 and annul a law by Royal decree, since the Prime Minister lacked the power to do it by democratic and parliamentary methods.

It is an interesting phrase of Quick and Garran's: '. . . in harmony with the larger measure of self-government granted by the Constitution . . .'

We are told—particularly by Monarchists—that our Constitution is the constitution of a sovereign nation. But Quick and Garran didn't see it like that, nor does the text say so either.

The truth is that the Constitution as written was as much about guaranteeing Imperial power and British business interest in Australia as it was about founding an Australian Federation.

I hope you can you stand a little more constitutional mulling, as arresting as what we've already had?

Section 1 of the Constitution says that the lawmaking of the Commonwealth shall be invested in a Federal parliament consisting of the Queen, the Senate and the House of Representatives. Two pages earlier, in the British Act of which the Australian Constitution is a section, we are told that the provisions referring to the 'Queen' shall extend 'to Her Majesty's heirs and successors in the sovereignty of the United Kingdom'.

This is the insuperable problem for Australian nationalists, given that the Queen and her heirs or successors become our Heads of State without any input from us and without any assent from Australians. It is also the fundamental problems with considering our Constitution to be one appropriate to a sovereign nation, since one of the customary marks of a sovereign nation is that it finds from amongst its own citizens its own Head of State.

Despite all this we ordinary citizens have been taught that the Constitution is the document of a genuinely independent nation. Justice Windeyer casts it as 'the birth certificate of a nation'. And in his Murphy Foundation speech, Malcolm Turnbull took the ghost of Justice Murphy to task for a statement he made in a judgment in 1976, in a case to do with a shipping accident in Sydney Harbour and hinging on the question of whether the British Merchant Shipping Act of 1958, an act of the British parliament, applied in New South Wales. Murphy decided that it did not, on the grounds that 'any authority over the people of a State would be incompatible with the integrity of the Australian nation, which is an indissoluble union of the people of the Commonwealth'. Murphy then went on to argue, 'In my opinion (notwithstanding many statements and opinions to the contrary) Australia's independence and freedom from United Kingdom legislative authorities should be taken as dating from 1901.'

1901 may have served Justice Murphy as an honourable conventional date from which to mark Australia's independence. But there are plenty of examples to show that Australia wasn't independent in 1901. In fact, for a range of reasons which seemed appropriate to Australian leaders at the time, and to ideas of Australia's destiny, Australia didn't *look* to be independent.

Turnbull points us to a debate in the 1897 Constitutional Convention in Sydney, where Edmund Barton, the jovial liberal, argued that it was not correct in the Constitution to refer to any treaty-making power on the part of the Commonwealth. 'In as much as the treaty making power will be in the Imperial government, we shall omit any reference to the making of treaties by the Commonwealth . . .'

The gargantuan sensualist and liberal, Sir George Reid (once caricatured by Steele Rudd as a 'short, fat, broad-backed, big-bingied man, with hardly any legs and no neck') rushed to agree with this. 'This (the matter of treaties) is an expression which would be more in place in the United States Constitution, where treaties are dealt with by the President and the Senate, than in the Constitution of a colony within the Empire.'

It is little wonder that that fine soul, Alfred Deakin, who like George Reid and Edmund Barton would also serve as an Australian Prime Minister, should wonder at stages whether the Constitution expressed the colonial tendency towards 'groveldom'. In the Constitution as enacted in Westminster in July 1900 and proclaimed in Centennial Park by the Earl of Hopetoun on a broiling 1 January 1901 (the classically beautiful Lady Hopetoun bravely sweltering under a parasol), the Governor-General was to act as the representative of the Imperial power and of British interest, as well as being Australian Head of State. And again, what powers he had (and indeed has)!

Donald Horne again, *circa* 1977:

> According to the Constitution this unelected official is, in the Queen's place, the government of Australia, Commander-in-Chief of its armed forces and empowered to veto proposed laws. Under the Governor-Generalate, the position of the Governor-General, far from being 'above politics', is one that can be used to the advantage of one political party over the other; it can be seen as the destroyer of political consensus, a cause of civil discord, and as the principal constitutional enemy of political democracy.

Concerning Section 68, which makes the Governor-General Commander-in-Chief of the Defence Forces: In 1983 Sir Ninian Stephen said in a speech at the Joint Defences Staff College in Canberra, 'It seems clear that no question of any reserve power lurks within the terms of Section 68 and practical considerations make it essential, even were Constitutional ones not also to require it, that the Governor-General should have no independent discretion conferred upon him by that section.'

The Defence Act of 1903 vests the 'general control and administration' of the defence force in the Minister of Defence. 'Which demonstrates,' as the admirable Sir Ninian says, 'the Constitutional position that titular command of the defence force is vested in the Governor-General, and the actual command of the defence force is vested in the government, and exercised through the Minister for Defence.'

Even so, even though it would be unimaginable that a Governor-General as sane and democratic as Sir Ninian would not claim any discretion to order out the troops, the Constitution actually says the Governor-General can do so. The Constitutional Commission did not see why what the 1903 Defence Act said, and what Sir Ninian said at the Staff College, shouldn't be made clear in Section 68—namely that the Governor-General was merely titular head of the defence force the way the Queen is titular head of the Commonwealth of Nations. But nothing has yet been done to make that distinction clear in the Constitution itself.

As we have seen, the early twentieth century was an age of white Australian race frenzy, of racism on such an unabashed and unquestioning scale that the term racism only palely captures the hubris and terror of our precious little Anglo and Celtic enclave in the South Seas. So, as Turnbull points out, it was aptly and characteristically a question of race which led to the suspension of the Royal or Imperial disallowance of Australian laws.

> Britain had forged a military and naval alliance with Japan, and the Japanese, seeing themselves as the champion of equality of Asians, objected strongly to the white settler society in Australia trying to limit or prohibit Asian (predominantly Chinese) immigration. Indeed in 1905, the Colonial Office in London instructed all Australian State Governors and the State Governments and the Governor-General to reserve for Royal (ie. British) assent any legislation aimed to restrict Asian immigration. Alfred Deakin, the Australian Prime Minister, objected at this interference and the instruction was withdrawn.

(It is interesting too that Billy Hughes's enthusiasm for Imperial federalism and support of Great Britain ran out in 1919 when he opposed the Japanese government's attempt to introduce a racial equality clause into the Peace Treaty. The defeat of the proposal, to which Hughes was the most fullblooded opponent, would be used in Japan by militarists as an example of why the West could be dealt with only by force. 'Sooner than agree to it,' Billy had fulminated, 'I would walk into the Seine—or the *Folies Bergère*—with my clothes off.')

In the earlier stages of Federal Australia's existence, Australia was not seen as independent enough to communicate directly with foreign governments. Communication between the Australian government and Westminster or Whitehall was not through the High Commissioner at Australia House (the

Australian High Commission was not established until 1910, and even then not as a full-fledged diplomatic office), but through the Governor-General and the Colonial Office.

In 1907, for example, Prime Minister Deakin wanted to communicate his concern about the transportation of French convicts to New Caledonia to the French government. He was not able to speak to the French Ambassador in London or to go to Paris and speak to the French government, or even send them a cable directly. Turnbull says, 'As the Prime Minister of a dependency he could do none of these things.'

And so he had to ask the Colonial Office to inquire of the Foreign Office whether they would ask the United Kingdom's Ambassador in Paris to inquire into the matter. The answer (that France didn't intend to use New Caledonia as a political penal settlement) came back from the French Government to the British Ambassador in Paris to the Foreign Office to the Colonial Office to the Governor-General and on to Deakin. It took from 20 April until 15 July for Deakin to get his response.

Similarly with the 'Great White Fleet'—the US Navy sent round the world by Teddy Roosevelt to show everyone that if they were considering war, they should take into account the existence of America as a naval power. When it came to Sydney, Sir Edward Grey, Foreign Secretary of the British government, told Deakin that 'invitations to foreign governments should not be given except through us'.

The executive independence which came to Australia and the other Dominions as a result of the Statute of Westminster in 1931 had not been as actively pursued by Australia as by Canada and South Africa. For one thing, Canada and South Africa had large white minorities to come to terms with—the Boers in South Africa, the Quebecois in Canada. Whereas most of Australia's population of the day had its origins in the British Isles (which geographically, if not politically, included the Dominion and soon-to-be Republic of Eire). Then, because it was so far from Europe, Australia had peculiar defence requirements which made it feel cosier with the idea of dependence. The British Fleet was still our umbrella, and anything which hurt the British was seen to hurt us. A memory of early childhood is from 1940, an aunt in Kempsey sitting on the floor by Old Mick's cabinet radio and weeping at the news that Hitler's Panzers had broken through the Maginot Line. No matter what her passionate father's view of the Monarchy might have been, she like other Australians believed the Empire had its uses. (This belief would not be tested until nearly two years later, when Singapore fell to the Japanese.)

And as well as that there was still the belief in a kind of Imperial federalism which would generate an Imperial or world-wide British defence policy. The impossibility of applying defence capacity uniformly throughout the Empire would be shown up cruelly in World War II, when Churchill and Roosevelt decided on a save-Europe-first, Pacific-second policy. But in any case not all our politicians of the 1930s wanted resources to be uniformly applied.

Sir John Latham, the Federal Attorney-General, at a League of Nation's Disarmament Conference in the year of the Statute of Westminster, voted with Britain to prohibit bombers. 'We regarded the preservation of London as the nerve centre of the Empire as of greater value to Australia than the advantages which Australia would derive locally if bombing . . . were to be continued.'

The Statute of Westminster did not put an end to the right of the Imperial parliament at Westminster to legislate for the Dominions, but it did declare that British legislation would apply in Australia and other Dominions only at the 'request and consent' of the particular Dominion. This was willy-nilly, whether Australia enthusiastically sought it or not, another item in the country's growing sovereignty.

But Australia did not have judicial sovereignty whilever appeals were available from Australian courts to the Privy Council. Such appeals would only be ended by the Australia Act of 1986. To the Australia Act, the British parliament needed to pass what a layman like myself thinks of as an echoing bill, bringing the possibility of Privy Council appeals for Australian cases to an end.

It is hard to escape the fact therefore that the Australian Constitution was never intended to be the founding document of a sovereign nation, and that Australia has undergone a long process of gradually devolving power to itself and its own institutions. In that process, the Monarchy stands out as the last yet massively surviving item, one which tethers us to our colonial identity. All logic and the drift of events indicates that it must be removed by the will of the Australian people at referendum. As the Statute of Westminster put an end to the arrangement by which the Governor-General's chief role was that of representative of Imperial interests, the Governor-General thereby becoming suddenly *more* Australian, so ultimately the mystic and constitutional sovereignty which lies cherry-like atop the great cake of state will ultimately become *more* and definitively Australian.

To pretend that the situation was, is and can be static is to ignore the realities of the way things have gone for us so far in this century.

At the National Press Club in Canberra in March 1992, Malcolm Turnbull had the good grace to argue against any facile condemnation of past Australians for their ready identification with Imperial interests.

I agree with him. There is little doubt that the overwhelming ethos of Australia defined us as Britons in the South Seas. Some Australians of Irish derivation may have resisted such a labelling, but perhaps purely in emotional and internal terms. For Australian society, in spite of its massive and savage sectarianism, delivered certain unheard-of equities and prosperities to its white population.

So there was a pragmatism in the way politicians like Curtin accepted and even seemed to cherish the Imperial dimension And again there was always the hope, expressed by politicians like William Morris Hughes and Stanley Melbourne Bruce, that there would be a single Imperial voice reached through Westminster's consultation with the Dominions.

It took some hard experiences to show Australians that as interested as *they* might be in Imperial federalism, the British were not interested at all.

Take for example an instance detailed by the historian Peter Spartalis in his book *The Diplomatic Battles of Billy Hughes*. This case involved the fallout from the Treaty of Sèvres which ended the Allies war against Turkey in World War I, a war in which the Australians at Gallipoli and in Palestine had played a massive part.

In 1922, Mustapha Kemal's Turkish forces were advancing on the Gallipoli Peninsula against a weak Greek defence. Billy Hughes believed that the Dominions had not been properly consulted over the Treaty of Sèvres, which had set up the basis for this new crisis by letting Greece and Romania extend their ambitions into Turkey. Outside Smyrna, the Greeks were routed, retreated across the Hellespont into Europe, and were chased by the enthusiastic Turkish forces. All at once the war graves on Gallipoli were about to fall to the Turks.

Lord Curzon, Colonial Secretary of Great Britain, put it thus: 'It would be an abiding source of grief to the Empire if these were to fall into the ruthless hands of the Kemalists.'

The British cabinet then announced to the press that the Dominions were being invited to participate in an expeditionary force. This press statement was made before either the New Zealanders, the Canadians or Billy Hughes actually received the invitation to do so. Mackenzie King of Canada said that the announcement prior to the British request reaching him had put him in an impossible position. Billy Hughes agreed to contribute Australian troops, on the basis that the 'price of Imperial support when Australia should ask for it was support of Britain'.

Billy Hughes, Australian patriot, did not blithely and reflexly go along with the British line though. His complaint is that of the Imperial Federationist doomed to perpetual disappointment at Westminster's and Whitehall's hands.

The point the [Australian] Commonwealth Government desires to emphasise most strongly is this, that consultation with the Dominions ought to take place before any action is taken or irrevocable decision is made by Britain, as then and then only can our voices be heard and our counsels heeded. Either the Empire is one and indivisible or it is nothing. If it is only another name for

149

Britain, and the Dominions are to be told that things are done after they have been done ... and are often asked whether they wish to be associated with her and to stand by her side, when they have in fact no other alternative, then it is perfectly clear, the relations between the Dominions and Britain being what they are, that all talk about the Dominions having a real share in deciding foreign and imperial policy is empty or air.

I feel I ought to speak quite frankly and say that the unity of the Empire is gravely imperilled by such action.

Lloyd George was stung into making sure that Hughes and Mackenzie King were thereafter provided with daily summaries of the situation in the Dardanelles.

Billy Hughes made a statement in the Australian parliament then, calling on Mustapha Kemal to remember the size of the army Australia had put into the field in the Great War. The day after the statement was published in Europe, the Turkish forces withdrew from Chanak. An armistice between the Turks and the Allies was reached in October 1922.

But when it came time for a conference at Lausanne on the issue of the Dardanelles, Japan was invited but Australia was not. 'Dominion governments will be kept informed from time to time of the general lines of policy on which British pleni-potentiaries propose to proceed, and of the course of the negotiations, and as in case of other treaties arising out of the Peace, they will of course be invited to sign new treaty and any separate instruments regulating status of the Straits.'

The Colonial Secretary's office then informed Billy Hughes after the Lausanne conference that 'you will see that Lord Curzon fully maintained rights of Dominions'.

To that Billy Hughes replied in his normal, headlong prose in which there wasn't always room for 'a's' and 'the's'.

I cannot quite appreciate your point ... what it all means is quite clear. We are to go on in the same bad old way. No part whatever was taken by us in making Treaty of Sevres. We signed it when made ... The Commonwealth Government did not approve of many of the provisions of the Treaty of Sevres, nor of British policy towards Greece, which seems to have been one of the factors that led to recent crisis. The Commonwealth Government was made to sign the treaty when it was made and when it could not be modified ...

This habit of asking Australia to agree to things when they are done and cannot be undone and when there is only one course open to us in practice, and that is to support Britain—is one which will wreck the Empire if persisted in ... In foreign affairs the Empire must speak with one voice: but whose voice is that to be? Surely not only that of a British political party! ... In the face of all this you tell us that we are not to have representation at this Conference, and that Empire will be represented by two Englishmen: that we shall, of course, be kept fully informed of how things go, and that we shall have rights to sign the treaty or decline to sign it. All I can say is that it is most unsatisfactory.

The British did manage to stand up to Turkish demands that in particular the Australian burial sites on Gallipoli were too large and should be reduced. This would have required the movement of bodies. Perhaps Lord Curzon and Churchill, the two British delegates, knew that to consent to such a demand would produce an even more astringent set of messages from Billy Hughes.

The news from Lausanne was welcome to the Australian prime minister, but of course it once more left his Imperial Federationist expectations totally unsoothed and unrequited. Billy did not seem to learn from the experience that Imperial federalism was not only a dead, but a non-existent duck. He kept believing the British could be chastised into it.

The continuing Australian fixation on race encouraged the view of ourselves as South Seas British. Well into Hughes's old age, Australians saw in British values and in immigration from Britain a hedge against Asian immigration to Australia.

Curtin, addressing a meeting of members of the House of Commons during a visit to Britain towards the end of World War II, said,

We carry on out there as a British community in the South Seas, and we regard ourselves as the trustees for the British way of life in a part of the world where it is of upmost significance to the

British Commonwealth and to the British nation and to the British Empire—call it any name that you will—that this land should have in the antipodes a people in the territory corresponding in purposes in outlook and in race to the motherland itself.

Geography and our vulnerability made us willing players therefore in what was in reality the game of colonial dependence. If we were to believe that Curtin was speaking with the absolute glowing fealty of a William Morris Hughes or a Sir George Reid, we would be naive, since one has only to look at the bitter anti-Imperial cannonades he unleashed in his writings and his speeches during the anti-conscription campaigns of World War I. It would also be naive to think he was a dissembling Irish Australian. He was speaking from what Australian nationalists considered the orthodoxy of his day. A younger Australian than John Curtin, my father spent two and a half years as a member of the Australian forces in Egypt, Libya and Palestine, and his photographically reduced letters, about the size of a human hand, came in envelopes marked *On His Majesty's Service*. Though his great-great uncle was a Fenian transportee, he would have agreed with John Curtin at that time. (These days, my father is an eighty-five year old Republican, since that is the reasonable temper of this time, just as Curtin's pronouncements were seen as the reasonable temper of *that* time.)

In this regard, think too of the great Antarctic explorer Mawson, newly landed in Antarctica in 1930 by the remarkable Antarctic navigator Davis, standing with his men beneath an Australian red ensign and a Union Jack. From pole to pole we were British.

Not that Mawson or Curtin or my jaunty, slouch-hat-wearing father were in any way slaveys. Curtin might say one thing in the House of Commons. His messages to Churchill when he wanted the Australian troops home in 1942 were however rigorously unambiguous. My father may have served the idea of Empire-interdependence, but his chief tales of adventure are all about not saluting British officers. It would be a brave contemporary Republican who would claim himself a more vigorous Australian than Curtin or the men and women of his time.

The shift in Curtin's expressions of loyalty and affection were all part of the struggle of Australians to define what they are.

We have it easier. No Empire exists. We have just the one barrier ahead of us.

And in this matter of interpreting the attitude of Australians, given the subtleties of our constitutional and psychic history: I am sure that the day will come when our own energetic espousing of the idea that we can remain in the Commonwealth, of which the Queen is titular head, might look as quaint and apparently reprehensible as the literal statements of Australian politicians and leaders of earlier times. For it may well be that as Australia develops new trade and diplomatic relationships and as Commonwealth countries pursue their own interests, the Commonwealth, already in decline, could face a limited future indeed.

Turning playful at the Press Club in Canberra one day, Malcolm Turnbull attacked the former Leader of the Opposition, John Howard, for saying in a debate that the Monarchy had given us decades of stability. Turnbull's argument, and mine, is that the political stability of Australia is due in large part to the political creativeness of Australians.

By way of illustration of the primitivism of the monarchical view of Australian history, he quoted from the poem the Australian Victor Daley wrote after witnessing Queen Victoria's sixtieth anniversary of rule in London in 1897, the same year that the Constitutional Convention met in Sydney.

> Sixty years she's reigned a holding up the sky
> And bringing round the seasons hot and cold and wet and dry.
> And in all that time she's never done a deed deserving jail
> So let joy bells ring out madly and delirium prevail.
> Oh, the poor will blessings pour on the Queen whom they adore.
> When she blinks with puffy eyes at them, they'll hunger
> nevermore.

Victor Daley was not the only one to express his Republican bemusement at Monarchist pietism. Henry Lawson wrote a similar and even more hostile verse.

The Queen has reigned for fifty years, for fifty years and five,
And scarcely done a kindly turn to anyone alive;
It can be said, and it is said, and it is said in scorn,
That the poor are starved the same as on the day when she
  was born.
Yet she is praised and worshipped more than God has ever
  been—
That ordinary woman whom the English call 'the Queen,'
  Whom the English call 'the Queen,'
  Whom the English call 'the Queen'—
That cold and selfish woman whom the English call 'the Queen'.

CHAPTER NINE

THE GOLDEN LANDS OF AUSTRALIA

IN THE PAST year as the Republican debate made ground, I have begun to get together a small Republican library, and reading into it has been a bracing and surprising experience.

The assumption is often made that Australia has been always monolithically and happily Monarchist until now, and that the Republican Movement and others have crudely raised other disruptive possibilities at a late date and for no good reason and, above all, on no historical base.

None of us had this view of things challenged in the school rooms of our childhood. The teaching of Australian history when I was a child, even in the schools of the Christian Brothers of Ireland, was as seamlessly Loyalist as any Orangeman in the working class slums of Belfast could have wished for.

But the very fervour of Australia's official attachment to the Royal House of Great Britain meant that there had to be, underground, a strong river of Australian feeling which—on occasions far more frequent than the Monarchists would like to believe—broke the surface of Australian discourse.

Not only that, tides of Republicanism rose and fell in individual lives—though the fact that Sir Henry Parkes started a Republican and ended a devout Monarchist is sometimes used to show that Republicanism is something Australians recover from as they get older and more reliable.

In any case, Republicanism was always the *other* Australian sentiment. For surely we are permitted to believe it was there in some primitive form in the men and women of such ships as the *Anne* and *Minerva*, leaving Cork and arriving in Sydney in early 1800, and full, both above decks and below, of gentlemen and peasant Irish rebels of the 1798 uprising? Again of course it would be improper to describe their feelings as 'Australian' Republicanism, but it is certain that they left traces of the Republican idea in Australian society. Many of them of course would be hanged at Toongabbie after an 1804 uprising and pitched battle with the New South Wales Corps. But some were pardoned, and were able to add to their Ireland-based dislike of the House of Hanover, appropriate antipodean experiences and further Republican animus. These men (Joseph Holt, Michael O'Dwyer, the so-called Wicklow chieftain) saw America and France as the countries which might be willing to help them—given the gross violations of their human dignity in Sydney and elsewhere. For they knew that had they been Americans, they would have been called Minutemen. Only in New South Wales were they, or more accurately their anonymous supporters, flogged miscreants. General Joseph Holt, Wicklow rebel leader himself, and like a number of the rebels a Presbyterian, described for example the administration of the thousand lash punishment handed out to a convict named Fitzgerald (the description forms the spur for Robert D. Fitzgerald's great poem 'The Wind at Your Door'). I doubt that in Holt's or many other *Anne* and *Minerva* convicts' heart, there was an unqualified love of George III and the Prince Regent.

In the early nineteenth century, the insensitivity of such viceroys as Governor Darling inspired amongst the Currency classes the dream of an Australian separation from viceregal hubris. Even William Charles Wentworth, in his freshest hours, was beguiled by such an idea. In founding the *Australian*, his newspaper, in 1824, he described the character it wanted to adopt: 'Independent, yet consistent—free, yet not licentious—equally unmoved by favours and by fear—we shall pursue our labours without either a sycophantic approval of, or a systematic opposition to, acts of authority, merely because they emanate from government.'

Like Henry Parkes later, Wentworth would get over his independent and Republican-leaning tendencies, and would a quarter of a century later be proposing a New South Wales franchise heavily based on property ownership. He would push too for the establishment of a New South Wales House of Lords—what the son of convicts, Dan Deniehy, would satirise as a 'Bunyip aristocracy'. His political trajectory, as detailed by most historians, was influenced by the fact that his own mother was a convict, and this was the most intimately dreaded yet publicly known thing about him. He did not like the democratic mob in the end, perhaps because their dubious origins reminded him of his own. And like many a colonial politician, he managed to suppress his independent tendencies out of a certain desire for preferment under the Imperial menage.

Most Australians know about the Republicanism of the Eureka Stockade in 1854. This is seen as the one tiny tear in Australian Loyalism. It was deftly repaired on 3 December by the musketry of a Somerset infantry regiment.

Eureka is part of Australian consciousness. But the Republican speeches and writings of Charles Harpur (1813–68) and Daniel Deniehy (1828–65), sons of Irish convicts, and of the Reverend John Dunmore Lang (1799–1878) became virtually suppressed items in the colonial history of most ordinary readers—until Manning Clark referred to them in his multivolume history.

David Headon, who is putting together a new edition of the writings of Deniehy, says that the editions of the work of Deniehy and his friend Charles Harpur, which came out in the 1880s, some fifteen years after their deaths, and which were edited by A. E. Martin, were heavily cut and—to use Headon's term—'corrupted', to do away with Republican references.

Two men in particular, the dwarf orator Deniehy and the

turbulent Presbyterian minister Lang, had been much influenced not by dreams of Imperial pomp but by news of European rebellion in 1848, and by the whole lineage of democratic and individual rights as developed in America and elsewhere. Like modern Republicans, they saw the equities of civic life as deriving not from the Monarch but from the democratic tendencies of ordinary people.

These two dazzling spruikers believed and argued—during the debates over the New South Wales Constitution in the 1850s—that the obvious option for that decade was Federation and a Republic. They were both the favourite voices of small traders, craftspeople and goldminers.

Other sons of emancipated convicts, like Deniehy's friend Bede Dalley, acknowledged the political reality that Loyalism lay at the base of all pragmatic, colonial politics, but Deniehy remained a Republican, whether on the floor of the New South Wales parliament or in the Sydney and Goulburn press, until his premature, unhappy, politically disillusioned death (speeded along by alcoholism) in 1865.

Throughout the 1840s and early 1850s, Deniehy had been exhorting Harpur and Charles Tompson (again the child of a convict) to assume to themselves national characteristics and to create 'a literature national and Australian'. In this regard he was influenced by the American promoters of a native literature: Emerson and Channing.

Very little of Tompson's work is ever anthologised, but a grateful elegy he wrote on the death of Lachlan Macquarie is both poignant (in view of his convict origins) and nationalist.

> Deep in the warm recesses of each heart,
> His lib'ral values held a grateful part.

You can certainly see Harpur's renunciation of the national icons in his poem on Wellington.

> And if, as Englishmen are proud to boast,
> He was their greatest countryman—alas!
> For England's national sterility! . . .
> Besides, he was not England's son at all:
> He was an Irishman, with whom the name

Of Ireland was a scoff! An Irishman,
Who for a hireling's meed and ministry,
Could tear away from his inhuman heart
The pleading image of his native land.

When John Dunmore Lang started the Australian League, Deniehy gave the opening speech in which he called for a Republic on the basis of the fact that there was 'a parallel state of government profligacy in North America before the revolution and in Australia at the moment'.

When for the sake of his profession he moved to Goulburn and began to publish in the editorial pages of the *Goulburn Herald*, he developed the idea that Australians were 'trustees' for Australia. That was why the land had to be unlocked and put into the hands of ordinary and decent immigrants. For that purpose 'Australia must become a Republic soon'.

It was impossible to write off Deniehy's Republicanism on his having been a season in Ireland as a youth, during which he met some of the leaders of the Young Ireland Movement, who would soon enough be in Australia as transportees. His arguments were based on local, Australian concerns.

Deniehy also foreshadowed Federation—he wanted it in part as a means of getting a Federal Court of Appeal from the local supreme tribunals of the various colonies. This new Australian court would supersede the main appeal at that time existing to Australians—to the Judicial Committee of the Privy Council. Given his melancholic tendencies, it is just as well he could not foretell how long it would be before appeals to the Privy Council would end.

John Dunmore Lang was likewise an expressed Republican for most of his adult life. He was the founder of Presbyterianism in Australia, but yet was obviously a turbulent man, expelled from the Presbyterian Church at one stage by the Synod of Australia. The populace always loved him better than the members of his congregation did. He had played a crucial part in the separation of Victoria and Queensland from New South Wales, he had been a great promoter of immigration from Scotland, and had travelled in and written about *ante bellum* America. Lang combined extreme Protestant liberalism with a horror of the Roman Catholic Church, and he would at one stage accuse Earl Grey of trying to 'Romanise' Australia by sending out too many Papists, or the product of mixed Papist-Protestant marriages. Yet he passionately disapproved of the civil oppression of the Irish in their own country. It was a fallacy, he said, to believe that 'it was expedient and necessary, for the maintenance of the Protestant institutions of this country, to deprive at least one fourth of our fellow subjects of their political rights and privileges, and to degrade them into the condition of a pariah caste in their native land'.

In Sydney in April 1850, Dunmore Lang began to lecture on the values of a coming Australian Republic, one which did away with rule from a distance, and one which explicitly opposed the privileges on which the British caste system was founded. With Henry Parkes and others he founded the Australian League 'to encourage a sense of national identity, to resist any further convict transportation, and to promote by moral means exclusively, the entire freedom of the Australian colonies and their incorporation into one political federation'.

That year he published *The Coming Event: Or the United Provinces of Australia*, which was a prophetic document in the history of Australian Federation.

In London in 1852, he published another and very impressive work, *Freedom and Independence for the Golden Lands of Australia*. Lang and the young Henry Parkes seemed to see Republicanism more or less the way modern Republicans do: as being inherent in the nature of Australia's society, its distance from Europe, and its geographic location. Neither of them of course bargained for the long reign and extraordinary popular success of the Widow of Windsor.

The idea of 'Red Republicanism' was sometimes used in Australia though as a political lever. The consummate Henry Parkes advised the Premier Charles Cowper that for the privileged land owners to go on calling for more convict transportation—to break the demands of labour for high wages—would be to play into the hands of these 'Red Republicans'. Such pressures upon Cowper and upon the former Young Ireland radical, Gavan Duffy, Premier in Victoria, would lead to the quick granting of universal manhood suffrage.

On the goldfields at Turon Lang's idea was that the Australian future lay in its being far more than a mere dependency of a far-off country, in its ceasing to be 'a despised colony', and in the inevitable end of the relationship between Australia and the Colonial Office struck a response from many of the diggers, Yankee, Irish, Canadian and British. The Australian nation, he said would require 'no Botany Bay baronetcies to place them on equal terms with the noblest and proudest statesmen of Europe and America'.

Republicanism was of course strongly voiced anyhow on the goldfields of New South Wales and Victoria in the 1850s, where miners took up the American revolutionary cry of 'no taxation without representation', and where radicals such as the newspaper editor George Black, the Scottish agitator Tom Kennedy, and Raffaello Carboni of the Young Italy Movement assured miners that because of the stubbornness of the authorities there would probably be no ultimate option but the American one—a bloody uprising.

I had always thought of Dunmore Lang as a dour fulminator. His bitter fights with his Presbyterian fellows in New South Wales and his sectarianism sometimes made him appear as such. Yet it was a bracing and lively experience to read his neglected work *Freedom and Independence for the Golden Lands of Australia*, published in London in 1852. This book too I acquired through the rare bookshop at Newport Beach, bearing it in my library sack back over the lovely headland between Newport and Bilgola, aware that I had found a treasure.

It was on his way to Britain to press the claim of Moreton Bay for separation from New South Wales and to drum up Colonial Office support for Scots immigration to Australia, that unquenchable John Dunmore Lang prepared his book for English publication by Longman Brown. He had recently formed the Australian League with Parkes, Deniehy and others to lay a basis amongst the citizenry for the coming Republic. Now, aboard ship, he was writing the book to match his intent.

'Although I anticipate much personal abuse, I expect no answer at all worthy of the name ... My proposal to establish free institutions throughout the Australian colonies on the basis of universal suffrage and equal electoral districts will probably be regarded in certain quarters with scornful contempt . . .'

Lang saw the basis of nationalism arising from the immigrant's experience: 'A strong attachment to his adopted country arises insensibly in his mind; and, as time wears on, and the new interests with which he has become identified are multiplied and strengthened, this feeling gradually ripens into a spirit of what could perhaps be designated colonial nationality.'

There was a divine purpose in all this.

> The spirit of colonial nationality, which necessarily arises in the circumstances I have described, is no accidental feeling: it is unquestionably of Divine implantation and designed, not for evil, but for good . . . In one word, a British colony, properly so called, and especially a group of such colonies, will infallibly become a 'nation', provided there is ample room and verge enough for its due development.

It is not just a matter of a group of colonies which has attained their political majority being able to *desire* entire freedom and independence. It is, according to the sea-borne Lang, the law of nature and the ordinance of God that such a group should have freedom and independence.

> I maintain, moreover, that Great Britain, the parent state, being an interested party in the matter, has no more right to constitute itself a judge in the case, and to put forth an adverse decision, than the unreasonable and tyrannical parent who withholds his freedom from his own child.

He quotes Milton as saying that what is required for a state or commonwealth is 'a society sufficient in itself and all things conducible to well-being and commodious life'. That, in his argument, was a definition of the Eastern Australian colonies.

Both John Dunmore Lang and Daniel Deniehy believed in fact that Australia was the best hope of a great Republic, a much greater hope than was America. The Australians were the 'Sons of Morning' to use a favourite phrase of Deniehy's, and America had lost its chance to be a child of morning through the institution of slavery. The energy Parkes and Lang and Deniehy threw into opposing transportation in the Anti-Transportation League was based on the belief that convict transportation was Australia's 'peculiar institution', and that it was an unjust imposition.

> The convict origin of these colonies has entailed on their present inhabitants an enormous additional expenditure, for the maintenance of their police and judicial establishments, beyond what would have been required for these services, had they been originally free settlements.

Any expense that Great Britain had put forward he does not consider to be germane to the question of whether Australia should be independent or not.

> Although Great Britain had never received any pecuniary or other compensation for the expenditure she incurred in the establishment of the Australian colonies, this would in no way have affected the right of those colonies to their entire freedom and independence, on the attainment of their political majority. The slave has an *absolute* right to his freedom . . . the son, who has completed the twenty first year of his age, has an absolute right to entire freedom from parental control . . .

Lang does not include the colony of Western Australia or Swan River, which had recently been transformed into a penal settlement, in his Australian Federation. 'It is more than possible that the Imperial Government will form a series of such settlements along the west and northwest coast. There is, therefore, as complete a separation of the eastern and western divisions of the continent as if a wide ocean had rolled between them.'

Dr Lang then examines all the Australian colonies he has in mind and concludes, 'Surely then a community of such extent, especially when separated by half the circumference of the globe from the dominant country which professes to have both a right and ability to govern it, must form, "a society sufficient in all things conducible to well-being and commodious life".'

His independent Australia therefore consisted of New South Wales, Victoria, Tasmania, South Australia, Cook's Land (present southern Queensland), Leichhardt's Land, and Flinders' Land—the Cape York Peninsula. He projected for these Seven

United Provinces of Australia provincial Senates and Houses of Representatives, and then a general national legislature, made up of a House of Representatives and a Senate, all open to popular franchise. This is an extraordinary foreshadowing of what was to happen in the end.

He saw all this as the only solution. He had decided from reading Benjamin Franklin that even Westminster parliamentary representation for the colonies would not work. 'Only think how the Honourable Member for Botany Bay would be sneered at on the floor of the House, and what small affect anything he could say would be likely to have on the affairs of the nation!'

At the stage John Dunmore Lang was tossing about at sea, William Charles Wentworth and others were—as I have already said and as most Australians know—touting the idea of a New South Wales House of Lords. Lang seems to anticipate the mockery Dan Deniehy would later pour on such a proposition. 'Are we to have colonial Peers of Parliament as well as colonial members of the Lower House—the Marquis of Parramatta, for instance, Lord Wollongong and Viscount Curraducbidgee?'

He is conscious as modern Republicans are that there will be cries that he is somehow offending a mother country and a Majesty which has done so much for them. He says that he has respect for the Queen.

> But what has all this to do with the *previous* question, as to whether we, as British colonies who have attained our political majority, have or have not, an inherent and infeasible right, under the law of nature and the ordinance of God, to our entire freedom and independence ...? For if we have such a right ... the right of Her Majesty the Queen to reign over us necessarily ceases and determines.

He is 'not against Her Majesty individually ... but simply as the imaginary political impersonation of the State ... Do we owe such allegiance in the sense in which the term is used in the charge, as implying that we have no rights in the case? To which I unhesitatingly answer, No.'

The form of independence will therefore be a Republic. 'There is no other form of government either practicable or possible, in a British colony obtaining its freedom and independence, than that of a republic.' He says that Charles James Fox's definition of British government as a 'disguised republic' (the way Monarchists now use the term Crowned Republic), raises the inevitable question: why not make the state legally and unambiguously a Republic?

He deals then with the problem of the Imperial defence of Australia, and utters a prophecy which turns out to be—barring the Japanese break out in the Southwest Pacific in 1942—close to the truth.

> The only chance we have of hearing of war in any shape in Australia for a century to come, lies in our connection with Great Britain, as a group of her many dependencies. And considering the warlike propensities of our worthy mother, and the character she has so long sustained of being the prize fighter and pay mistress of the world, our chance of peace under her wing is at best very precarious.

I began to feel a lot of fraternity with John Dunmore Lang when he complained that people would rebuff his ideas with the tedious old claim that 'the *future* time can be the only proper time for the consideration of so grave a question. Let us hear no more of it, therefore, for half a century to come.' This cry could justly be described as congenitally Australian, since the opponents of Federation regularly used it, and I and other Republicans are heartily sick of hearing it in this age.

Lang writes a considerable amount on the history of Greek colonisation, and above all on British colonisation in the Americas.

In proving that there are no benefits in remaining a colony, Lang lambasts the Colonial Secretary Earl Grey, accusing him of trying to foist the transportation system again upon Australia and of having permitted the Legislative Council (one third of it unelected) to apportion its electoral districts and to control the sale of waste lands. Anti-transportation and anti-squatter Sydney went without democratic representation. Citizens were forced to appeal for recourse to the Colonial Secretary, who ignored their pleas. Lang therefore compares Earl Grey, 'as the Autocrat of all colonies of Britain' to Lord North, the British Prime Minister whose unhandiness generated the American revolution.

Then he moves on to Governor FitzRoy himself, whom he accuses—not quite as cogently as in some of his other argument—of having got the daughter of a pub owner in Berrima pregnant during a viceregal progress!

He predicted correctly though that the miners arriving in Australia for the goldrushes would not long put up with a system of government which involved Earl Grey's temporising and attempts at continuing transportation on the one hand, and on the other, people like FitzRoy going in progress as a sort of submonarch throughout New South Wales and impregnating honest native women.

So fed up was New South Wales as he wrote, said Lang, that it did not even bother getting together an exhibit for the Great Exhibition in London in 1851. He recounts that various New South Wales worthies 'considering the discovery of gold a fit and proper occasion for getting up a public demonstration of loyalty towards Her Majesty, doubtless for their own glorification, proposed to have a Royal diadem of Australian gold constructed . . .' But, there was so much public disgruntlement at the British government, that 'the proposal was groaned upon at a public meeting held for the purpose in Sydney, and the idea had consequently to be abandoned'.

Out of touch aboard his ship, Lang has further complaint still against Earl Grey. He knew that the Port Phillip branch of the Anti-transportation Association had sent a delegate to petition Earl Grey to discontinue transportation to Van Diemen's Land, but up to the time Lang had left Sydney, no word had come of this delegate having been treated with any courtesy by the Colonial Secretary.

Lang asked why in the inevitable adjustment of the unfair electoral laws of 1850, there would not arise in New South Wales not just a colonial constitution but a full Treaty of Australian Independence. One of the clauses of the Treaty of

Independence would be that Great Britain should be entitled to one half of the land fund—from the sale of Australian land—to promote immigration from Great Britain. This would give the Australian colonies for fifty years a somewhat tributary status, but they would benefit from it by the arrival of fresh immigrant stock.

Lang's reason for this proposal is the fear of Chinese immigration. 'This Chinese immigration—disguise it as its advocates may—is merely a peculiar form of slavery! It is introducing into the country an inferior and abject race; and there are other evils attending it which I cannot venture to mention.'

His astounding book of 335 pages finishes by looking at the validity of penal colonies, but only in remote places—the west and northwest of Western Australia perhaps. Lang saw ultimate Federation not stretching to these places, but extending instead to various islands throughout the Southwest Pacific.

Freedom and Independence was written in a month, according to John Dunmore Lang.

> I am now writing its concluding paragraphs at latitude 42 degrees South in the Southern Atlantic, the interval having been chiefly a succession of violent gales, sometimes fair and sometimes foul. This will doubtless account sufficiently for occasional defects of style ... for it is scarcely possible, in such circumstances, to arrange either one's thoughts, or papers, as in a comfortable parlour or library on shore.

The book was obviously a white heat task. 'After the gross injustice which the Australian Colonies have so long experienced from the Mother Country, and the unworthy treatment they have received at her hands, I am decidedly of the opinion that there is nothing really worth struggling for in Australia but entire freedom and independence.'

Manning Clark says that when the Australians read John Dunmore Lang's book, 'they rebuked him. For the colonial bourgeoisie was bound by more than ties of sentiment to the mother country. The British provided the capital for all those enterprises—railway building, roads, public buildings, schools, universities, churches—which brought profit to the colonial bourgeois.'

Hence the Constitution of New South Wales, as an expression of this colonial bourgeoisie, sought to combine material progress, equality of opportunity, and 'abolish the privileges of birth while remaining loyal subjects of Her Majesty'.

The beginning of the post goldrush suburbs of Sydney and Melbourne, says Clark, was the visible sign of the validity of their faith.

The Crimean War in the early 1850s seems to have produced a slightly ambiguous reaction in Australia, but it brought forth a highly non-Republican effusiveness towards Britain and the Queen, and a sympathy for the common soldier. This was mixed with firm statements even in the *Sydney Morning Herald* that the British system of drawing room appointments for generals must come to an end.

Lang, Parkes and Deniehy spoke at a public meeting gathered to discuss the outbreak of the war at Maxwell's Circus, which I think—though I may be wrong—was near Circular Quay. Parkes gave certain signals that he would not come out for a Republic or oppose the tide of British jingoism. Deniehy wrote to Lang sadly of Parkes, 'There is too much Englishman-ism about him.'

It has to be acknowledged again that there was a greater flexibility in Australian colonial institutions than had existed in colonial America. One of the hardest tasks Australians have with Americans is to explain our slow ascent to our own identity, to explain why our so-called 'bourgeois democracy' won out over American-style Republicanism. Many Americans naively think it shows a lack of spunk in Australians that we never rebelled. In a sentimental view, in the grand world, the world in which the highest events were the French and American Revolutions, a world like that for which Henry Lawson would yearn, this Australian capacity for flexibility and compromise was to be deplored. In the world of real and imperfect practical politics, it was I believe to be applauded.

It saved bloodshed, it gave Australians leisure time to devote to practical, progressive movements which, above all, were the Australian forte. The great Australian tragedy was though that this very flexibility became associated in the minds of many Australians, even to this day, with the positive influence of the dreary Widow and that whole subsequent dreary House of Windsor.

In 1887, in Henry Lawson's youth, meetings were held in Australia to propose celebrations for the fiftieth anniversary of Victoria's reign. In Sydney the meeting—meant to be solidly Empire Loyalist—was hijacked by Republicans, who were described as being either 'English socialists' or members of the 'old Convict Leaven'.

At this Sydney meeting then, an extraordinary motion was passed by these unruly elements. 'That in the opinion of this meeting, the proposal to impress upon the children of the colony the value of the jubilee year of a Sovereign is unwise and calculated to anger the democratic spirit of the country.'

The Republicans who stole the meeting were much denounced by the by-now-Monarchist Sir Henry Parkes, by Sir Frederick Darley and Sir William Manning, who probably all agreed with the utterance Manning Clark reports as falling from Loyalists' mouths at that stage, 'Thank God there is an English fleet in the Harbour'.

New meetings were therefore organised to which admission was by ticket.

That same year saw the birth of a monthly newspaper called *The Republican*—the first issue appeared on 4 July, the anniversary of the Declaration of Independence. 'We are today,' said the first issue, or more accurately, said the editor, Henry Lawson's wonderful mother Louisa, 'in a far better position than America when she turned Boston harbour into a teapot and her peasants into patriots.'

And the very same day as the first issue of *The Republican*, the Australian Republican Union was founded in the Temperance Hall in Sydney. Manning Clark writes,

> The venue was symbolical because like their predecessors in popular movements in Australia many republicans were characterized by a craven servitude to wowsers, puritans and prudes. For the most part they were renegades from Catholic Christendom and

the Protestant churches, men who had lost their faith but not the morality often associated with that faith ... Children either of Jansenism in the Catholic Church or of Calvinism in the Protestant churches.

The erratic and brilliant William Lane in Brisbane was influenced by these events in Sydney. 'He wanted the Republican kiss to pass from one to another until loving-kindness reigned all over the world,' writes Clark. But like most of his day he didn't want Asians to participate in that loving kindness.

The young Henry Lawson, who had seen toughs used at a Loyalist meeting in Sydney to keep Republicans from participating, wrote a number of Republican-cum-Utopian-idealist poems.

Sons of the South make choice between
(Sons of the South choose true)
The Land of the Morn or the Land of E'en,
The old dead tree or the young tree green,
The land that belongs to the lord and the Queen,
Or the land that belongs to you.

As Padraig Pearse, leader of the 1916 Easter uprising in Dublin, is accused by writers such as Ruth Dudley Edwards of toying with the idea of blood sacrifice, so there is in Lawson's work the same superheated expectation of blood in the streets.

But freedom's on the Wallaby,
She'll knock the tyrants silly,
She's going to light another fire
And boil another billy,
We'll make the tyrants feel the sting
Of those that they would throttle;
They needn't say the fault is ours
If blood should stain the wattle.

He saw himself as earning the regard of women by immolating himself on the Republican barricades.

It is generally understood that at this stage of history when Henry was selling his early poetry to the *Bulletin*, that magazine was busily engaged in parodying the Monarchy, the English class system, and the Imperial impulses of Great Britain. Joseph

Furphy and William Lane likewise urged their listeners and readers, whether in the pages of *The Republican* or elsewhere, to embrace the new Australian identity. Such voices were all but smothered in the great Imperial-colonial effusions in the centenary of European settlement in 1888. 'Groveldom', was the cry of the *Bulletin*.

Republicanism ran counter to the *gemütlich* spirit of white Australia at its first centennial, yet remained a strong enough concept throughout the 1890s for the Republican Union to be invited to send delegates to the People's Federal Convention at Bathurst in 1896.

Republicanism after Federation found a preposterous and primitive voice in the notorious John Norton's *Truth*, which attacked all Establishment figures from the Crown down to Sir George Reid and Dame Nellie Melba. But Federation had satisfied a lot of nationalist feeling. And the common belief in Imperial federalism and the fear of Asia, which seems to have pervaded virtually all Australian thinking in the early twentieth century, even the most radical thinking, favoured the Monarchy.

Unlike Lang and Deniehy, some twentieth century parliamentarians were severely and directly punished for expressing Republican ideas. Loyalism was dogma and was seen as connected to Britain's great sea power which Australia needed for its safe existence. The early twentieth century was never to be the Republican era the nineteenth was.

One reason for that was that the labour movement went after more proximate aims. Stephen Murray-Smith wrote in one of Geoffrey Dutton's collections of Republican essays:

George Black, the prominent New South Wales labour leader who led his Republican League out of the Republican Union in 1888 to protest against the former's lack of socialist vigour, afterwards claimed that he wasted much time on trying to spread the gospel of Republicanism and was 'side tracked temporarily' from the major political tasks facing the labour movement.

As with the pushing of the Republic today, there is inertia amongst some ideologues. 'One of the major contributions of the ideologues in the labour movement was the view, which gained particular weight after the disillusionment of the strikes, that social oppression would continue whatever the ostensible form of government.'

Melbourne became 'the city of dreadful knights', and any assault on the Monarchy was punished, especially if Ireland was invoked. In 1883 the Home Ruler, Francis Longmore, signed an address congratulating the Irish people on struggling clear 'of the heel of the foreign despot'. He was forced out of Victorian parliamentary life for the next ten years.

When in 1901, Edward Findley, the Labor member for Melbourne, published an imported article from Britain in the *Tocsin* criticising Royalty, Peacock, the Victorian premier, moved Findley's expulsion from State parliament. The motion was passed.

That was the period of reaction too in which the New South Wales Crimes Act, which Ruxton wanted brought down on the heads of Republicans, was passed.

The spectre of the association of Australian Republicanism with pro-Irish feeling panicked others in 1920, when Hugh Mahon, Member for Kalgoorlie in the House of Representatives, spoke of the death in British custody of the Lord Mayor of Cork, Thomas MacSwiney. 'Mahon,' writes Stephen Murray-Smith, 'was reported to have expressed the hope that "the sob of the widow on the coffin would one day shake the foundations of this accursed Empire".'

Billy Hughes obtained Mahon's expulsion from the Commonwealth parliament.

'The era,' (again Murray-Smith) 'was one of hysterical protestations of loyalty of this order, and one wonders what kind of a hollow at the heart of Australian life such hysteria did and does suggest.'

Experts can probably fill in the next forty years, but there does seem to be a Loyalist hiatus. I referred earlier to the causes for that in the 1940s and 1950s.

In 1963 then, the Republican voice surfaces again in Geoffrey Dutton. While serving as a visiting professor at Kansas State University, Dutton wrote an article for *Nation* about the

Republic. It happened with Dutton, as with many other Australians, that the Monarchical connection we took for granted in Australia looked particularly grotesque when seen from a distance and through the eyes of foreigners.

As I have already indicated, Dutton had a Republican lineage anyhow. A great-uncle of his who had been premier of South Australia had also been a Republican, and had ridden through North Adelaide on horseback bearing a Republican flag.

A hundred years had passed since that small North Adelaide Republican rally, wrote Dutton, and yet no modern public figure had stood up to challenge the Monarchy.

> If one raises the Republican issue, the identical arguments appear from right and left. The Queen is above politics and therefore the ideal head of State; better her for the women's magazines and the mob than Jackie Kennedy or Marilyn Monroe; Australia's traditions are with England; the Queen is a fairly cheap luxury; the whole issue is not really an open issue at all, so let's forget all about it.

By 1963, the tenth year of the reign EIIR, Dutton complained, such robust sentiments as those published in the *Bulletin* in the 1890s and early 1900s were not only out of style but would have been considered blasphemous. Menzies was still in power, and he had declared us—in a then much applauded utterance—'British to our boot straps'.

'The Queen, however, is only at the top of a system which degrades us as much as it puzzles foreigners,' Dutton asserted. Dutton parodied the formalities of Government House as 'the stucco-ed portal of ancient pomposity'.

Reading Dutton's article, you begin to realise again what we had once taken for granted. That as late as the 1960s, Government House and perhaps even the government houses of the States were staffed by British aides-de-camp. We were still seeking Britons for the chairs of our universities, for our radio and television production, and frequently as editors for our newspapers. Dutton said it was time to end these habits and closed his piece by calling urgently for a Republic.

Not only did this article lead to Geoffrey Dutton being blackballed at the Adelaide Club, but even the man (the father of a friend) who had nominated him for membership was urged by a committee member to resign. The Adelaide *News* featured a banner headline quoting the state president of the RSL: SEND DUTTON BACK TO RUSSIA WHERE HE BELONGS.

Geoffrey Dutton would ultimately edit and publish a book on Australian Republicanism, *Australia and the Monarchy*, full of intelligent argument on both sides of the question.

The Dutton article was the first time since World War II that the Republican issue had gained such visibility, and the visibility of the issue was soon increased by the publication of *The Lucky Country*. Donald Horne says that he was influenced by Geoffrey Dutton to give a certain Republican emphasis to *The Lucky Country*, and this element of the book drew the passionate attention of commentators.

In that famous tract, Horne attacks the idea of our automatic Britishness.

> Almost every Australian feels a sense of difference when arriving in England. Yet a Prime Minister of Australia has taken pleasure in allowing the Queen of Great Britain (also constitutionally the Queen of Australia) to make him a Knight of the Thistle as if he was some great Scottish gentleman, and allows himself to be surrounded by those who jostle for honours with some of the energy of nobles in a petty German court in the eighteenth century. There is no Australian National Anthem, only 'God Save the Queen' . . .
>
> Migrants who come from European Republics have to swear allegiance to the Monarch before they can become naturalized. Service officers still draw their commissions from the Queen as they did in the first settlement. The ceremonial clinging to Britain is part of the delusional structure of the people who now run Australia . . . The momentum towards concepts of independent nationhood has slowed down or stopped. Perhaps the world has become too puzzling to Australians . . . To many Australians of fifty years ago, this present pause would be unbelievable.

But though Horne mocks the British privilege structure for its own inanity, particularly when transplanted to Australia, he also saw, in those placid, lazy early Sixties, the likelihood of ruin in our habits of dependence. 'Whatever the inconveniences to Australia [of the European Economic Community]

the psychological shock of being dumped might have has-
tened that dramatic reorientation, of admitting where in the
world Australia really is and doing something about it, that
must be a necessary condition for Australia's survival.'

For expressing these opinions, Horne, like Dutton, would
be treated with astounding abhorrence by other members of
the community. In an essay written in 1966, he recounts how
after the publication of *The Lucky Country* a guest of his at a
drinks party took him aside and told him

> that he had refused to read any more of my book after reaching
> the bit that said that Australia would become a Republic and that
> this would be a good thing. He then spent a little time warning
> me of the dangers of Republicanism. Amongst other things he
> recalled the aftermath of the French and Russian regicides—and
> concluded by imploring me to stifle my revolutionary urges and
> to consider the future of my wife and children.

Similarly, a man who had had dinner with Horne prior to
the publication of *The Lucky Country* now complained to a
friend of Horne's about his outrage at having found himself
sharing a dinner table with someone who had 'subsequently
been revealed in print to have filthy disloyal views ... Another
Monarchist with whom I was supposed to do some business,
refused to see me.'

The Dutton-edited *Australia and the Monarchy* was a vigorous
book, as was *Republican Australia?* published eleven years later.
Horne was a hearty contributor to both.

> A Republican Australia would be forced to enter into a dialogue
> with itself on the question of what Australia was supposed to
> be about. For the moment the government speaks as the voice
> of the Crown. A Republican Australia would speak as the voice of
> the People. An officer in the defence forces would not hold the
> Queen's commission: he would hold the People's commission ...
>
> If the simple title of 'Mr' was not good enough for a man he
> could go and live in England and try his luck there ... The ideal
> that men are more the same than they are different is held to be
> true by most Australians ... It is time that we showed official
> confidence in this principle.

In the first Dutton book, Peter Coleman spoke for the continuance of the Monarchy, and as fresh as Horne's arguments now seem, Coleman's eloquence is partly undermined by changed circumstances. I am sure the arguments of today's Monarchists will age even worse. Peter Coleman argues in 1966 the 'irreplaceable value to Australia of the British alliance in South East Asia'. (Now of course a vanished factor.)

We see in Coleman the point put forward by modern Monarchists, although they speak now of economic rather than ideological bogeys: 'Why on earth divide Australians on an issue which, compared with our mutual interest in defence against, for example, Communism, is trivial?'

Coleman at least concedes that, 'There are those Anglophiles who do not understand that Republicanism does not mean Anglophobia.' This is an awareness today's Monarchists do not yet seem to have achieved. He concludes by suggesting that the Republican–Monarchist debate will not become a real issue 'until the decision that will have to be made seems an obvious and natural one, involving the minimum of crisis'.

That day is approaching, and that is exactly the sort of natural transition the ARM is now proposing.

The urbane Coleman does better in 1966 than Professor Daniel O'Connell did in 1977. The only basis on which O'Connell can foresee an Australian Republic is as a cataclysmic one.

> The United Kingdom might break up, the Imperial Parliament vanish, or a People's Democracy arise on the ashes of the British heritage ... The future of Australian government would be in the melting pot, for it would still be true that the abolition of the Monarchy, or even the dismantling of the Imperial Parliament, would have a catalytic impact on the federal balance of Australian government. That is why the constitutional destinies of both countries remain inextricably entangled.

Or perhaps, Professor O'Connell (a reasonable reader might ask), Australians might peaceably take the recourse open to them under Section 128 of the Constitution, and turn their nation into a Republic without incurring the immediate mayhem you take for granted.

The Royal Styles and Titles Act of 1973 explicitly endowed the Monarch with the title of Queen of Australia, thereby seeming to turn the Monarch into an 'Australian', as distinct from a British, institution. It worked well enough to give Australian Monarchists their own national title under which to pursue their fealty.

The dismissal of the Prime Minister Gough Whitlam in November 1975 (despite his generosity to the Monarch in the Styles and Titles Act) will inevitably in retrospect be seen as the greatest blow the Crown suffered in the twentieth century here, and—through no malice of the Monarch—threw up all the most dangerous questions.

What is the Crown? What is its relationship to the constitutional Monarchy in the form of the now middle-aged but still estimable Elizabeth II? What sort of democratic Constitution allows such seignorial powers to an appointed official, who lays about him in the name of the 'Reserve Powers of the Crown'?

The event led to the creation of an organisation called Citizens For Democracy, of which I was for a time a member. I remember appearing on platforms with Donald Horne and with Lionel Bowen, a Federal Attorney-General and deputy Prime Minister ultimately to Bob Hawke. Meetings of Citizens For Democracy in various parts of Australia were also addressed by Manning Clark, Patrick White, and the then Leader of the Opposition, Bill Hayden, who would later create some controversy by assuming the Governor-Generalship and those same reserve powers, which of course he happily forswore ever using.

Hayden's assumption of that office—kindly interpreted—is an index of the strange permanence of the relationship between Australia and the Crown. He shows a whimsical sense of the Governor-Generalship itself as only having a limited future as an institution.

In Brisbane in 1977, Patrick White confessed to the obvious dichotomy of the Australian soul of which Hayden's later taking up of the Governor-Generalship is a symptom.

> I am also a man of divided loyalties. Brought up partly in Australia after the First World War, partly in England (school and university) in the Twenties and Thirties I can see both points of view. I've been torn apart many times over, tossed on waves of

sentimentality, almost seduced by tempting offers. Above all, we must not allow ourselves to be seduced ... We must not be blinded by the theatre of pomp and circumstance on which our social structure in Australia continues to depend— on an outmoded Constitution, outmoded Governor-General and cohorts of supporting knights, some of them on the distinctly murky side.

We are assured the Monarch has no power to regulate these embarrassments. And would it not be better to have our own powerless figurehead rather than one in another hemisphere—a head of state elected by the Australian people?

Patrick White's speech in Brisbane coincided with the Monarch's and Prince Philip's first visit to Australia after Whitlam's dismissal. The official stress was not upon that aspect of the tour, but rather on the fact that this was the Queen's Silver Jubilee year. Gough Whitlam was at that stage still Leader of the Opposition, a ghost at Parliament House feasts. Max Suich, editor of the since deceased *National Times*, had commissioned me to do a piece about travelling as an avowed Republican with the press corps who were covering the Royal tour. I remember sharing a seat in the press bus with Janet Hawley, typical of a new generation of young journalists who were likely to describe Royal events at something less than a full pitch of frenzy.

Packed in the press bus, we went out to Fairbairn airport in Canberra and saw the Royal jet touch down and the Queen progress down the stairs. We had already been reminded by protocol officers that Royal press protocol required that the Queen not be directly quoted, that the 'sources close to the Queen' device always be used instead of direct quotes. A veteran journalist from the *Mirror* had his photographer take some fifty shots of the Queen in her progress down the steps from the plane. His story was headlined in the *Mirror* that night—'Sources Close to the Queen' said that they doubted her capacity to last a strenuous tour.

He told me in the bar at the Northbourne Hotel that he ran that story every Royal tour, and it was getting easier the more the dear lady aged. 'If you take fifty shots of anyone, she'll look ratshit in half a dozen of them and then you just run this "sources close to the Queen line".'

This *Mirror* journalist was a typical rough Sydney proletarian, turning—as Sydney proletarians will—the protocol to his own persistent advantage. Being more of a young Turk then, I vowed I wouldn't use the 'sources close to the Queen' convention. Rightly or wrongly, I decided that in the *National Times* the Queen would have to be democratically responsible for her own utterances, as innocuous as they might be.

It was apparent during that tour that there would be never again anything like the fervour of the Menzies era. A small, polite, scattered crowd—certainly far less than 10,000—lined the route from Fairbairn to Yarralumla. I am sure that at some level of her being even the Monarch was saying, 'Not another bloody viceregal residence!'

The great centrepiece of that visit was the opening of Parliament. Just before it occurred, Donald Horne addressed the National Press Club on Republicanism, but it was obvious to me when I dashed from the Press Club to Parliament House that no one in the Senate or the House of Representatives was interested in what Horne had had to say. At the stage of this first post-Dismissal Royal visit, the parliamentary Labor Party, which Gough Whitlam was soon to leave, was trying to regroup. I mentioned Horne's speech enthusiastically to a darkling young member called Paul Keating, but there was no response.

The Queen opened Parliament in the Senate, with members of the House of Representatives crowded in in their usual way, and their wives in the gallery opposite the press. Sir John Kerr, whom Patrick White had called the Macbeth of Yarralumla, was not there, but even so many of us expected some subtle protest from those who felt democracy had been disadvantaged by his actions. However, all the members had their eyes firmly on the electorate which was still solidly Monarchic and wanted to forget 1975. I admitted even then that that was reasonable enough in political terms.

That night there was a reception in the square-columned Great Hall of Parliament. Though April can be glacial in Canberra, this was a steamy night. The ladies and gentlemen of the press were the only ones permitted to appear in street clothes.

All the other guests were heavily ball-gowned and dinner-suited, and wore handsome decorations.

The Queen would speak, and the Prime Minister would respond and announce what gift the Australian government had in mind to celebrate the Queen's Jubilee. Gough Whitlam was then to join his congratulations to those of Malcolm Fraser.

The Queen's speech is hard for me to remember—but then her speeches were crafted for that effect. I know that there were expressions of affection and kinship; the joy of her association with the Australian people over twenty-five years.

Malcolm Fraser, Prime Minister by controversial line of descent, uttered his congratulations to the Monarch and announced that the jubilee gift of Australia to her would be a race horse. The race horse did not in fact exist yet. What the Queen was being offered was a foal to be conceived at the next standing of a named champion stallion with a named champion mare. As normal as such gifts might be amongst thoroughbred racing folk, to the irreverent press the idea of a gift as biological as this became a basis for a lot of ribaldry. Afterwards, talking to us, Gough Whitlam said he had never heard a horse so fulsomely praised since Caligula made one a Consul.

On the platform Gough Whitlam spoke after Malcolm Fraser. He too congratulated the Queen but seemed to be guilty of flippancy. 'Even now your kingdoms abound. Last week you were declared Queen of the Solomons. What could be next? Queen of Sheba?'

This little *mot* of Gough's would become the first instance of a statement about Royalty by an Australian politician to be considered in appalling taste by those well-known arbiters of sensibility, the British and Australian tabloids.

Later that year, I received a letter from Yarralumla offering me a Commander of the British Empire (CBE). I wrote Sir John Kerr's secretary, David Smith (later Sir David), a polite letter of refusal. I was in mid career in Australia, and after an initial period in which I had experienced great generosity of spirit from the literary community had now begun to receive some fierce treatment from the literary high priests of Australia, in part because I was writing books like *Gossip From the Forest*, which lacked any overt Australian content (even though I would argue that only an Australian could have written it).

But though I still argue my work at that stage was in its own way Australian (except perhaps *Confederates*), I would not however claim any great nationalist virtue for having refused the perceived honour. It was the truth that if I had accepted it I would have needed to accept a system of sovereignty which I had never identified with. I would have had to change my self-definition, and probably my friends.

In our little house at Clareville, amongst massive angophoras, we had a little refusal-of-CBE party anyhow. Much, much later I received another letter from David Smith offering an Order of Australia. Its documentation mentions that the honour comes from the Governor-General with the Monarch's approval. Not a perfect set-up in Republican terms; but it left open the reasonable interpretation that the Order came from Australia, and is altogether less Byzantine and feudal in its terminology than the documents covering the CBE.

That one I took with gratitude, since it will be around and mean the same after the Republic as it does now.

It seemed throughout the Eighties that Citizens For Democracy—for whatever reason—gradually lost their ability to call on prominent commentators in the big debate. If the organisation had retained its prominence and its validity in this matter, it is unlikely that there would have been any need for the creation of the Australian Republican Movement.

While Citizens For Democracy still exists and gives a yearly award to leading promoters of the Australian Republic, there was a belief amongst the founding body of the Australian Republican Movement that the running could no longer be left to that organisation.

There had also existed from the late Seventies onwards an organisation known as the Australian Republican Party, led by Peter Consandine, a former alderman of Strathfield Council. Consandine's group encompasses in its overt concerns a spectrum of issues, none of which the movement quarrels with, even though again they are usually the sort of issues on which it is hard to achieve a general consensus.

What seems more disturbing is Consandine's stated intention of standing candidates for the Federal Senate. I am sure that this is a waste of resources—it was not a method used in the drive to Federation in the 1890s. A number of us could possibly credibly stand for the Senate, or even take a Senate seat given the approval the Republican proposition now has. That might bring an initial surge of publicity, but it won't produce the bipartisan support which will be necessary to bring about the change.

I suppose our attitude is: convince the people, and the politicians will follow.

Consandine himself has been joyfully unabashed in hitching his destiny to the publicity the ARM has brought to the issue. I am not maligning him in saying that—he told me himself. He told Malcolm Turnbull the same thing in Western Australia when he turned up at an ARM event to distribute Republican Party material.

One night at the Opera House, when Consandine and I both happened to be going to the same performance of David Williamson's *Money and Friends*, he clapped me on the shoulder, complimented me for having done so well as his public relations wing, and bought me a glass of champagne on the strength of it.

In July 1992 the *Good Weekend* photographed some of our committee and some of Consandine's and put us both on the cover. An article within did its best to prove we had factionalised, and despised each other. It didn't manage to show that. I was quoted about Consandine's wildly frank manner and his partially winning larrikin ways. In that and other interviews I said that there was no way that we owned the Republican proposition or had exclusive rights to the Republican mansion. Just the same, if Consandine makes it into the Senate on the strength of the visibility of the debate in the past year, it will be at best an embarrassment and, at worst, a side show on the road to genuine independence.

CHAPTER TEN

*

MEMOIRS FROM A YOUNG REPUBLIC III

ON THE FIRST of October 1991, I went off to California to take on the job at the Graduate Writing Program. We had rented a little cottage at a beach called Laguna, which had both fax and telephone for ease of communication, and which looked out on the same Pacific which fronted our place on the Northern Beaches of Sydney. I felt exiled here though, specifically because the ARM was so successfully involved in a debate which in my absence daily took on new directions and subtleties.

And as so often happens in situations which seem to leave the individual a lot of freedom, I found the reality of UCI a little more complicated than it had first been depicted to be. The graduate fiction writers were somewhat demoralised. A visiting novelist from New York, Lynn Sharon Schwartz, had written an article attacking UCI as having a cold, corporate feel and calling the graduate writers mediocre, accusing them of being more concerned with selling film options on their work than producing good fiction. The day I arrived, the *LA Times* carried an article about the Schwartz accusations and dealt with my arrival and the hopes UCI placed in my appointment. It was not an article calculated to make me feel that my task at UCI was straightforward or that I would easily be able to take all the time I needed to work on this book and on ARM business.

In my outer office was a woman named Shirley Cox who had recently moved from Atlanta, Georgia, with her husband. She had taught art at Georgia State, but had been unable to find a teaching job at any of the Southern Californian universities which were just beginning to feel the impact of the recession. We made an alliance to try to raise the morale of the graduate writers and make them feel that again, as under Oakley Hall and MacDonald Harris, there was a direction to things; that their work would be sympathetically but professionally read, and that efforts would be made to get them published. That was one side of the problem addressed. As well as that, Shirley began word processing this book and—though a Democrat—became a devout Republican in the Australian sense.

I knew that it would be a turbulent time commuting between Australia and the Writing Program. But at least UCI knew about the Republican Movement and were—in their way—quite proud of it, many academics sporting the Australian Republican Movement sticker on their notice boards and office doors.

My first commute home came in early November. It coincided with the publication of a travel book on Ireland I had written the previous year, so that interviews covering that were part of the itinerary as well. The centrepiece of that trip back was a Republican dinner in State Parliament House in Macquarie Street, Sydney. I was a little astounded that the Speaker of the Legislative Assembly and the President of the Legislative Council both gave permission for the use of the dining room for this purpose. This dinner was marked by a high representation from the Italian-Australian community, an index of the influence of both Franca Arena and Franco Belgiorno-Nettis in that community, but also of the fact that the Italians had so frequently in Australian history seen themselves as Republicans and spiritual descendants of Raffaello Carboni, the Republican of the goldfields, participant at the Eureka Stockade and Italian unificationist.

The second group who were noticeable were the Chinese

business community. The Chinese might have been counted out of the Republic of the *Bulletin*, Henry Lawson and William Lane, but they were part of *this* Republic.

Geraldine Doogue acted as master of ceremonies, an auction was conducted by Ian Chapell and Mark Day, and amongst the items sold was—through a certain inspiration of Mark Day's—a copy of the speech I had prepared for that night, put together in a fog of jet lag on a word processor at Malcolm Turnbull's offices that afternoon and then delivered in that same jet-lagged, strung out, mildly confused and elated condition.

The dinner in that dining room looking out over the Domain was the first chance I had to reflect aloud on the fact that the debate had entered a new phase, one in which most Australians could be unabashedly Republican without feeling they ran great social and political risks.

Since the blackballings and the pariah-doms of the past had not operated so strongly in our cases, the air at the dinner was celebratory. It was all the sign that the Republican idea was accepted by a large part of the community as a reasonable one.

There was no denying though that a diminishing number of people in Australia were so mentally outraged or even traumatised by the Republican proposition that they could not listen to the argument with any calm at all. The Monarchy was so much part of their central definition of Australia that it was genuinely painful for them to imagine Australia without it. Senator Kemp, for example, had claimed that the speech at the North Melbourne Football Club Grand Final Breakfast had been delivered to 'to attack Australia's legitimacy, to impugn the worth of our institutions and to denigrate our achievements'. He would always continue to be unappeasable about our intentions.

Kemp was a great promoter, too, of the idea so popular with Monarchists that we are a 'Crowned Republic' anyhow.

Since the turn of this century, there has been a radical transformation of the position of the Monarch in Australian affairs. Originally the Governor-General was the representative in Australia of the British Government. The Governor-Generalship has now separated itself from this role and exclusively operates on behalf of Australians.

To people like Senator Kemp, this is the end of the argument. As John Dunmore Lang complained, we are required to be acquiescent about having a Governor-Generalship, a sort of junior Head-of-Stateship under the Crown. Though many good men (as yet no women) have filled that role, everything about that office—the oaths connected to it, its public rhetoric and ceremonial—is directed not towards the Australian people but towards the Monarch.

The message from people like Senator Kemp was that we be happy to continue as an independent dependency; that we should remain in some limbo condition partway between Imperial subjects and genuine citizens. That we should continue to believe that our institutions owe everything to the Crown and nothing to us; that we have been able to eat the pabulum of liberty only when it is delivered from another place, and that we cannot find it amongst ourselves. And that if we were asked to make our own way, it would create such a disturbance in the chemistry of our own inadequacy that it would all lead to tanks in the street and bloodshed!

It was obviously time, by the night of that Parliament House dinner, to say to people with some conviction that we—not the Kemps—were the ones building rationally on the past, on the whole history of gradual attainment of sovereignty which had gone on in the Australian colonies and in the Federation from the start.

And if it was true that the Governor-Generalship exclusively exercised its power on behalf of Australians, then what was wrong with taking that extra step and allowing Australian officials the means to identify themselves as unambiguously Australian?

The only demonstration against the Republican dinner that evening was conducted by two stalwart women of more than sixty years of age who set up posters by the gate of Parliament House and carried on a spirited debate with arriving dinner guests. While I was talking with them they enlisted the support of a couple of pleasant English tourists who politely wondered why we needed our own Head of State now, after their Head of State had served us so well? I said to them, 'Well, look, when we have our own President, we can loan him or her out to you, and see if you like having a Head of State who isn't a British citizen.' They didn't think that was a point. Whyever would the British want an Australian Head of State?

The two protesters had a particular rancour for Franca Arena, because she had taken an oath to the Queen and was now betraying it. I said that Franca had tried to make special arrangements with the President of the Legislative Council to take an oath to Australia, but was told no such adjustment could be made. The system made people such as Franca take ambiguous oaths. A Republic would make all oaths honest ones, I said, and was desirable for that reason.

They were two strong women and they howled that down.

I left Australia the following week again and went to London for the publication of the Irish book. The launch party took place at the Irish Embassy, a circumstance which Senator Kemp would probably find immensely sinister. As in July, the British still seemed passionately interested in the question of what Australia would do.

But there is no single opinion in Britain about Australia's gradual drift towards a Republic. I have met Britons who applaud the direction Australia is so obviously taking, and others who are outraged by it. Some of them are angry as if we are attacking *their* possessions, and this can only be explained by a supposition that *their* possessions include us. A BBC World Service man asked me, 'What are you trying to do to our Queen?' as if his own heritage was under threat. All I could tell him was that *his* Queen was safe. Needless to say again, he just didn't get that. His mind was full of the map of Empire, and the sovereignty of the Monarch of Great Britain had to extend to every last centimetre of it.

In speaking of such primitives, though, I do an injustice to the larger numbers of British journalists whose attitudes range from the politely curious to the positively supportive.

And after Britain, back to the Writing Program. But again without a lot of composure of soul, since it was obvious that the debate was racing along in Australia. I could only take part in it through the fax and the telephone, and I was frustrated by that.

The Writing Program itself seemed by now to be back on an even course. The relationship between the young writers and Shirley Cox was excellent, and they now felt they were dealing again with people who were interested in their careers.

On top of that, as they had promised to do earlier, the University of California found a writer from Boston named Judith Grossman who was willing to come and administer the program at UCI from early 1993 onwards. I knew that the Queen was coming to Australia in February 1992, and—since I had no specific teaching in that quarter of the year—that I would be coming home for most of that month, particularly the period prior to the Monarch's visit for the celebration of the sesquicentenary of the Sydney City Council. The City Council had been founded by Royal Charter of the young Queen Victoria, so there was an historic basis for inviting the present Monarch to attend. Nonetheless, as 1992 began, opposition to the idea grew amongst both the public and the press. The Australian government was bearing the expense of transporting the Royals and their retinue, and this created some anger at a time of Australian recession. The British press had laboured the fact too that the Queen paid no British tax.

I was asked to comment on all this even before I left Los Angeles. It seemed to me that this sort of dependence on the Royal presence was more the fault of Australians and Australian governments than it was of Monarchs. If the Sydney City Council couldn't celebrate its one hundred and fiftieth anniversary without an entire Royal retinue, then of course we had to foot the bill. There are many universities and corporations in the world that began with Royal Charters—from Harvard to the University of North Carolina to Trinity College Dublin. Most of them seemed to be able to manage their anniversaries without demanding the attendance of Royal persons.

Naturally, it was not solely because of this specific historic incident that the Monarch was coming. The Monarch was also coming as sovereign of Australia. It was probably the case that the Queen, given her obvious sense of duty to the institution, saw the tour as a chance to mend fences with her partially disaffected Australian subjects.

This fairly routine Royal tour was generating the same degree of interest, particularly in New Zealand and Great Britain, that our original launch had. I went up to Los Angeles International and caught the plane, saying goodbye to Judy again. She believed in the ARM and agreed with my degree of commitment, and her main concern was the impact of all this travel on my general health. Since the late 1960s, when she had taken it bravely for granted that I could support us and our two daughters on my writing, she had been tolerant of my enthusiasms. I hoped I was as tolerant of hers.

Back on the northern beaches of Sydney, I would no sooner be finished a day's debating on the Australian media than the British would begin to call up, anxious to know what we had planned for the Royal visit, perversely disappointed when we said 'nothing', that we wished the Monarch a happy time in Australia, that we had no argument with her. We did however have an argument with our fellow Australians who fostered the culture of dependence. 'Our fictional allegiance to the Queen,' Horne had written at the time of an earlier Royal tour, 'does not make us provincial. It is our provincialism which maintains our fictional identity with the Queen.'

The ARM were still conscious that nothing could happen without Melbourne. We were already perceived as a Sydney operation, and it harmed us. I kept saying in interviews with Melbourne stations that we realised up there in Sydney the fact that Melbourne had been the cockpit of Australian politics, the champion of Federalism, the crucial State in the emergence of the Federation movement, and in modern times the centre of the anti-Vietnam movement. We assured people we understood this and meant to try to find a few prominent Victorians to found a Melbourne committee as a matter of first priority.

But Melbourne people have a way of not quite believing Sydneysiders who express pieties towards them, and it was a relief to be able to go to Melbourne that February, before the Queen's arrival, and greet a Melbourne committee in that Great Hall of the National Gallery, beneath Leonard French's great glass mural. On a platform beneath the mural sat a remarkable Melbourne group. It was headed by Dr John Hirst, academic and author, who had written a perhaps decisive article in *Quadrant* on the conservative arguments for a Republic. There were Max Gillies the actor and comedian, Alison Broinowski, diplomat and author, Fred Schepisi the film maker, Bob Ansett, the historian Peter Spearritt, and many others, including the publisher Sandy Grant.

The planning of this launch was not meant to coincide with the Monarch's Australian visit. The Queen's visit in any case was focused mainly on Sydney and Canberra. By this stage though invitations to Royal levees had gone out to many Australian worthies in all areas of—as they say—'the national life'. Much of our membership had declined the invitations, and some were bound to be present at, say, the reception at Sydney Town Hall, because of the professional and other groups they represented. Some again considered these events good social fun. It would have been churlish and counterproductive for us to call on Republicans to stay away. For the first time in two decades I did not have to make that choice myself, since there was little chance of an invitation coming to the chair of the ARM.

And yet I did remember that a particular writer who had approached me after the Republican Movement was launched and complained that he had not been asked to join, was happy to agree to dine at Yarralumla and to drink the loyal toast. There's nothing particularly wrong with drinking a toast to the Queen, and I would be willing to do it myself once Australia is a Republic. But in my speech in Melbourne, I did raise the question of Republican demeanour in the face of Royal tours. I argued that, while acknowledging all those Republicans who *did* need to attend the events because of their professional or parliamentary or some other standing, others of us who didn't need the Royal levees should ask themselves whether it was fair to send such cross-messages to this genial English grandmother. She was entitled to presume that all those who met her, drank to her and called her 'Majesty', acknowledged her as their sovereign.

There were people who had championed her—Doug Sutherland, Senators Bishop and Kemp, John Howard, Peter King of the Liberal Party—and they had earned the right to look her in the eye and do the allegiance dance. But a lot of Republicans were playing both sides of the street.

In the next day's Melbourne papers some Royalists were affronted at our calling the Queen 'a pleasant English grandmother'.

The most telling thing said at the launch was said by Max Gillies. Max had the typical comedian's sombreness when asked to speak on such matters as distinct from sending them up. He said that it was in one sense a shameful thing for us to have to take up this cause so late in the twentieth century. There were pressing matters that we would only be equipped to deal with once this agenda matter was disposed of. What a pity, he said, it had not been dealt with by earlier generations.

After the meeting, Fred Schepisi asked me out to his place for a hit of tennis and a barbecue. It was obvious that to him the events of 1975 were the determinant. But some people at the lunch, including a young Melburnian woman from the film industry, were by no means convinced and kept asking me what harm had the Queen done? In my post-speech, post-tennis, post-lunch state, it was hard to crank out the argument that this was not an adversarial matter or a personal one, not a matter of the Monarch doing Australia wrong but of Australia itself choosing to be diminished now by this improbable association. It was in no way a case of the Queen having committed crimes against Australia. It was more a matter of Australians having used the Monarchy to commit a crime of deliberate dwarfism upon themselves.

I argued to the film industry woman that we ought in the end to separate out the institution from the face on the stamp or the cover of *Women's Weekly*.

Twice in that week I debated the Opposition politician, John Howard, once on the ABC in Sydney and once on the BBC in London by telephone hook-up. The admirable thing about John Howard was that he put a case for the Monarchy which was at least internally coherent, and which did not draw for any of its validity on the tanks-in-the-streets hysteria of Senator Bronwyn Bishop. But that was a weakness too, since the attachment to the Monarch depended so much more upon what was visceral than on thought-out positions. In a way, Bronwyn's tactic had a sort of an intelligence to it. She knew what she was doing with her fearmongering, and that only fearmongering would work.

The experience of debating John Howard on the BBC was very different from the debate in the ABC's flash new studios in Ultimo. The BBC convenor told me that we would each basically state our case in a minute and a half, and that we would then enter into general debate. He asked me if I could be careful about limiting my opening case to a minute and a half.

Like a typical colonial sucker, I obeyed that rule. Then John Howard spoke and went for close on four minutes, with my attempts to protest or intrude probably turned heavily down on the volume knob. John Howard had the referee of his choice. His best chance of winning was a foreigner. The only tragedy was it was someone who won't vote in the ultimate referendum. My London agent Tessa Sayle called to tell me that she had felt the convenor had been appalling, and asked did I want her to protest?

My main consolation over that debate, apart from the fact that British public opinion would not be the determining factor in Australia, was that the press were aware of John Howard's proclivities. The day after our debate, a Tandberg cartoon in the *Sydney Morning Herald* and the *Age* showed John Howard excitedly telling John Hewson and Peter Reith, 'If an election was held in Great Britain tomorrow, we'd win in a landslide.'

As the date for the Queen's arrival in Sydney approached, we were worried that Peter Consandine's Republican Party group would engage in some piece of street theatre against the Monarch and that we would be tarred with his brush, as he was only too happy to be tarred with ours. To do him credit, that fear proved unnecessary. The truth was that it was members of her own camp who embarrassed the Queen, most notably the Reverend Fred Nile, a member of the Legislative Council in New South Wales.

I had met Fred often as an opponent, since he had been heavily engaged for some years in a campaign to get certain

books off the Higher School Certificate. With some excep-
tions, they were basically Hoover's list of anti-American books:
D. H. Lawrence's *Sons and Lovers*; J. D. Salinger's *The Catcher
in the Rye*; Joseph Heller's *Catch 22*. Peter Schaeffer's play
Equus was also on Fred's adapted list, as was David Williamson's *Don's Party* and my own *The Chant of Jimmie Blacksmith*.
George Johnston's *My Brother Jack* also enjoyed seasons on the
hit list. I once admitted to Fred that I had not written *The
Chant* for school children, and that of course if I had I would
have used somewhat less uninhibited language. I said that I
hoped teachers made alternative arrangements for those youths
who found anything offensive with the book. The Reverend
Fred, in his primitive way, had seized upon this as a total
admission of culpability, and what was worse he said he respected me for it. As the Queen would discover, to be respected
by the Reverend Fred was an undesirable experience.

Fred and Mrs Nile had recently told the press that they had
had to sell their house in Sydney and move to the country
because of what they owed on their last election campaign.
But now Fred announced that he had found $50,000 to mount
a committee to save the Monarchy. A number of commentators unkindly suggested that this was not simply a save the
Monarchy committee. It was a save the Reverend Fred Nile
endeavour as well.

At the cocktail party at Government House, which was boy-
cotted by five members of the Legislative Council, Reverend
Fred tried to ambush the Queen with a large address of loyalty
signed by a number of his supporters.

The most vocal champions of the Monarchy were not people
like Nick Greiner, the then Premier of New South Wales, who
took the address of loyalty from Fred's hands and tore it up to
prevent embarrassment to the Monarch, nor John Hewson,
nor any neo-Menzies. The House of Windsor got its most
vocal defence from the Reverend Fred and from Bruce Ruxton.

Otherwise, gone was the old passion of Royal visits. The
fervour say which Richard Walsh satirised in *OZ*, in a day by
day diary of the Queen's 1963 tour of Australia and New
Zealand.

February 6th. The Queen arrived in New Zealand. Local and imported Maoris applauded wildly when the Queen spoke a few words to them in Maori: 'Araha-nui kia ora kou-kou', meaning 'love and good luck to you all'. Fifteen of the imports were unluckily killed when the bus in which they were returning home toppled two hundred feet into a valley.

February 7th: The Queen arrived in Auckland and attended an opera in the evening. In the foyer fifty people were treated for shock and heat exhaustion.

February 20th: Nine thousand five hundred people turned Adelaide's Royal Garden Party into a free-for-all. Fashionably dressed women with shoes off clambered onto chairs for a better view of the Queen.

February 21st: At Adelaide's Victoria Park Racecourse sixty five thousand children were packed in for a rally. Seven hundred collapsed in the heat.

Such fury, passion, faithfulness to the limit as the tragically killed Maoris had displayed, had well and truly gone from the Monarch's Sydney visit twenty-nine years later. The press covered the tour at something less than the incandescent ardour of the old days. There were no Menziean pledges of love unto death. I believe that commentators who wrote on the matter during and after the tour shared the perception we had—that this was more like the visit of a Head of State of another country than a progress by the Head of State of one's own. Admittedly the *Sydney Morning Herald* estimated that fifteen thousand lined the streets of Sydney to see the Queen's progress from Admiralty House to the Town Hall. But everyone knew that George Bush, or even the Monarch's daughter-in-law, Princess Di, could have drawn a larger crowd.

What the Monarch herself must have been aware of was the calmness of Australia's attitude towards her. She too must have known that something as irrational as her Monarchy in Australia could not long survive an attitude of polite and tranquil respect.

On 24th February, at a reception for the Queen and the Duke of Edinburgh at Parliament House, the Prime Minister Paul Keating, made a speech of welcome which Loyalists irrationally chose to find blasphemous, which most of the young considered to be polite and realistic and which, because it

showed none of the accustomed servility of Australian politicians towards the Monarch, sent the British tabloids into a
frenzy. Especially so since—with the Queen's express approval—the Prime Minister's wife chose not to curtsey to the
Monarch.

'Your Majesty,' said Paul Keating,

we have all changed in that time [the forty years of the Queen's
reign]. The men who sat in the Australian parliament on your first
visit . . . had memories of Empire. Not a few of them saw the
world through Imperial eyes. Many of them had been born in
Queen Victoria's day and remembered the several monarchs in
between.

But I daresay a good many members of this parliament are like
the majority of Australians and have known only one monarch,
Queen Elizabeth II.

This is an altogether different generation, reflecting the profound change in our two countries and the relationship between
them. As our constitutional relationship has evolved so have the
circumstances of our economic and political lives . . . we must also
face regional realities. Just as Great Britain some time ago sought
to make her future secure in the European community, so Australia now vigorously seeks partnerships with countries in our
own region. Our outlook is necessarily independent. That independence in part was reflected in your becoming, in 1973, Queen
of Australia. In 1992 it is reflected in our growing sense of national
purpose.

That such a modest assertion of national identity should seem
sacrilegious to many is an indication of the pseudo-religious
potency of the Monarchy in some minds.

In view of the reaction to his speech before the Queen, on
her departure Prime Minister Keating had a backbencher called
Mellam ask him a question as to whether the 1950s, the apogee
of the Monarchy, were a time of great advancement for Australia, a golden age? Would the Prime Minister tell the House
whether it was the Government's intention to pursue similar
outcomes?

In his response, Keating attacked the Menzies era. For one
thing, he argued, commodities then occupied 85 percent of
Australia's exports.

That was the golden age when Australia stagnated. That was the golden age when Australia was injected with a near-lethal dose of fogy-ism ... when they put the country into neutral and where we very gently ground to a halt in the nowhere land of the early 1980s, with a dependency on commodities that would not pay for our imports.

That was the golden age when vast numbers of Australians never got a look in; when women did not get a look in and had no equal rights and no equal pay; when migrants were factory fodder; when Aborigines were excluded from the system; when we had the xenophobes running around [talking] about Britain and bootstraps; and that awful cultural cringe under Menzies that held us back for nearly a generation.

I said today at the Press Club that one of my colleagues, the Minister for Administrative Services, Senator Bolkus, has always been at the cabinet about the future development of the old Parliament House and about whether it ought to be a constitutional museum or museum of Australian cultural history. We thought we could basically make the changes and put some of the cultural icons of the 1950s down there. The Morphy Richards toaster, the Qualcast mower, a pair of heavily protected slippers, the Astor TV, the AWA radiogram. And of course, the Honourable Member for Wentworth [Mr Hewson] and the Honourable Member for Bennelong [John Howard] would go there as well. When the kids come and look at them they will say, 'Gee, Mum, is that what it was like then?' And the two Johns can say, 'No kids. This is the future.'

I am told that I did not learn respect at school. I learned one thing: I learned about self-respect and self-regard for Australia— not about some cultural cringe to a country which decided not to defend the Malaysian [sic] peninsula, not to worry about Singapore and not to give us our troops back to keep ourselves free from domination. This was the country that you people wedded yourself to, and even as it walked out on you and joined the Common Market, you were still looking for your MBEs and your knighthoods, and all the rest of the regalia that comes with it. You would take Australia right back down the time tunnel to the cultural cringe where you have always come from ...

You can go back to the Fifties to your nostaligia, your Menzies and Caseys and the whole lot. They were not aggressively Australian, they were not aggressively proud of our culture, and we will have no bar of you or your sterile ideology.

There was a certain spirit of truth in what Keating said, even though a number of British journalists and commentators would later complain to me, during a book tour in Britain in July 1992, that losing sixty thousand or more men into the Japanese pen and sacrificing the two great British battleships, *Prince of Wales* and *Renown* was hardly the equivalent of abandoning Malaya. It was nonetheless true that Roosevelt and Churchill did forge a Europe-first policy—mainly at Churchill's insistence—which was not in Australia's best interests, and which of course was the spike through the heart of Imperial federalism. It was true too that Churchill tried to prevent the Australian divisions from leaving the Middle East and coming home to defend Australia, and that Curtin had to stick very much to his convictions of Australia's best interests to resist the claims of British Eurocentricity. I don't think I am alone amongst commentators in thinking that if the Great Eurocentric himself, Menzies, had still been Prime Minister in 1942, he would have succumbed, or cut his cloth, to Churchill's argument of liberating the centre of Empire and Europe first, and only thereafter of attending with energy to the periphery where Australia stood.

Whether accurately or not, Keating saw his speech to the Queen, and his apparently more *ex tempore* but—in some ways —planned outburst in the House, as being in a line of descent from Curtin's 1942 speech in which he signalled that the British alliance might not continue to be the dominant Australian alliance. Keating saw his outburst too as being integral to his Australia First concept.

The tragedy for him and for Australia was that he had not followed such an independent line in his economic thinking. There he had been the captive of the economic rationalist cadres of the Australian Treasury, who, like the colonial and derivative thinkers they are, have followed the directives of economic fundamentalism so popular in the United States and the United Kingdom, and so favoured within the Organisation for Economic Co-operation and Development. These men have chased cold economic indicators with a subservience which reminds one of Bob Menzies' servility in accepting, while still Prime Minister of Australia, the bizarre ceremonial post called the Lord Warden of the Cinque Ports.

The fundamentalists of the OECD early won Keating's loyalty by declaring him the world's most accomplished treasurer. In Australian history Labor men have always had a weakness for the praise of economists and bankers. As depression Prime Minister James Scullin could stand up for an Australian Governor-General yet succumb to the demands of the Bank of England, so Keating could assert Australian identity as regards the ancient, dead teguments of British Loyalism, but had not yet found an Australian way of managing the economy of an affluent nation in a sea of industrialising cheap labour economies. 'In these circumstances,' wrote Henry Rosenbloom in an essay in the Australian edition of *Time* magazine,

> Australia will remain a relatively high cost island in a hostile world . . . It is likely that manufacturing will survive only if moderate tariff levels are maintained and there is a high degree of strategic government involvement and intervention in the economy. There needs to be much closer links between the bureaucracy and business, as well as a return to the humanity and common sense of the older generation of economic planners.

Many Australians wished that Keating could have cast the ideologues out of the Temple as vigorously as he was exorcising the phantoms of Empire. I was just one who was hoping so, because he had produced a combination of high interest rates and low economic activity. He had not done it out of malice—like many of life's disasters it had arisen out of the fascinating amalgam of love and vision and vanity which characterises this extraordinary man.

I was just one who, as small time entrepreneur and partner in Echoes guesthouse, was finding it hard to meet interest payments on the basis of diminishing business. I dreamed of old-fashioned pump-priming leaders like Roosevelt. No one was priming the pump in Australia. They had soldered up its mouth, and a particular kind of clever economic journalist, both in Australia and in the United States, told us daily that any sort of interventionism was the sin against the Holy Spirit and could not even be thought of because of the deficit in each country. And yet, 'Sir,' I wanted to say, 'America and Australia are both in desperate need of rebuilding and renewal, or even, in Australia's case, building the first time around (the Alice Springs–Darwin railway, for example). And if you ran up the deficit a little to initiate all that, wouldn't you start to get it back in revenues from the taxes on newly booming industries and newly employed citizens?'

In the twin hopes that Keating would cast off both the derived monetarism *and* the Imperial connection, we watched in fascination. Grandeur on the independence theme seemed to conjure up the hope of a spacious economic vision, something transcending the old economic fundamentalism.

Some Republicans were worried that Keating was overdoing the British bashing, not that after two hundred years of slavish adulation of Britain by Australian officials, Keating's attitude wasn't a refreshing change. But Republicans did not want to bring the conservative parties out in defence of the Monarchy.

Everyone asked what was behind Keating's championing of Australian identity. The accusation that he was trying to create a distraction from Australia's economic griefs is a glib but improbable one. Unlike the prime minister he followed, Robert J. Hawke, Keating believed genuinely that there *was* a connection between this question and the total national milieu. Whereas Hawke saw the Republic as something to be attended to only in an ultimate, settled season.

Keating had a new set of advisers too—Hawke's *Grey Eminence*, Senator Richardson, being in decline. According to politicians I spoke to, Richardson had always been opposed to raising the Republican issue. To the electorate, Richardson believed, it was an ogre. But younger advisers like Senator Chris Schacht argued that there was nothing to be lost through asserting the prospect of the Republic, about asserting that aggressively Australian bias of which the novelist Joseph Furphy had written.

It was interesting that in debates Keating kept using that Furphy-esque adverb—'*aggressively* Australian'. The Australia First program, of which Keating's 'aggressively Australian' statements were part, brought a revival—at least temporarily—of Keating's political standing. It will probably count for a large part of his support in future elections, however they go. It is my belief though that they may not go well unless the economics of the Treasury and of the government likewise become inventive and 'aggressively Australian' in their own right.

Not that his opponents, the conservatives, could hope for better long term success than Keating, given that their main concern for a large part of 1992 was a debate over which economic grave was better—New Zealand's or Australia's?

In 1992, two attacks on the economic fundamentalism as practised by Keating and promised by the Opposition were published. One was a collection of essays edited by Donald Horne (*The Trouble with Economic Rationalism*), the other by Mr Robert Manne (editor of *Quadrant*) and Dr John Carroll (*Shutdown: The Failure of Economic Rationalism*). In the Horne book, Dr Elaine Thompson, a political scientist who was a member of ARM and had frequently spoken to us as a private group and in broader seminars, a woman who combined scholarship with pithy good sense, who spoke in a level, forthright, Australian intonation, wrote up to her usual standard.

> ... the economic problems that many of us see are quite different from those defined by the economic fundamentalists who have been setting Australian policy. They are defining them in their way. We have a right to define them in ours.
>
> ... The economy does not exist as a thing. It is a wicked error to raise it above all other perspectives. When the present economists decide to fight inflation first, they have made a decision that they are not interested in the human costs of the unemployment they create ...

In *Shutdown*, Hugh Stretton, economist and historian, argued that there was a need to get rid of the Treasury ideologues, to 'identify the people who advised the deregulation and predicted its effects ... remove them from positions of influence and discard the theories which misled them'.

Tom Fitzgerald, who had attacked the Treasury high priesthood in his Boyer lectures, greeted both books enthusiastically in the *Sydney Morning Herald*.

According to these commentators then, it was obvious again that the Monarchy was not the only dead hand on Australia's heart.

CHAPTER ELEVEN

★

HANOVER, SOUTH PACIFIC

ONCE AGAIN I had returned to UCI and to the little house by the Pacific. I was frankly exhausted from the Australian campaigning, and from trying to keep up with my writing.

In Laguna, small saltbox houses began thirty yards inland, and were mixed in with classic Southern Californian architectural follies. Our own view of the sea was partly obstructed by a French-style manor Bette Davis had built across the street. Here she had been unimaginably miserable with her alcoholic husband the actor Gary Merrill, who had been a mean drunk, savage to her, brutal to her children. The place was tranquil now though, occupied by a very orderly Newport Beach property developer, and the sea was tranquil off Laguna too, where a hopeful spring was in progress.

Over it hung obvious and nameable clouds. The residual reports of George Bush's Gulf War soured the days with rumours of war atrocities and of the President's prior involvement in an arms deal. On the domestic front, between Laguna and the airport there were certain exits you couldn't take for fear of assault, humiliation and death. America had large police

202

forces to guard the free market, trickle-down propositions of the Reaganite religion from rioters, and while the ghettos were violent, it seemed the trouble was contained and would go on being contained indefinitely. It was a concern though that the alienated Latinos and blacks and poor whites availed themselves of their constitutional right to carry weaponry of equivalent force to that of the armed forces. That was about the only civil right they could be sure of.

From Australia came news that Keating had made a speech to an Italian group in Sydney, saying that an Italian (Raffaello Carboni) had designed the Eureka flag, and that it would soon be time to call on such talents again. But it became apparent that the question of a new flag did not have the same popular support as did the Republic. This again was mysterious, but another illustration of the fact that the 'merely symbolic' is far more than merely symbolic. Like most members of the ARM, I continued to get my calls from everywhere on this subject. Certainly in the popular imagination the flag question and the Republic question were linked, and it was hard to imagine a Republic which did not have its own flag.

Nonetheless while the flag makers were energetic, and kept sending their fine designs to Tony Pooley and various members of the committee, it was obvious that the question could become a quagmire if improperly handled, at least in terms of the number of possible options. The Republic was a simpler issue, and it was also a constitutional one. Whereas the flag could in theory be changed simply by act of parliament, though it would be a rash government who did it without consensus and long consultation.

The economic indicators for which the government and the Opposition and the parliamentary press corps lived, exclaiming like ancient augurs looking for indications of the future in the guts of chicken, kept going badly for the government. There was talk that Keating was going to do what America so badly needs to do but was almost theologically opposed to— spend money on building and rebuilding infrastructure. But the idea seemed to be played with rather than implemented. 'Job training' was the favourite term in both nations. It would fill in the time until some economic miracle occurred.

No suggestion of an infrastructure binge came from the

Bush government, and as the gritty California temperatures rose, so did the chagrin of the underclass of South Central Los Angeles.

In March I drove with Judy east from Los Angeles to do a reading in Santa Fe. I had written a small book on the southwest of the United States—*The Place Where Souls Are Born*, based on a winter journey through that wonderful geographic and cultural and ethnic region.

Every time I ventured into that country the experiences which went into the book returned to me. One thing that fascinated me about that area, apart from the god-struck and impossibly grand landscape, was the resemblance to Central Australia. Not only in the sense of isolation, but in the presence of an alternative America.

For at least a thousand years before the arrival of Columbus in the New World, this region—Utah, Colorado, Arizona, New Mexico—was farmed by communities of Indians generally lumped under the name Anasazi. Large townships developed in the Montezuma Valley in southwestern Colorado, and at Hovenweep on the Colorado-Utah border, and then of course thousands occupied the great cliff dwelling sites of Mesa Verde, Canyon de Chelly and Chaco.

On Mesa Verde you can see the energy of these vanished farmers everywhere in architecture, in pottery, in the remaining check dams and terraces. Their cliff dwellings were like tightly packed adobe blocks of flats, with ceremonial chambers called *kivas*, generally underground, in their midst. From a vagina-like notch in the floor of the kiva, the souls of those born of clan women emerged. The notch was called *sipapu*. The *sipapu* was the place where souls were born.

Amongst the descendants of the Anasazi are the Pueblo and Zuni of New Mexico —the Taos pueblo and its surrounds were made famous by D. H. Lawrence, and Pueblo dwellings and mission churches were one of the staples of the paintings of Georgia O'Keeffe. Other descendants of Anasazi live on the Hopi Mesas in northern Arizona, just below the Painted Desert.

In the ancient Hopi towns towards the end of the winter, when we were there researching the book in early 1990, the dazzling Kachina spirits, who had spent the winter in the San Francisco Peaks near Flagstaff, reappeared in the various villages. Hopi villagers in places like Oraibi or Walpi indicate the arrival of the Kachinas by dressing in Kachina costumes themselves and dancing for superhuman lengths of time, manifesting the hero ancestor in their own bodies. Like the Aborigines, the Hopi have no tradition of kingship, but rather a rule by elders who possess ritual knowledge. In our society Monarchy and priesthood had long past diverged from each other, though not entirely, since even in Australia the Monarch was until 1973 Defender of the Faith, and of course titular head of the Anglican Church.

The Hopi and Pueblo and Zuni have the normal problems of contact with outside culture so familiar amongst indigenous Australians: imported disease, demoralisation and liquor. But having been sedentary people for at least a millennium, they have the advantage over former nomads like the Apaches and Utes and even the Navahos—at least in this regard, that they have been occupying the mesas and the various pueblo dwellings along the Santa Fe since long before the arrival of the Spanish. Therefore sedentariness and town-dwelling and farming didn't have to be forced on them, and they were in their own country all the time, whereas other tribes tended to be driven off their land. Or else, like the Navaho at the time of the Long March of 1867, were dispossessed of it for a cruel time. (Some Navahos, rather than lose land, had stayed on the floor of Canyon de Chelly and been slaughtered there by the US Cavalry led by Kit Carson.)

These days the Navaho Nation lands completely surround the Hopi freehold, and that makes for grievous border and other disputes, particularly since the nineteenth century surveys on which the grants are based were so inaccurate.

Anyhow, in these and other ways, when you are in the Southwest you are aware of no longer being in two-dimensional America, just as in remote Australia you can also get a sense of unsuspected dimensions. Just the same two-dimensional America intrudes here. There are an Arby's Hamburgers and a Kentucky Fried Chicken in Tuba City, the biggest town in the Navaho Nation.

And then of course, on top of the various Indian issues,

there are the Yankees, and the Mexicans arriving from over the border looking for jobs. And the Mormons, who have a special sense of mission towards native Americans, given that the Book of Mormon sees American tribes as a lost tribe of the chosen, the Lamanites.

Because of all this complexity, the Hopi having to cope in one day with the Navaho, the divine Kachinas, the black doctor at Keames Canyon who comes from Massachusetts, and the software salesman who wants to make a deal with the tribal council, I was fascinated by this country. I enjoyed very much writing the book. I'm afraid that in the American press it was reviewed mainly by New Mexico and Arizona locals, who found plenty to carp at, but gave it a B plus, or in some cases an A minus, for effort and—dare I say it?—passion.

It was this book I was reading from in Santa Fe.

On the way back, we got beyond Flagstaff in a late winter mid afternoon. Barely a hand-sized patch of black cloud lay behind the San Francisco Peaks, the twelve thousand foot high stumps of a volcano which covered the area in ash in a ferocious eruption in the eleventh century.

West of Flagstaff is a small town called Williams. From it the old Grand Canyon rail spur used to run, and since I wrote the Southwest book, the rail has been reopened. The earlier time we went through Williams, doing research for the book, an almost instantaneous blizzard had descended on us, forcing us to creep along to the Williams exit and try to find accommodation in the snowdrowned town. When we managed to find a room in a motel, we had put on our cross-country skis and skied up the main street to buy dinner.

But *that*, I told Judy, wasn't going to happen this time through Williams. The only limitation on the breadth and broadness of that sky was that tiny cloud on the shoulder of the mountains. Again, as last time, in a few minutes the thing grew like a succubus and raged down on us and began dumping snow. The visibility was not as bad as the first time we had been forced to find succour in Williams, but it was pretty ferocious. *Again* we crept down the Interstate 40 and took the Williams exit. For old time's sake, we tried to get a room in the low slung little motel we'd stayed in in the blizzard of two years before. But it was already full of motorists who'd been bullied off the highway by the storm.

In the end we found a room at another motel, called up Laguna Beach to check on our messages, and found that Tony Pooley had called from the ARM desperately looking for someone to replace Malcolm Turnbull at the launch of a South Australian branch of the ARM.

Business had crowded in on Malcolm and made his journey impossible. Could I come back? Never had the impossibility of my living arrangements been better shown up than this. Never had it been more graphically displayed as well that Republicanism wouldn't leave me or Australia alone. The launch was to be the following Sunday.

Once I would have liked the idea of jazzing back and forth over the Pacific as much as anyone. Once, in 1983, I had made a similarly short trip to Los Angeles (in this case Tuesday to Friday) to sign a film contract on *Schindler's Ark* with Stephen Spielberg, and that had been an exciting trip, since after all he flew me at the front of the plane (where all film people fly, it seems), and in any case the only mental effort required of me was to remember my own signature. But I dreaded the sort of journey Tony Pooley proposed. I hated the feeling of making jetlagged speeches while feeling remote from the dais, as if my body were still out there, catching up to me; the feeling of giving jetlagged interviews, and wondering if I made sense even in my own terms. Then before getting over the journey home I would need to make a return journey.

Since I wouldn't be able to go to Sydney until Thursday night, which would get me into Australia on Saturday morning, I would go straight to Adelaide, do the launch on Sunday, do some Adelaide press and radio, return to Sydney on Monday, then go back across the Pacific to Laguna Beach on Tuesday.

I don't remember much of that journey, although I will always remember the launch. Not only was Daniel Thomas there to represent the arts, along with Mary Beasley and Louise Mitchell, but Graham Cornes, the coach of the Adelaide Crows, presented himself as well, a sign if you needed it that Republicanism was out of the enclaves and salons and right out there on the paddock.

At the end of the session a woman of Czechoslovak origin rose up and told us that her children and grandchildren were Australian citizens, but that she could not take that oath. 'Make it possible for me to die an Australian?' she pleaded. The meeting ended there, and to many of those who attended her question summed up the Australian dilemma.

It is generally believed that the great number of non-British immigrants contribute to Republicanism. It is probably so. But the 1988 conclusions of the Constitutional Commission on the impact of ethnic migration on Republicanism are interesting in that regard:

> It is a commonplace of prognostications about Australia and the Monarchy that, as the ethnic composition of the population changes and as the older members of the community die out, support of a Republic must increase. This paper offers nothing to sustain this sort of demographic determinism. This is less because of its failure to address itself to patterns of support by country of origin or age; more because of its failure to detect any secular decline in support of the monarchy ...
>
> That it does not appear to have done so should alert Republicans to the need to see Australia and the Monarchy in a broader social context. In particular, Republicans would do well to open their papers and magazines, turn on their radios and televisions, and heed—as Monarchists have long done—the 'propaganda of the deed': royal births, royal visits, royal weddings.

It was true that in 1988 the Monarchy seemed set for a long Australian tenure, despite the ethnic population. It is probably true too that there will not be a Republic until people see it not as a denial of grandeur but as an assertion. In that regard it is obvious yet again that the debate carried further in the first four years of the new century of European Australia than in the past two centuries. It was as if in the intervening few years something like a critical mass had built up. One can see the impact of the change in 1992, but remarkably it was not evident in 1988.

In the change, there can be little doubt but also little available proof that the immigrant community took a large hand.

I suppose we'll find out at the referendum.

Meanwhile, the President's Club of the University of California, a group of Californian tycoons and their spouses, were due to meet at a retreat at a resort in Cabo St Lucas, on the tip of Baja California in Mexico, on the Thursday the Los Angeles riots started. Jack Peltason, the President of the University of California, had asked me to tell these largely male entrepreneurs about the famous graduates of the program, and how the program was run, and to hope that from this would come endowments for reading and lecture series and for scholarships for out of state writers.

California was now, post-Cold War, not quite the rich and bountiful economy it had been, and its governor, Wilson, had little enough interest in generating jobs in the ghettos let alone endowing the arts or humanities.

It was ironic that that weekend at Cabo, we had fled the unstable United States and were watching the deep azure of the Sea of Cortez and the Pacific in relatively stable Mexico, even as the burning and rapine continued in Los Angeles. We had had to get there by taking the back door, catching the plane from San Diego, Los Angeles International being surrounded, as I mentioned earlier, by disputed territory. The United States was a Republic which wasn't working. But the reason it wasn't working was not that it was a Republic. It was not working because of its *laissez-faire* assumptions. It was not working because the institution of slavery still haunted and damned and limited it.

The Bush administration was beginning to fail because it had no understanding of the texture of black history or of the reality of society in the ghetto. When the riot ended, Bush and his vice-president would exhort America to return to solid family values as a guarantee against future civil disturbance. Of course they were right in a detached sort of way, but about as helpful as a doctor who tells a patient that the way to health is to feel better. In the President's rhetoric, the lack of understanding of the connection between economic disadvantage and civil unrest was of an heroic scale. But I was interested to find that the men and women who surrounded the pool at dusk in Cabo St Lucas for the first margaritas of the evening showed a greater and more uneasy awareness of the complexity of their Republic.

At this stage Ross Perot engaged in his first run at the presidency (he would temporarily retire and then return to the race), and Bill Clinton had still not picked up much from the universal discontent with the Bush presidency. But at least amongst these men and women there were signs that Bush's glib formulae were running out of credit.

And indeed later in the year one of them, founder of an immense computer services organisation called Western Digital, and a lifetime Republican in the American sense, would declare himself against Bush precisely for reasons of the sort of policies Bush was pursuing in the recession and when faced with the civil unrest of Southern California.

I would notice that back home Australians tended wrongly to attribute the Southern Californian disturbances to inherent faults at the core of the American political proposition, as if all this was the great Republic's punishment for dividing the executive from the legislature, or even perhaps for passing up the benefits of a constitutional Monarchy.

About this time, as I was getting close to the end of the academic year at UCI, the Reserve Bank announced that it intended to produce a new, small plastic five dollar note on which the face of Caroline Chisholm, the nineteenth century's champion of the immigration of working class women from the United Kingdom to the Australian bush, would be replaced by the visage of the Queen. The news produced another flurry of phone calls from press and radio stations in Australia. It would seem that even Monarchists like John Howard wanted Caroline Chisholm retained. This showed again that questions to do with national identity would now go on occurring with cyclical force, and produce plenty of public debate bearing directly or indirectly on Australia's future and on the Republican option.

An occasional small fragment of the Australian ferment would wash up in the *Los Angeles* or *New York Times*, two highly Americo-centric journals. In the northern spring and early summer, tales of Royal impropriety were having an apparent impact both in Britain and in Australia, and even in America. The Royal family was suddenly no longer as embraceable. It was known that the Queen paid no British tax. There were accusations that Fergie, wife of one of her sons, had been blacklisted by the rest of the family, and that Charles had mistresses, and that Princess Di had been miserable enough to try to throw herself down a stairwell. The same British tabloids which had lambasted Keating for his supposed over-familiar treatment of the Monarch were now belabouring her and her extended family.

It has to be said that compared to the sins of his forefathers, Charles's were fairly bourgeois sorts of crimes, though to his wife they were probably intimately hurtful, and the anguish, for once, transcended class and privilege. Just the same it seemed as if the Monarch was now paying for a sort of social contract which had grown up between her and her subjects everywhere during her reign and the reign of her father. The idea being that the subjects would support the Monarchy in high style and permit it its untaxed wealth and its civil list as long as it reproduced in its family life the values and assumptions of the British middle and working classes. Its dress was to be either respectable or regimental, and its marriages were to be ideal.

I remember that in Homebush in 1951–2, when the future Queen was being courted by Prince Philip and when by the railway line to Parramatta, all the adults up and down Loftus Crescent (except the dissenting Old Mick), seemed anxious to discuss their future Monarch's marriage, people would say, 'It's definitely a love match'. Love matches were what the Monarchy owed the populace. That was the deal democracies came to strike with their constitutional Monarchs.

Under the cruel scrutiny of the British press and of various biographers, it was now seen that the deal had been violated. The two-dimensional princes and princesses were showing the all too three-dimensional discontents of real marriages— all exacerbated of course by the preposterous lives they were both required and privileged to live. The Monarchy, which had not been destroyed by the philandering of Edward VII or VIII, by the outrageous philistinism and carnality of George IV, could in the end be seen to be brought undone through the extreme respectability of George VI and Elizabeth II, and the assumptions people drew from it.

The truth is though that for the Australians the question of the morality of the Monarch and her family is not the essential question. The essential question is the difference in our character from what the Monarchy represents; the reality of our geographic and diplomatic and commercial orientation compared with that of Britain. As far as I care the Monarch is welcome to go on enjoying all the arcane gestures and great wealth A. J. Marshall once detailed in a whimsical article in one of Geoffrey Dutton's collections of essays on the subject.

It is a matter of indifference to most Australians whether the Civil and Consolidated Lists will go on being voted to the Monarch and the Royal family by the British parliament, even though the Consolidated List might be trimmed as a means of disciplining unruly and sexually miscreant Royal children.

The Royal yacht *Britannia* is welcome, and very likely to sail on, the Royal flights to continue, the Royal train to continue to chug around the British countryside. The Crown properties of Buckingham Palace, St James's Palace, Hampton Court, Holyrood and Kensington Palace will remain as Crown properties, and the Royal fortune, which got a fillip in the reign of Edward VII through that Monarch's friendship with Baron de Rothschild and Sir Ernest Cassel, will continue to burgeon. The Royal plate will remain, and the Koh-i-nor and Star of Africa diamonds. And all the paintings, the income from land in the five counties known as the Duchy of Lancaster (the methods of royal agents in evicting tenants in the Eighties and Nineties raised flurries of scandal in 1992), Sandringham and Balmoral Castles.

The Monarch will continue to receive a silken tricolour from the Duke of Wellington as his quit rent, and a fleur-de-lis from the Duke of Marlborough for Blenheim Palace. The Duke of Argyle will send a red rose. The Monarch will continue to own all the unmarked mute swans, and to have title over all sturgeons, the Royal fish, captured in her waters.

Perhaps it can still be argued in straight economic terms that the British get more out of the Monarch in tourism than it all costs, though it never seemed that that is proven. But maybe there are hidden and immeasurable benefits. A. J. Marshall writes, 'To the bulk of the British people it [the Monarchy] is as necessary as aspirin and in a general way serves much the same purpose.'

To us, according to a submission of the RSL to the Constitutional Commission, it is also an anodyne. 'At the simplest level, the monarchy adds a touch of ceremony, tradition and splendour to the life of the community. At a more complex level, the monarchy satisfies that basic human necessity to attach sentiments of loyalty and solidity to some appropriate person, symbol or institution.'

A. J. Marshall then, asking himself in 1966 whether the British would ever abolish the Monarchy, decided, 'It will need a combination of an economic depression like that of 1931, a succession of winters like that of 1947, and a Monarch like George IV to make them do it.'

Matters of expense and economic tables won't solve the thing for Australia. If the Monarch had no establishment and walked through Westminster with no expensive retinue, it would still be utterly inappropriate for Australia to invest its fealty in such a distant figure.

In my last month or so in California, before coming home for a proper stay of four months, I got news that a pro-Monarchy group had been founded in Sydney. It was called 'Leadership Beyond Politics: Citizens for a Constitutional Monarchy'. Its membership included Sir Harry Gibbs, a very genial former Chief Justice of the High Court; Michael Kirby, a prominent jurist from the Appeals Court; Dame Leonie Kramer, the Chancellor of Sydney University and a former holder of the Chair of Australian Literature there. Another supporter was Helen Sham Ho, a member—like Franca—of the Legislative Council of New South Wales and—to put paid to Senator Bishop's theory that all Australians of Irish background were *ipso facto* Republicans—two Christian Brothers boys, Doug

Sutherland, former Lord Mayor of Sydney, and Barry O'Keefe, QC, brother of the renowned late rock star, Johnny O'Keefe.

My first reaction was one not of any threat to the Republican dream but of wistfulness. It was sad to see eminent Australians running the risk of seeming ridiculous to future generations; lashing themselves to the mast of HMS *Britannia*.

Dame Joan Sutherland, the great diva, sent her fax of support from the Helvetian Republic, again saying—her turn of phrase perhaps influenced by Grand Opera—that we should all be imprisoned on Pinchgut.

A source close to Sir Harry Gibbs said that what worried him were the legal complexities, and the reasonable fear that removing the perceived copestone, the Monarchy, would bring the whole structure crashing down, requiring the rebuilding of another and more dangerous one.

I am not competent to speak on the level of constitutional knowledge which Harry Gibbs has, though there are other lawyers of equal distinction who believe that a Republic *is* inevitable, and that most of the constitutional problems associated with it can be cleared up either by a Constitutional Convention of the kind which in the 1890s solved much more diverse and severe problems, or simply through constitutional amendment. The amendment, though based on a simple Yes or No vote by citizens, would do away with the sorts of Royal prerogatives mentioned in Section 59 and elsewhere. The amendment might also empower the Federal government to make laws on matters such as the terms on which a president could retire, or the basis on which he or she could be removed if necessary. But none of this will be insuperable.

There have been at every stage of Australia's constitutional growth tribes of experts to tell us why the proposed move will be a disaster. In the Geoff Dutton edited book of 1977 entitled *Republican Australia?* Daniel O'Connell, Chichele Professor of International Law at the University of Oxford, argued in favour of appeals from the State Full Courts to the Privy Council of Great Britain. He saw any other proposition was both legally disruptive and dangerous to the Federation. Continuing such appeals was a protection which State governments had against Canberra's autocracy!

It may be worth looking at this mysterious institution, the Privy Council. It was an ancient inner group of advisers to the Monarch. Indeed, at the emergence of parliamentary 'government', the British cabinet itself had originated as the political committee of the Privy Council. Under an 1833 Act, the cabinet could refer matters for decision by what was called the Judicial Committee of the Privy Council. So things stood at the time of the enactment of the Australian Constitution. This Judicial Committee is the same as the Privy Council in the sense in which generations of Australian lawyers and lay folk have understood and used the term. The Privy Council in this sense was a committee of judges—Quick and Garran listed them as Lord President of the Council, the Lord Chancellor, such Privy Councillors as held or had held office as Lord Keeper of the Great Seal, Chief Justice or Judge of the Court of the Queen's Bench or Common Pleas, Chief Baron or Baron of the Court of Exchequer, the Master of the Rolls, the Vice Chancellor, the Judges of the Prerogative and Admiralty Courts, and the Chief Judge of the Court of Bankruptcy. One or more cabinet members—as well as the Lord Chancellor— would also attend the Privy Council's meetings.

Where to put it in the constitutions of the Dominions, the terms on which people and governments could appeal to it, was always a large question. The Constitution of Canada in 1867 (the British North America Act until the Canadians repatriated it in the 1980s) made allowance for appeal to the Privy Council. But both the Canadian and Australian Constitution gave the Federal governments power to limit appeals. The Canadian Supreme Court became the final Canadian court of appeal by 1949, and no disaster occurred. And yet in Australia in the 1970s people like Professor O'Connell seriously argued that to do away with appeals to the Privy Council would be a massive blow to the Australian system.

The Federal government of Gough Whitlam wanted in the 1970s not only to bring an end to appeals to the Privy Council of Great Britain, but also to cut out direct contacts between State governments and the Crown and route them through the Governor-General. According to O'Connell Queensland adjusted its affairs to combat this. He wrote approvingly,

The renovation undertaken by Queensland has made subversion, by constitutional means at least, impossible as far as the powers of the Crown are concerned. The Queen is now brought into the [Queensland] parliament as one of its elements, as she is in Westminster, Canberra, or others of the monarchies of the Commonwealth. Her representative is stated to be the Governor ... and his instructions are put beyond the reach of capture by Canberra ... He cannot be dictated to in these matters (appointment and dismissal of ministers and so on) by the Governor-General ... A Whitehall postbox is, apparently, thought to be more secure against being rifled politically than is a Canberra one.

O'Connell seems quite ecstatic with this arrangement and with its rationality. It meant too, of course, that Queensland would retain its right of appeal to the Privy Council no matter what the Federal government decided.

Appeals to the Privy Council in Federal matters had already ended in 1968. From 1974 onwards you could not appeal to the Privy Council from the High Court, but until 1986, if you had a case before the Supreme Court of any State, you could choose who to appeal to, either to the High Court of Australia, or to the Privy Council, whichever your lawyers thought you would have a better chance with.

It happens that in 1986 an end to appeals to the Privy Council came about without the constellations falling from their position in the heavens and without Australian federalism being destroyed. And why it came is that as legalistically impressive as Daniel O'Connell's arguments might be, there was a fundamental absurdity to the situation. This absurdity is stated by a more broadminded lawyer, Sir Zelman Cowan, in an essay in the very same Dutton book. Cowan writes, 'The metaphysical notion of the liberated Australian in his Commonwealth capacity and a colonial Australian in his State capacity is untenable.'

The Monarchy will also ultimately vanish because of the metaphysical absurdity inherent in it, the metaphysical and almost theological absurdity of personal union of two crowns, one in Australia and the other in Europe, very nearly poles apart.

Daniel O'Connell, like various members of today's Leadership Beyond Politics, joyously maintained that the whole question of dependence on the united Crown of the United Kingdom 'is as irrelevant to the question of independence and sovereignty of Australia as was the machinery linking the Crowns of England and Scotland between 1605 and 1707, or between England and Hanover between 1714 and 1837 to the mutual independence of those countries.'

The England and Hanover connection ended I believe with the accession of Queen Victoria. The mutual interest wore out. It is wearing out here.

Yet in the Monarchist view Australia is meant to stay sempiternally linked because Hanover and England, for a fixed time, a time somewhat less than the history of European Australia, had a joint Crown! This is meant to satisfy legitimate Australian yearnings. This is meant to be a coherent argument to put up in our region and to explain ourselves to the world.

And then there is the supposedly impenetrable problem frequently raised by Alexander Downer, at the time of writing this, Shadow Minister of Defence (perhaps he will *be* the minister by the time it is published). The Queen is the Queen of Queensland, of Tasmania, of South Australia, says Downer, and would still continue to be so even if the Monarchy was abolished in the Federal Constitution. This is very like the argument which Zelman Cowan found untenable in relation to the Privy Council. The Queen is a sensible woman. If the majority of Australians in a majority of States don't want her, would she demean herself, having lost the whole, by consenting to stay on as a regional sovereign? Could say a Tasmanian be a Republican citizen on the Federal side of his being, and a Royal subject on the State side? And what ridicule such an absurdity would bring both to Australia and the Monarchy?

So O'Connell's ultimately fatuous scholarship has since been swamped by reality. That fact is a demonstration of the limits of all the legalistic arguments which, in the end, despite Sir Harry Gibbs's eminence, will come up short when set against the genuine aspirations of the Australian people.

Leadership Beyond Politics issued *A Charter for the Defence of the Australian Constitution*. Amongst its sentiments were found the following: 'We should not disrupt our nation with a divisive debate founded on ignorance of its history and institutions, based on outdated, phoney nationalism or drawing on imported prejudices.'

To me this is an almost pathological sentence. Firstly, the reality of the debate in the past eighteen months flies in the teeth of the claim that it is a dangerously divisive question.

One of the drafters of the Charter, Lloyd Waddy, QC, still regularly claims we have been seamlessly independent since 1901. For him therefore to accuse the Republicans of ignorance of Australian history or of Australian institutions is a little rich. And rich too to fall back into a last constitutional redoubt to defend the British Monarchy with cries that the Australian thirst for identity is 'outdated, phoney nationalism' or 'imported prejudices'—the latter an attack of course on the larger part of Australian immigrant community who are now opposed to the Monarchy. It is curious that whenever an Australian Republic is mentioned, the cry is of dangerous nationalism. When British heritage, and the worship of British identity, is invoked, this is somehow an authentic and reasonable form of nationalism!

I found it both typical yet particularly tragic to think that the founding Professor of Australian Literature, Dame Leonie Kramer, could associate herself with such guff. The acerbic Patrick White expressed certain excessive opinions about her in *Flaws in the Glass*, and although Patrick was known as a misanthrope, it is nonetheless true that others, myself included, thought that she had very little regard for Australian writers. As someone whose position would inevitably lead to her receiving a certain amount of attention from historians, it was the final act of her essential un-Australianness that led her into this assembly made up largely of antipodean blimps.

What is significant though is that even the Charter aforementioned recognised the possibility of change in the future.

Some of us, whilst willing to contemplate the possibility of a different form of government at some future time, oppose the attempt to raise such a debate at this time. Those of us consider that there are many other issues facing Australia now which have far greater urgency: reconciliation with Aboriginal Australians; reduction of unemployment, especially amongst the young; improved relations with our Asian neighbours; restructuring of the economy ...

And then the argument of the 'Crowned Republic' is raised, and the claim that Australian Republicanism is a personal attack upon Her Majesty. 'Some of us simply admire Her Majesty the Queen of Australia. We are hurt and angry at the attacks on her in recent times, despite her exemplary lifestyle of service to her people including the people of Australia.'

This is an instance of the Monarchy-as-an-exemplar school of thought. Of course, we could not possibly find an exemplar amongst ourselves.

Since Republicanism is described as 'provincial nationalism', one can only conclude from this accusation that Monarchists consider Australia a province.

In a summary of arguments in support of the Charter, the countries which are constitutional Monarchies are invoked. The Netherlands, Denmark, Norway, Sweden, Spain. The Asian nations, Japan, Thailand, Malaysia. Not once is it mentioned that the Monarchs of these countries are also citizens of those countries.

The tired imagery, 'If it isn't broken—don't fix it!' is again brought forward—this from people who regularly upgrade most things in their lives, from computers to, in some cases, spouses.

The tired poverty of these claims, the idea that sharing a Head of State with Canada, New Zealand, Papua New Guinea and many other countries is a 'proper source of pride' will serve ultimately only to provoke an indulgent laugh from citizens of the ultimate, coming Republic.

Back home, we settled into Bilgola as familiarly as if we had never left it, and I found myself going off with enthusiasm to Chifley Square to chair the sorts of robust and rugged committee meetings you'd expect from a committee which included folk like Donald Horne, Malcolm Turnbull, Franca Arena, Franco

---

Belgiorno-Nettis, Neville Wran, Jenny Kee etc.

We found that people wanted to know what sort of Republic we had in mind, even though we always said it was a decision for national debate. And so after some argument we came up with a suggested model of the Republic, and of the way a president could be elected.

The sort of presidency we were talking about was obviously not like the presidency of France or the United States. In both those cases the presidency had enormous executive powers we would not look to an Australian Head of State to possess. Secondly, the parliamentary democracy which was our version of the Westminster system would remain in place. The powers of the President would be equivalent to those of the Governor-General and obviously—as the Constitutional Commission urged in its report in 1988—there could at some stage be some reasonable adjustment and redefinition of these powers. Part of the redefinition could be to make it clear for example that the Governor-General would be titular and not real Head of the armed forces.

The biggest question was how should the President be elected? Nearly everyone in Australia uttered the sentiment that they didn't want the position to be a convenient siding for old political hacks. At first sight it might seem the best way to prevent this would be to have everyone vote for the President at a popular election. That was originally my suggestion. But where this system exists, as in the Republic of Ireland, it does not always prevent the election of political veterans (some of whom have been competent enough in the role nonetheless). The ARM ended by suggesting that the best way to prevent one party using the post for its convenience may ironically be to have both houses of Federal parliament electing the President. Given the usual disparity of each house, it would be difficult for one party to get a jobs-for-the-boys nominee up, and therefore the President would need to be a product of consensus, a person whose talents transcended mere party affiliation. The question would then be whether the majority electing the President should be a simple majority or a two-thirds one? Some argued that the building of a two-thirds majority for a particular candidate might lead to minor deal-making (you support the candidate and we'll support legislation we want passed). Simple majorities were less likely too to produce two nominees whose votes became deadlocked, leading to the election of a compromise candidate. But the two-thirds majority has its champions. It *would* really mean that no party could use the post for their own direct convenience.

This indirect way of electing a President would leave the people the option of punishing politicians at the next election if they make the wrong choice. But the point is, whichever method you use—direct popular election or indirect election by both houses of parliament—the place of the people in the whole process would be immensely more democratic than in the present system, where our Head of State is handed to us willy nilly by Westminster. We *can* get a Head of State who is above party politics, about whom the people feel comfortable, and we can do it without fuss or bitterness. And at the end of the process we will have someone who can speak for us alone.

But even though in discussion we had nearly settled on a suggested model of the Republic, the final arbiter in all these matters will be the people engaged in popular debate, making their expert and lay opinion available to the Federal government. And as we constantly argued, these arrangements would obviously be a relatively small adjustment to the Australian political system, yet would have a massive impact on the way Australians saw themselves, and on the way the world saw Australia.

As well as attending to ARM work, I was writing flat out in the little computer room at home. Every writer has a different rate of work and a different desired daily output. People said I was fast, but to me I seemed very slow indeed. No sooner had I begun a book than I felt an urgency to get it done, and a year seems to me a long time to have a book on the premises. I was writing this book and another, a novel called *Jacko*. I had written like this since I was young, spiralling down obsessively into each book I was working on. In keeping sane I had found the demands my daughters Margaret and Jane had made on me when they were young had been a saving distraction. Children don't give a damn whether their father's writing good prose or not. They want to go down to the beach when they want to go down to the beach, and they want to go with someone whose attention they can claim.

My research library for *Memoirs From a Young Republic* spread the length of a trestle table—biographies and memoirs of William Lane, Henry Lawson, John Dunmore Lang, Dan Deniehy; various histories and anthologies; Quick and Garran (about which I shall speak soon), the reports of the various committees of the Constitutional Commission, *Freedom and Independence for the Golden Lands of Australia*, and so on; and at one end various encyclopaedias and histories of Rugby League. They were there because the great Manly Warringah utility player Des Hasler, had asked me to help him get his memoirs together. I was delighted with the sort of Australian sportsman Des was. In my sport-besotted childhood, I had naively identified skill at Rugby League with human virtue, and it was wonderful to find in Des's case that there was some truth to the idea. He was a wiry, indomitable, magnificently sane and fundamentally serious fellow who had played frequently for his country. Now the close of his career was at least in the middle distance. He had suffered a severe leg injury which made it not quite as sure as it used to be that he would get through gaps. He still lived an almost monk-like regimen of training and intense consideration of his craft. He seemed to be a man with an interesting family too (one of his brothers had been working for the past three years in Port Sudan, in the disastrous nation of the Sudan). His lack of neurosis made him a quiet, self-contained man. I liked the way he obviously took his schoolteaching so seriously. I liked him too because he was a pro at what he did. He could live with failure, but he hated failure brought on through taking half-measures. Manly were having an ambiguous season— the normal thing for them: winning games that seemed beyond them to win, losing the ones they should have won. Referees were tough on them too. But I still loved watching them at Brookvale on Sunday. And then Des would come around, generally on Wednesdays, and dictate his memories of astounding State of Origin games, or of Test matches in England, France or New Zealand. It was a perfect break from reading the reports of the various committees of the Constitutional Commission.

It was obvious now that the universities were going to be strong in support of Republicanism. A young woman called Stephanie Pribil had already opened a branch at Adelaide University. Since the previous year there had been flourishing branches at University of Sydney, where Michael Fullilove, a law student, had got together a committee, and at New South Wales, where another law student, Lorand Bartels, was active with a strong committee to support him. Bartels and Fullilove had been attending our committee meetings for some time, and in Orientation Week in February, just previous to the Queen's visit, I had spoken on the lawn of Sydney University for the Republican body there. Malcolm had debated the Republic for Lorand's branch at New South Wales. In Canberra at the ANU a group called Republic 2001 had formed independently.

In Sydney again, I found everyone was still talking about the five dollar bill. Even Bronwyn Bishop and John Howard wanted Caroline Chisholm retained. People were crossing out the face, writing *Republic* across it, or working to remove it with chemicals such as nail polish remover. The committee in Sydney looked upon such events as—to use Tony Pooley's frequently repeated phrase—'a free kick'. We didn't think we wanted to join in the general defacing, but the fact that it existed was a perverse demonstration that the Monarchy was in eclipse.

The Melbourne committee had gone into a more pro-active mode than us and had manufactured little Caroline Chisholm stickers which could be applied over the top of the Queen's visage. This would cause minor friction with some of our committee in Sydney, who thought that we should keep it clear that we were opposed to the Australian attachment to the Monarchy, not to the Monarch as a person.

When the Reserve Bank was not giving us free kicks then,

the extended family of the Monarchy continued to. Charles's mistresses had now been named, and Lady Di's friends queued up to speak about the poor woman's unhappiness and even of her suicidal impulses. Andrew and Fergie were in the process of splitting up, the motherly Queen of the five dollar bill was said to be mean to Fergie, Fergie was on with a Texas oil millionaire, etc., etc.

We were in a position to say repeatedly what was the truth: that if the entire extended family of the Monarch behaved impeccably, there would still be overriding reasons for Australia to become a Republic.

I have to say that I have never taken much interest in that family and its fairly pedestrian talents, and of who was being kind to whom. The irony was that most of the British media were dancing on the Monarchy's spine, reporting the latest source close to the Queen, or to Princess Di, or to Prince Charles *ad nauseam*. They were making more of a meal of all that than the Australian Republicans, whom they regularly despised in their columns, ever had.

I kept on saying that far more significant than all the Monarchical unhappiness and rutting was the fact that the Monarch had gone to the European parliament on behalf of her Government at Westminster, and had committed herself to 'the great European fraternity'. In the speech she gave in Strasbourg, Australia, Canada, and New Zealand got no mention. Only her Government of Westminster. But weren't her governments also the governments of New Zealand, Canada and Australia?

This incident more than any other, I argued, showed that we did not have someone at the apex of our government who was bound to speak for us and us alone. You could say that the Governor-General undertakes that task for us, and in many instances since World War II that is true, even though I don't think men like Viscount De Lisle cared much whether Australia got spoken for or not. Besides, the three tiers of government mentioned in Section 1 and expanded upon in Section 61 of our Constitution—the Queen, the House of Representatives and the Senate—give no standing to the Governor-General except as the Queen's representative.

In any case, I kept saying I thought that her European Parliament speech at Strasbourg was far more significant than anything that happened in Royal bedrooms or on Royal staircases. Close to so many Australian hearts as she was, where was her mention of Australia, where her expressed concern?

CHAPTER TWELVE

*

THE FAD OF FEDERATION, AND AN HONEST NAME

WHEN I BECAME involved in the Republican issue, like most ordinary Australians I harboured only a few simple propositions, ideas however which I was sure in my blood had to be achievable.

Out of a necessity to debate the matter, sometimes in ways as robustly populist as I could make them, but sometimes with lawyers and politicians, I needed to read commentators. So again I came across, as during the days of the Constitutional Commission, the two talismanic names: Quick and Garran.

I knew that Dr John Quick and Robert Garran had written a monumental and habitually quoted work called *The Annotated Constitution of the Australian Commonwealth*, which had been published in 1901 to go along with the Constitution itself, but I thought that given a hectic life, I might try to avoid frontally reading Quick and Garran's more than one thousand pages. Surely only Constitutional scholars read the thing. It was good enough to encounter these two remarkable Australian lawyers of the Federation period through quotes in the writings of Sawer or Winterton, or in the speeches of Malcolm Turnbull. I only wanted to know *enough* about Quick and Garran. I didn't want the intimacy of their close text.

I knew in my blood though that I had an appointment with them. In the end I walked one brilliant winter's day over the South Bilgola headland down to Newport, and asked the people in the rare book shop there to track down a 1901 Quick and Garran. I had little idea how richly I would be rewarded. For no one had really told me how well, or with what a dramatic grasp of all constitutional history, particularly our own, these two men wrote.

The two of them were virtually part of the Federation process, so that they were, as Malcolm Turnbull puts it, 'eminently well placed'. John Quick as a Bendigo barrister and a delegate to a citizens' Federation conference in 1893, had devised a plan (the Bendigo Plan) by which the States of Australia could proceed to Federation. Quick then represented Victoria in the official National Australasian Convention of 1897–8. Robert Garran was a New South Wales barrister who had written a passionate book about Federation *The Coming Commonwealth*.

Not least of the glories of Quick and Garran is their 252 page historical introduction, a lively presentation of the steps by which Australia defeated its own inertia, cynicism and sense of impotence and managed to federate.

In 1883, to mark the laying of the last section of the railway line between Sydney and Melbourne, a banquet was held in Albury at which Victorian and New South Wales speakers dealt with that era's ghost of the future that would not go away—Federation. The statements at this dinner do remind the reader very much of the way people speak now of that other ghost of the future, the Republic. Most of the speakers, for example, talked about Federation as 'a far off divine event' rather than a practical policy. The New South Wales Premier, Alexander Stuart, was worried by people who believed that Federation should be 'precipitated in a moment' (no one was trying to do that anyhow), but Mr James Service, Premier of Victoria, which would always to its glory be the most federalist State, said, 'We want Federation and we want it now. I have been now thirty years almost in public life, and I decline to ascribe to the doctrine that I am to die before I see the grand Federation of the colonies ... *We imagine there are supreme difficulties in the way, but I believe they will crumble into dust.'* (My italics)

Again, today, in the matter of the Republic, there are cries of supreme difficulties.

The meeting at the joining of the railways in any case led to the calling of a convention of State politicians, which met in Sydney and in which all the Australian colonies and New Zealand and Fiji were represented. The Federationists (including of course Service, Parkes, and Samuel Griffith of Queensland) were much moved by questions of mutual defence, quarantine, and matters of general Australasian interest. Two other matters raised were 'the relations of Australasia with the islands of the Pacific', and 'the prevention of the influx of criminals' (specifically French criminals from New Caledonia). Other issues were fisheries in Australasian waters, the enforcement of judgments and criminal processes beyond the limits of an industrial colony, and so on. The Federationists argued too that since all the States made their separate representations to London, their voices were weakened and diffused.

This convention produced a Draft Bill of the Constitution of the Federal Council which defined 'the matters upon which united action is both desirable and practicable at the present time'. But it also recognised 'that the time has not yet arrived at which a complete federal union of the Australasian colonies can be attained'.

One of the cries of the anti-Federalists, who included many prominent men, one of the most notable being Sir John Robertson, was that the large States would become tax and customs milch cows to pay for the smaller ones. Sir John mistrusted the other colonies. He wrote, pretty much as Monarchists and inevitablists write now,

> Is it not better to let the idea of Federation mature, to grow in men's minds, until the time comes when we can have a solid, enduring Federation? No good object can be served by creating a body such as this Council. It will add to our strife, it will add to our dissatisfaction with the workings of our institutions, it will lead to endless complications, and it must result at an early stage in an entire breakdown.

Again, at the risk of labouring the point, this last sentence was the sort of thing uttered nearly one hundred and ten years later by Alexander Downer in a debate I had with him in Adelaide in 1992.

And then this, the final cry of men and women who do not want to be troubled by vision: 'Considering the proud position in which we stand now—as free as any country in the world, with power to govern ourselves and maintain an attitude which commands the respect of great nations, we would better avoid joining in making a spectacle before the world which would cover us with ridicule.'

Sir Henry Parkes believed that the Federal Council was too narrowly set, and so he persuaded the diffident new Premier of Victoria, Duncan Gillies, to consider a National Convention. After a preliminary conference in Melbourne, the Convention met in 1891 in Sydney. It consisted of government members and former ministers of the six Colonies and of New Zealand, which was only remotely interested but felt that it should be apprised of what the Australians intended to do.

This Convention split into Constitutional, Finance and Judiciary committees. I was delighted to read that the final stages of drafting a proposed Constitution occurred on board the pleasure boat SS *Lucinda* on the Hawkesbury River on a weekend in the early autumn of that year. It is just that Pittwater and the Hawkesbury are so exquisite in an Australian way that they were a supremely appropriate place, beneath the great sandstone terraces and on those robust waters, to frame a major Australian document.

All these men—there were sadly no women—knew what the main compromises between the various colonies had to be. Quick and Garran wrote, 'The serious "lions in the path" were of course the differences of population, and the differences of fiscal policy; and accordingly the chief issues in the Convention were (1) between large States and small States and (2) between high tariff policy (in some States) and a low-tariff policy (in others).'

Modern Monarchists talk about the serpentine mesh of legalities which will prevent us achieving national identity. Somehow serpentine meshes of legalities always evaporate before the reasonable intentions of a given national group. But it has to be said that these no-doubt-flawed men (none more flawed than Sir Henry Parkes with his weakness for younger women and for overdrafts and political opportunism; a man tired from a recent British junketing and in ill health) bravely launched themselves at a more intricate set of questions than anything which faces us now.

There was the question of the form of the Federal government, of the Federal supreme court—which would in the final event be called the High Court; of finances, trade and commerce, the location of the Federal capital, the method of amendments of the Constitution—a far less severe version was drafted on *Lucinda* than that which ultimately turned up in Section 128. There were questions of the basis for the Federal franchise, what was to be done with rivers, the powers of the Senate, responsible government, the position of State governors, due process, etc., etc. The draft that was hammered out on the Hawkesbury would not ultimately be very far removed from our final Constitution as promulgated in 1901.

When the various delegates took their draft Constitution back to their State houses for discussion, they ran into delays and objections. One of the objections was from the Labor Party in New South Wales, who worried that the draft Constitution conferred 'enormous powers' on the Governor-General. 'It was steeped in "Imperialism"; it meant the crushing of the workers by "a military despotism".' One cannot blame the Labor men, given that the Constitution—literally interpreted—does pay lip service to such ogres.

But the main delay was the same delay as operates now with the Republic: inertia, timidity and lack of a national imagination. The Commonwealth Bill, as the draft Constitution was called, was at least approved of generally in the Victorian House, whereas in New South Wales, George Reid attacked it for trying to tether free traders in New South Wales together with Victoria's protectionists. Sir Henry Parkes saw the question of Federation written off as a 'fad', and everyone cried for the whole question to be postponed in favour of 'urgent local legislation'.

One asks what would have been the ultimate force and value to the Australian community of the 'urgent local legislation' if Federation had not taken place. But cynical George Reid compared New South Wales to a teetotaller who through Federation contemplated keeping house with five drunkards. And everywhere, the Commonwealth Bill languished in the houses as governments fell and sessions ended and the vision went undiscussed.

Sir John Robertson, the land reformer, was able to boast in New South Wales that 'Federation is as dead as Julius Caesar'.

And as the Houses of Parliament let Federation dangle, the cry went up, as it does now, that there were no identifiable economic benefits from the move, and that therefore there was no urgency for it. Indeed that there were only unseen dangers.

It is worth quoting Quick and Garran at some length here, as they discuss the point in the late 1880s, early 1890s when Sir John Robertson was so confidently declaring Federation dead.

> But as a matter of fact the Federal spirit was only just beginning to awaken. The Commonwealth Bill, though neglected by the Parliaments, had helped to educate the people. Since 1891, public interest in the question of Federation had been steadily gaining ground; from 1892 onwards it began to advance rapidly, as a result of the collapse of the 'land boom', the financial panic, and the resulting commercial depression. The crisis showed plainly that the prosperity of each colony was bound up in that of the others; that disaster to one meant loss to all; and that strength lay in co-operation. These considerations helped to break down the spirit of isolation and mutual jealousy which prosperity had fostered, and to emphasise the dangers of disunion.

It is of course our argument that in similarly tough times, as a result of the collapse of yet another land boom, it will be plainly seen that the prosperity of Australia is not bound up in that of *others*, especially not in that of Britain, which to our shame left us before we had the courage to leave it.

'Federation began to appeal to the pocket as well as to the heart; and the people began to wake up to the fact that the "fad of Federation" with which politicians and parliaments had been dallying so long, meant the salvation of Australia.'

This growth in popular federalism was spurred on by an

organisation of the Australian-born, the Australian Natives' Association. The principle acted on by the association was that citizens would have to carry a lot of the debate and lead the politicians. (This was the same basis on which the Australian Republican Movement would operate in the 1990s.)

> It had long become apparent that the parliaments would accomplish little without a stimulus from their constituents; the conviction grew that Federalists must create a public organisation, with the twofold object of demonstrating to the parliaments the strength of the Federal sentiment, and of further solidifying and educating that sentiment.

Under the aegis of the Australian Natives Association (which was primarily a medical insurance scheme), Federation Leagues were formed throughout Australia. The founding of a Sydney Federation League made Sir Henry Parkes feel that his thunder had been stolen. But Sir Henry could not have disagreed with the stated purpose: 'to advance the cause of Australian Federation by an organisation of citizens owing no class distinction or party influence, and using its best energies to assist parliamentary action, from whatever source proceeding, calculated to further the common aim of Australian patriotism.'

It was at its meeting in Corowa in 1893 that Dr John Quick himself, a citizen member of the Australian Natives, came up with a procedure by which Australia could advance to Federation. First, each colony should elect on its parliamentary franchise ten representatives to a Federal Congress. Second, the Congress should frame a Federal Constitution. Third, on a day to be arranged between the governments, the Federal Constitution should be referred to the electors of each colony for acceptance or rejection. And fourth, if the Constitution was accepted by majorities in two or more colonies (again less draconian than Section 128), it should be forwarded to the Imperial government to be passed into law.

Wherever I go to speak on the Republic these days, it seems that someone rises to argue that a major cause of all Australian griefs is that we are not a unitary government. This is especially so now, when the South Australian government is stuck with the enormously expensive follies of its own State Bank, and the Victorian government can hardly afford itself. It is apparent to any intelligent citizen that talent begins to run thin on the back benches or in the cabinets of our State governments, and is often thin enough in Canberra as well. It is interesting to find out from Quick and Garran that there was a unification scheme put forward by Sir George Dibbs, Premier of New South Wales in 1894.

'It would be easier first to completely unify the interests of the two great colonies of Victoria and New South Wales, and then to attract neighbouring colonies within the sphere of our extended influence.' Sir George believed that the expense of State and Federal establishments would not be warranted. Perhaps history will prove him correct.

But in terms of *Realpolitik*, of achieving Federation by one means or another, Quick and Garran saw flaws in the Dibbs argument. 'It deliberately contemplated dividing Australia into two sections—the large States and the small States—and denying to the latter any voice in the form of union.'

The citizens organisations brought off such events as the Bathurst Convention of 1896—'a People's Federal Convention', and it was followed by the final official Convention, which met first in Adelaide and then moved on to Sydney and Melbourne.

The first referendum on the Bill federating Australia was held in 1898, the draft of which, when presented to New South Wales people, was accompanied by a commentary by Mr Garran. Sir George Reid had voted for the proposed Bill, yet complained about its shortcomings. The New South Wales press was full of talk about Federation being based on a desire by small States to plunder New South Wales. South Australia and Tasmania by contrast worried that 'the rights and interests of the less populous States would be unduly subordinated to the mass vote of the majority'.

In the referendum two of the States taking part, Victoria and Tasmania, voted massively for Federation. South Australia had a two-thirds majority. But New South Wales did not reach the 80,000 target set by the Enabling Act. The affirmative vote was 71,595, more than eight thousand short.

Just the same, it was obvious Federation was inevitable now.

Sir George Reid, Premier of New South Wales, went back into negotiation with the delegates from the other States over the burden on New South Wales, with its great ports, of contributing customs revenue, over voting requirements of joint sittings of the Senate and House of Representatives, over the powers of the Senate in money bills, and so on. For if the small States felt the danger of being underpowered, New South Wales feared emasculation through the Senate.

A new referendum was called for June 1899. 'The Sydney Bulletin,' writes Quick and Garran, 'which—when it has a positive policy—is a great power throughout Australia, concentrated its unrivalled wealth of ridicule against the opponents of the Bill.' This time the majority was more than 25,000 in New South Wales, and easily cleared the required 80,000 Yes votes. The margin was nearly 150,000 in enlightened Victoria. Little South Australia had just under a 50,000 margin, Tasmania 12,000, and Queensland—where the matter had only recently begun to be debated—an honourable 7500.

Western Australia was still negotiating, wanting the right to go on imposing her own customs for five years and to be exempt from the intrusion of the Inter-State Commission, the body which adjusted matters between the States, for the same period. In 1900, while the Federal delegates were negotiating with the British at the Colonial Office, Western Australia voted, 45,000 to less than 20,000, to join.

New Zealand watched, but though the Australians made room for them in the Constitution, opted not to involve themselves in a federation. Their arguments were interesting. One was that New Zealanders were yeomen, and the Australians were of convict descent; or if not, the society was still tainted with convictism and the atmosphere it had generated.

The second reason was that Australia was largely in the tropics and the tropics were unsuitable for people of European descent, producing debilitation in European women, and therefore a recourse by men to locals from the neighbouring islands and from the indigenous race, all resulting in a 'mongrelisation', in which the New Zealanders did not want to participate.

The first argument, according to New Zealand historian

Tony Simpson, is a fancy, a pretension of respectability. According to him New Zealand and Australia were peopled by economic refugees, some of whom had come before the courts and some of whom had not. The second argument is even more fantastical, given that tropic Australia is now crowded with economic refugees from New Zealand.

In any case, lacking only New Zealand, the Federation was formed against all the gainsayers. New Zealand was careful nonetheless to tell the Colonial Office that it should 'reserve the right of joining the Commonwealth at any time, or within a specified time, on the same terms as the Original States'. New Zealand also sought the right of appeal to the High Court of Australia, and the option for Australia and New Zealand to enter into necessary arrangements for joint naval and military defence.

The modern terms of Closer Economic Relations under which Australia and New Zealand now live are based on ideas that came up at the time of the Federation debate.

The question of appeals to the Privy Council of Britain was one much fought over by a series of sessions of the Constitutional Convention, and then between the Australian delegates who went to London to argue it out with Colonial Secretary Chamberlain. Chamberlain was besieged by British companies with interests in Australia to ensure that the resolution of the Adelaide session of the Convention (1897) should not stand. Indeed the 1898 version of Section 74 was very different from the Adelaide draft. The Adelaide Convention had argued that there should be no appeal to the Privy Council, either from the State courts or Federal courts, 'except that the Queen may, in any matter in which the public interests of the Commonwealth, or of any State, or any other part of Her Dominions, are concerned, grant leave of appeal to the Queen in Council from the High Court'. This had not been broad enough to satisfy British commercial interests.

So much again for the idea that our Constitution is the document of a sovereign nation and it would have come as a surprise to the delegates in Adelaide to know that ninety years after their deliberations, Australian litigants would still be choosing between the High Court and the Privy Council.

I was only back in Australia two or three weeks when I had to go to England for the launch of *Woman of the Inner Sea*. On a stormy Saturday night before I left, I debated John Howard in the Great Hall of St John's College at Sydney University. It was a debate organised by the Tipperary Association, so that I had to pay public honour to John's willingness to debate the issue before a potentially anti-Monarchist crowd. However, John got more support than would have on paper seemed likely—there were a number of students of the college who supported the Monarchical attachment, even though they were somewhat outnumbered by members of the Sydney and New South Wales Universities' branches of the Republican Movement.

We debated beneath a painting of two men perishing, Burke and Wills-style, in the Central Australian desert. It was a reminder that there were Australian realities beyond what we were discussing. I remembered a little verse of William Butler Yeats on Parnell, the leader of the Irish parliamentary party in the House of Commons in the nineteenth century:

Parnell came down the road, he said to a cheering man:
'Ireland shall get her freedom and you still break stone'.

The only qualification being that there was reasonable hope of deliverance from the desert in the Republic, and none in the Monarchical connection.

The book tour of England and Scotland was interesting in that the curiosity about Australian Republicanism had not gone away, and only half of every interview was about the book. My being a Republican makes no difference to the attitude of someone like Melvyn Bragg, who runs the 'South Bank Show' on British television and who comes from the extreme north of England—a place called Wigton in Cumbria, where attachment to the Monarchy was never as strong as in the southeast of England. Melvyn simply sees no reason why Australia should share a Head of State with Great Britain, especially given that Australia's claim on the Monarch is somewhat further down the totem pole than Britain's.

Bragg is a fine novelist (*The Maid of Buttermere*, *A Time to Dance*), and at the stage I went to England had a new novel out, *Crystal Rooms*, about a young boy from a housing estate in the north who is dumped in London by his mother's lover and who is a focus for intersections between people in politics and the media and clubland and the prostitution of the young. It is a very Dickensian book, but then Thatcher's and now Major's London has become a very Dickensian place—the monetarists have worked their way back, through extreme devotion to the economic rationalist ideal as in Australia, to the nineteenth century.

I suppose you would call Melvyn a very affluent Hampstead socialist, still in his self-image a child of the northern mining towns, a player of rough old Rugby League in his youth.

For the past three times when I have gone to London for a new book, Bragg included me on his panel show on Radio Three, 'Start the Week'. This time I went to it straight from the plane. 'Start the Week' is a discussion with four people, and Melvyn works in tandem with a guest journalist, quizzing the panel members. Republicanism came up with the same ease on 'Start the Week' as it does in the Australian media. Baroness James (the detective story writer, P. D. James), who had recently been visiting writer at UCI, actually said (perhaps out of her habitual politeness) that she thought Australian Republicanism was 'a jolly sensible idea'.

Other British commentators found no problem either.

But below that stratum of sympathy or indifference—many British people have as little interest in whether we remain a Monarchy as they do in the fiscal deficit of South Dakota—lies a solid mass of Imperial presumption. It sees us as ungrateful children. I suppose that feeling is inevitable in a nation which still habitually calls itself 'Great'.

Some journalists thought that there was a deliberate alliance between Keating, the ARM and Murdoch, a strange freemasonry to bring down the Monarchy. Not only did this credit us, with our one-person office in Sydney, with a power of

237

organisation of which we were incapable, but it also did Rupert
Murdoch the credit of believing that he had an agenda beyond
selling papers. Besides, if Murdoch's publications led the way
in flaying the Monarch's family, there was no need for the rest
of the tabloids to fall into line. Murdoch's *Times* took a much
soberer attitude to the cavortings of the princes and princesses
anyhow.

In some of the British one encountered a paternal concern that
we could not get by without the Monarchy. One man, a senior
editor in a publishing company, asked me if it was likely that
we would fragment like Yugoslavia. If he had asked Bronwyn
Bishop that same question, he would have got the answer he
was looking for.

In a summer heat wave I went up to Scotland, accompanied
by two people from Hodder and Stoughton, my British publisher. We met up with a Scottish novelist who had been
involved in the attempt to get home rule for Scotland, a foray
which had been defeated at the last British elections. The
Scots novelist was very aggressive to the two London people,
berating them for their Englishness, fundamentally aggrieved
—in the way an assertive writer from one of the Commonwealth countries might be—at having to be published in London by people who did not understand him. I found myself in
an uncustomary Australian situation: defending the Brits from
unfair attack.

I asked him why the Scots vote didn't go the way he wanted.
'Tory lies,' he told me.

I told him that at least in theory the thing would be just as
hard in Australia. They'd had the advantage in Scotland of
needing only a simple majority.

As well as trying, along with those of my partners who
were willing, to keep Echoes going, the other hard decision
hung over me—I would need to arrange with UCI to take off
at least the whole of 1993. I would teach there from late September of 1992 till Christmas, but even that stay would be
interrupted by a return to Sydney for the launch of Donald
Horne's book on Republicanism and for a Republican dinner
in Parliament House.

I certainly felt hedged about, but the one lasting and glorious thing in my life—apart from the generosity and enthusiasm of my wife and two daughters, one of them in Dublin, the other with us—was the Republic, and the pace it was taking on in Australian minds, and the sense of its inevitability.

I remember telling some English interviewers that this was being done without rancour, without bitterness or denial. If they were used to and somehow perversely flattered by being kissed off with ambushes and hurled bombs, it was not going to happen in this case. In this case they would have to get used to the goodbye being said with the ambiguous nudge of affection which characterises the relationship between the two nations.

Returning to Australia for the rest of the Australian winter, I was able to fix up the UCI arrangement. Perhaps by the end of 1993, anyhow, the Republic will be such an accustomed concept that I will be able to take up the old commute again, at least for a year or two. Six months here, six months there. Like David Malouf with Tuscany. I hope I can talk Malouf in fact into coming to UCI one year, forsaking Tuscany for the gritty air beneath the Santa Ana Mountains.

The ARM held a little assessment seminar at the Clancy Auditorium at University of New South Wales. It was the height of the debate over the five dollar note, and one news report made it sound as if the main purpose of our meeting was to devise chemical ways to get rid of the Monarch's face from the five dollar bill. In fact we dealt with such issues as whether the conventions that affect the behaviour of the Governor-General needed to be written down in the Constitution or enacted in some other way, or whether they were an inherent and unquestioned part of the Australian political culture. The convention for example by which the Governor-General has the power to dismiss a Prime Minister who has lost the confidence of the House.

The present Federal Executive Council, which generally consists of the Governor-General and two ministers, would almost certainly need to be carried over into a Republican system. Its concern up to now has been basically to consider and ratify the making of proclamations and regulations, the creation and abolition of government departments, the issue of writs for the election of members of the House of Representatives, and the authorisation of entry into international treaties—all arising from result of legislation Parliament has already passed. Sir Paul Hasluck approved of the Executive Council and the Governor-General's role in it. 'The Governor-General could and did play a significant role by requiring ample and adequate explanations and reasons for what was proposed.'

That late July too, I spoke at the National Press Club, calling my speech 'Silken Shroud or Honest Name?' The rationale behind the title was that in eighteenth and nineteenth century Thailand, when courtiers were not permitted to touch the Monarch, if the need arose to assassinate him they would slip a silken shroud over him and beat him to death while he writhed inside it. This of course was what the British tabloids were doing to the Monarchy in the United Kingdom. But they could keep their silken shroud. We weren't interested in that mean stuff. All we wanted was our own honest name.

The speech ended perhaps a little sentimentally but with a pungent enough message.

In the hope of making the point, I shall conclude with a tale of two women, both of whom represent different sides of the Australian tradition.

Last Sunday, the genial wife of a Manly committeeman at Brookvale Oval, where Saints were not only humiliating Manly but not doing themselves much glory either, spoke about her English parents, and the obvious emotional, symbolic and spiritual nutriment they had drawn from George VI. When George VI, she said, broadcast on the radio soon after the start of World War II, her father had risen in his place and saluted. A similar scene occurred —by the way—in John Borman's brilliant film, *Hope and Glory*. This woman said she realised Australia had changed, but hoped that there would always be room for her tradition, for her memory.

Then in Adelaide in March, another Australian woman rose as we were launching a branch of the Republican Movement for South Australia. She said that her children were all Australian citizens and were urging her to become an Australian citizen, which she would dearly love to do. But she claimed that she could not in conscience take that oath to the Monarch which everyone in Australia has to take if they wish to serve in Parliament, in courts, the armed services, or to become an Australian citizen. Make it possible, she begged the Australian Republican Movement, for me to die an Australian.

In Monarchical Australia there is room only for one of these two decent women. In the Republican vision there is room for both. For Republicanism is not the slamming of a door on the past, but the opening of one on the future. The constitutional Monarchy is now a limiting factor on our national identity and the real scope of our society. That door which awaits us, that honest gate, must be opened in the end. There, beyond, in a new and—we hope— glittering century, knowing who we are, denying nothing, affirming all, no longer wearing the deceptive demeanour of a colony, we will have settled the most basic Australian question: who we are. Then perhaps we can go on to make something even further of ourselves, and to confirm, celebrate and redeem our remarkable history.

This is the day I finish writing this book—29 August 1992. By now, the ARM is a movement open to all Australians. We have hit on a pyramidal organisation, each State branch running its own affairs, all of us lending personnel to each other for special events, and membership being open to people for a joining fee of $25 or—in special cases—less. The founding membership fee of a hundred dollars (and sometimes much more than a hundred: Bruce Petty the cartoonist having been very generous to the movement) is still available to those who want to make a gesture of that size, but it gives them no more political power in the organisation than more modest joiners. State and university groups of the ARM will supply delegates to a national committee to meet occasionally somewhere in Australia to be decided on. We hope to help delegates with airfares, and so on.

They say in today's *Sydney Morning Herald* that at a reunion of Gough Whitlam's ministry tonight, the present Prime Minister Paul Keating is going to raise the prospect of the Republic again. 'He plans an escalating series of speeches and references in coming months to build support for the idea.' An alteration to the citizenship oath is likely to occur soon. If Keating succeeds electorally, then the pace will increase. I know that most of the conservatives—if in government— would be too intelligent to permanently paint themselves into the Monarchist corner. Keating's survival is however a large question, and by the time you read this book you'll know how it has been answered. The dreary monetarist vision of his government, different in degree only from that of the Opposition, in no way matches the visionary nature of the drive to the Republic. As it comes from him, the message limps. But it is still the message. It is larger in impetus than the destiny of one or two or three political parties.

Like Federation it is a matter for citizens, and citizens will get it home in the end. I have little doubt at all as an individual that having done so, we will use the Republic as the light by which we review everything, from our relationship to our antediluvian continent, to our position with its indigenous peoples, to the question of our international relations. Delivered of colonialism at last, and finally cured of the twitches of dependence, we will be able to see ourselves in a real light for the first time. We will have settled or at least embarked on the question which for so long has persecuted us: What is an Australian?

The fruits may be incalculable. Whereas we already know the staleness and limitations of the old way.